THE

EVERYTHING®

NUMEROLOGY
BOOK

Discover your potential for love,
success, and health through the
science of numbers

Ellae Elinwood

Adams Media Corporation
Avon, Massachusetts

EDITORIAL

Publishing Director: Gary M. Krebs
Managing Editor: Kate McBride
Copy Chief: Laura MacLaughlin
Acquisitions Editor: Allison Carpenter Yoder
Development Editor: Julie Gutin
Project Editor: Kate Epstein
Production Editor: Khrysti Nazzaro

PRODUCTION

Production Director: Susan Beale
Production Manager: Michelle Roy Kelly
Series Designer: Daria Perreault
Cover Design: Paul Beatrice and Frank Rivera
Layout and Graphics: Colleen Cunningham,
Rachael Eiben, Michelle Roy Kelly,
Daria Perreault, Erin Ring

An Everything® Series Book.
Everything® is a registered trademark of Adams Media Corporation.

Published by Adams Media Corporation
57 Littlefield Street, Avon, MA 02322 U.S.A.
www.adamsmedia.com

ISBN: 1-58062-700-5
Printed in the United States of America.

J I H G F E D C B A

Library of Congress Cataloging-in-Publication Data
Elinwood, Ellae.
The everything numerology book / by Ellae Elinwood.
p.   cm.   —(An everything series book)
ISBN 1-58062-700-5
1. Numerology. I. Title. II. Everything series.
BF1729.N85 E45 2003
133.3'35–dc21
2002009980

Illustrations by Barry Littmann.

This book is available at quantity discounts for bulk purchases.
For information, call 1-800-872-5627.

Visit the entire Everything® series at everything.com

Dedication

To Gregge Tiffen, master nu. ɔlogist—
healing and inspiring the u 'd,
one person at a time.

Contents

Foreword

MANKIND'S MOST BASIC ISSUE has always been its need to survive. A close second has been our need to communicate with each other and make ourselves understood. This need has created one of the great human struggles, as people have searched for an acceptable format and method that would cross all borders and reach all nations.

At the dawn of civilization, when languages were still in their primal and unformed state, the need to communicate was a critical necessity both within the inner tribe and as a means of dealing with external groups and individuals. Only one language that met all the criteria was available to those early people: the language of numbers! From sign language to pictures on cave walls, the language of numbers was understood by everyone.

Eventually this language of numbers was formulated into a system that coincided with an alphabet. This increased its meaning, regardless of the particular application, and the system known as numerology was born.

Ellae has efficiently delved into the ancient archives of numbers; the vision she presents here is unobstructed by the limitations of language or nationality. It offers the reader a panoramic view of the way human beings embrace numbers and how that embrace becomes a vital energy in our life, creating everything from the way we identify ourselves to the methods we use to reach our life goals.

This book makes for a fascinating read, and is sure to open ideas and dimensions that have been locked away in your mind. You will never see life in the same way again.

Gregge Tiffen
Dallas, Texas
February 2002

Introduction

WELCOME TO THE AMAZING SUBJECT OF NUMEROLOGY, the science of understanding the interaction of energies as they join together in a single unit. Today, people use numbers in math, which influences many aspects of our lives. We count, measure, estimate, and equate numbers. They are so much a part of modern life that it's hard to imagine our world without them. There was a time when the numerological aspect of numbers played an equally great role in human life, but we have gradually allowed numerology to lag behind.

For most people today, numbers are nothing more than mathematics, which they either love or hate. But numbers can be so much more—agents for more loving relationships, for more money, for better health, for personal growth, for spiritual awareness, and for greater luck. Maybe you, like other skeptics, say, "No way!" Well, it's time to clear your mind.

In numerology, each number is alive, a living energy that flows from and into infinity carrying positive and negative characteristics. When these energies combine, they create the spark of life. In ancient times the magi— early numerologists—became so skilled at directing and arranging these flows of universal life, they could shift the expected outcomes of events according to their wishes.

The magi used the power of numerology to shift reality in larger arenas. Today, you can do the same in your personal arena. Numerology will help you understand yourself through the wisdom of the numbers. Remember: The numbers are alive, they have personality. Beyond that, they are the substance of life and energy that empowers our spirit and soul. Use numerology wisely; it is the language form of the universe, and it has the power to show you how to live your life in joy and prosperity.

In beginning your exploration of numbers and their deeper natures, you are embarking on a journey that is filled with wonder and riches, betrayal and defeat, and the triumphant steady restoration of numerology, numbers as energy, numbers as universal communication, and numbers that live.

This book will take you back to the ancient times when amazing accomplishments were gained as math and numerology joined forces to create wonders. When you have completed your journey, you will have a better understanding of the amazing past, present, and future of numerology. You will be more in tune with some of the cultures that used it wisely to enhance life. You will have the tools at your fingertips to become a part of this lineage of wisdom. You can use numerology as a guide to help you make decisions as you seek

self-knowledge, establish satisfying relationships, improve your love life, and become more financially successful; in general, it will help you make your life more fulfilling than ever before. This life is at your fingertips.

Numerology as we know it today is designed to help you progress through life's dilemmas. If you're not satisfied with your life or areas of your life, you have the power to create different outcomes through what you learn from the numbers. Then, you can learn how to create and apply the true inner changes into behavioral changes that change your life to be the way you want it, every day.

What are your personal reasons for taking your precious time to learn this new skill? Do you want to improve your life? Have you always been curious about numerology? Maybe a good friend or a close relative has been encouraging you to learn more about this fascinating subject, and you are finally interested?

Experience improves when you focus your intent through action. Take the time to sit back and examine your reasons for getting interested in the subject of numerology. Decide what you want to get out of studying it. Then pick up *The Everything® Numerology Book* and keep on reading.

Your journey, any journey, starts with the first step, and it's always into unknown terrain. Stretch your mental muscles, shake out those cobwebs, and join in for a countdown to numerology. This journey will continue to expand your perceptions and add value to your life.

CHAPTER 1

The Birth of Numbers

Humanity's connection to numbers may be traced to the very dawn of human existence. Numbers came from symbols found in nature, making them our original language, and they continue to provide the common ground of communication for all people, in each and every culture.

The Perfect Language

Pythagoras, Einstein, and Merlin—among many others—have said that numbers, mathematics, and the metaphysical understanding of numbers and vibrations together form the perfect language. As you will see, numbers have connected us to our survival since the very beginning of human existence, and they continue to help us understand and describe our differences physically, emotionally, and mentally.

Numbers are our common root. Over time, they have expanded in usefulness from counting perils, to defining emotional differences, to clarifying mental skills and accessing spiritual qualities. Now numbers still lead us, show us, and give us the language to continue forward into uncharted terrain. They are now showing us how to complete the circle of evolution. This language from the humblest of roots has been sought, honed, and passed down throughout the generations by great men and women of many disciplines.

ESSENTIALS Humans have relied on numbers for thousands of years. Today, numbers are used today by scientists, mathematicians, I Ching masters, Tibet's holy teachers, Christian scholars (who follow Jesus' triune teaching), and ordinary people like you and me who are just trying to get a handle on it all.

At the Very Beginning

Life was very different for early humans two to three million years ago. The world was not made for humans to rule over. There were no cities, roads, medicine, science. Life consisted of two environments—the protective habitat inside the cave, and the unprotected outside world.

Early humans lived in nature in all her wild beauty, but it was a difficult life, full of dangers and the constant struggle for survival. Because there was safety in numbers, the well-being of the tribe ensured the safety of its individual members.

Early Forms of Communication

The issues of living and problem solving were more perilous, although less complex, than they are today. Many people died of disease or were killed young. Old age was unheard of. Life consisted of surviving, and little more. Many needs were predictable, repetitive, and needed no clear verbal communication: to survive, to reproduce, and to be included in the larger, communal group. As a result, natural individuality was suppressed to ensure the tribal communal rhythms of deep compatibility.

Much of interpersonal communication was carried out with eloquent body language, gestures, face and eye movements, and simple sounds. Together, these elements formed a rudimentary language that served the simple needs of those early tribes.

FACTS

Language need not be a system of words—in fact, it may be any system of communication that is shared among a group of people. Whether it's sign language or a written language, the system is a language as long as it allows people to communicate. Even communication through numbers, body gestures, clothing, and music may serve as a language.

However, in the world outside of the cave—the dangerous world of enemies, wild animals, the constant hunt for food, and the harsh environment—this rudimentary language began to grow in complexity as the humans came to rely more and more on it to communicate during the hunt.

Early humans had developed only the simplest physical tools to hunt for food as well as to provide protection: chunks of flint that were chipped into arrowheads and hatchet heads, rocks for throwing, fire for cooking and burning, and wooden shafts for anchoring arrowheads or hatchets or for sharpening into lances. It was risky to rely on such weapons, so the key to success lay in the number of fighters. Humans had to pick their battles carefully—if they miscounted, they would be easily overwhelmed by a larger number of prey or enemies.

Numbers became the agreed-upon language that provided them with an accurate way to communicate. The language of numbers also answered their need to define, understand, defend themselves from, and integrate with the world around them. Eventually, this communication allowed humans to gradually realize that each individual human being is separate and distinct from the other members of the tribe.

ESSENTIALS

At first, numbers were expressed through speech. Later, humans developed written symbols to represent numbers visually—on the ground, on cave walls, and so on. Most likely, the inspiration for these symbols—circles, semicircles, horizontal and vertical lines, triangles, cones, and other shapes—came from nature.

The Birth of Architecture

Some say that civilization began when the early humans left the caves and settled down in villages. We might never know how they first learned to build dwellings, but we do know that in order to build them, they had to understand numbers.

How did they figure out the size a structure needed to be in order to contain a family of five, ten, or however many? How did they manage to get poles of the same length in order to build walls? How did they know how many leaves, branches, sticks, or other materials they would need to cover their huts? How did they know how to build an entrance that allowed them to enter but kept out the wild weather and unwanted guests? Architecture.

FACTS

Architecture combined math, numbers used to measure distance and amounts, and the new, astonishing skill of building shelter. It was at this point that numbers hit the big turning point. They changed from symbols of communication into mathematical science.

At this point genius did what it usually does: It expanded and elevated the human understanding of what may be possible. Our relationship to numbers had changed—as it would change again and again. Before, numbers had stood on their own, each one unique and unblended with any other. With architecture, humans could manipulate numbers by combining and coordinating them for the benefit of their survival, for survival has always been the great driving force behind our constant drive forward, to grow and develop.

Numbers Attain Personal Characteristics

Meanwhile, evolution took its course. Human beings continued to develop their outer world, learning how to hunt with greater skill and preparation, mastering the powerful natural force of fire, and conceiving of and creating the wheel. They learned to domesticate animals and eventually settled down in villages, where they became aware of more emotional differences among themselves. No longer under the relentless pressure of untamed nature, they could relax a bit. As early humans grew more emotionally diverse, numbers evolved right along with this growth.

Numbers that had once been used to identify amounts and measure distances now had a new purpose. They could be used to describe personal characteristics, as follows:

- She wants to be number 1.
- They prefer each other's company only—they are a couple, a 2.
- Extra support means 3.
- A 4 is solid—4 points stand for strength.
- Your hand has 5 fingers that reach out into the world to get what you want.
- The family is 6.
- Gazing inwardly is a concept of 7.
- Adding two 4s gets you an 8, a number of great strength.
- A 9 represents the humanitarian.
- Two hands make up a 10, the highest number, which represents a full and rich person.

These ideas gradually became condensed so that each number came to carry a particular significance.

Significance of Numbers			
1	singular	6	harmony
2	couple	7	inner reflection
3	creativity	8	strength
4	structure	9	humanitarian
5	shaker-mover	10	completeness

How the Numbers Evolved

As human evolution continued, the challenges posed by nature only worked to further develop human skills and mental strength. Humans continued to improve their tools. They learned the art of healing through herbs and other techniques. They became more successful at providing themselves with food through better hunting techniques as well as by learning the arts of agriculture and domestication of animals. As an evolving species, they took their use of numbers to the next level as well, making the meaning of each number more complex and defining its positive and negative characteristics, like this:

1 an action-oriented originator, a leader or a fool

2 a balance of two things; a point of vacillation

3 fun or dilettantism

4 the ability to organize or repress

5 the one who created movement or inconsistency

6 harmony of health and home, or interference

7 the deep intellect of seeking, or aloofness

8 power and success, or ambition for self and material possessions

9 the one who expressed universal love or aimless dreaming

10 the one who saw the whole picture or imposed personal beliefs

The Evolution of Numbers Gave Us Numerology

The spiritual evolution of numbers led human beings to develop numerology, a way of using numbers to show them—teaching them, as living agents—how to define and understand that which already existed.

ESSENTIALS   The lion exists in life, but 1 defines it as a singular animal. Similarly, numbers help define and understand characteristics as they emerge, providing a bridge for us to bring into understanding that which already exists but is not yet defined, understood, or utilized.

As humans continued to evolve spiritually and came to wonder about the meaning of life and their place in it, numbers led the way to greater understanding. Numbers and numerology gave them the language in which to form their great questions and seek out their answers. Numbers helped define crucial relationships like these:

1	represents destiny, force, or dictatorship
2	loving; overly protective
3	inspired; overly enthusiastic
4	gives stable security; controlling
5	a number representing change; scattered
6	harmonious; eccentrically out of touch
7	psychic; withdrawn
8	unifying; possessive
9	universality; martyrdom
10	grasp of the whole picture; excessive attachment to one way

Numbers are a part of us. They have always been. That's because we have brought them right along with us, using them to help us understand the stage of the world we are stepping into. As we progress from stage to stage of our existences, numbers are the only constant, perfect form of communication.

Four Areas of Personal Growth

Humans developed one step at a time through each of the four levels of evolution: physical, mental, emotional, and spiritual. Even today, all individuals are faced with the necessity of integrating these four areas of themselves into inner harmony as they grow daily and live through all the experiences life sends their way. That is why numbers continue to provide a vital tool for understanding ourselves, others, and our place in the fabric of life.

The number 1, representing a single lion, became a single person who stood alone emotionally. That single person then became a single, unique thinker, then finally a single force for cosmic power. Numbers have always shown the way, allowing us to define our experience of life, one another, our relationship to life, and our place in this world.

FACTS

Numbers took a leap into coordinates and combinations, and it was then suddenly possible to duplicate the forms and shapes in nature with accuracy. Then someone could also pass on a skill in a way that it became easily repeatable. The vistas that opened, the enhanced possibilities for survival, the blossoming aesthetic values—it must have boggled the mind.

Our Flip-Flopped World

Our world today is radically different from that long-ago world of the early humans. In modern life, our time is centered upon lists of things we need to accomplish, and we judge ourselves and each other by our success in completing these goals. We buy much and long to buy more.

The dangerous outside world beyond the cave has diminished dramatically as humans have turned it into their own realm. We have medicine, science, psychotherapy, education, planes, heating, huge homes . . .

the list goes on. However, the deep inner rhythms of the tribe—what we now experience as the couple, the family, the community, the state, country, and the world—are a daily struggle to find, let alone maintain. Now it is the family circle—our tribe, so to speak—that we struggle with most, as people fail in their personal, intimate, and family relationships.

The New Challenges

We long to reinstate unity, harmony, trust, and commitment to others in our lives. These are all ideals that have been sacrificed one step at a time as humans worked to make nature safer and improve their lives physically and materially.

We pushed hard and grabbed at Earth's bounty, its space and resources, but we are about to reach the limits. We now need to complete the circle in this evolutionary process; we need to balance the outer development with inner unity. We must return to the inner harmony of the tribe. Of course, our tribe has grown to incorporate billions of people of differing skin color, religion, gender, sexual orientation, and many other characteristics. But it is in our power to regain our tribal oneness again, for our tribe is the world.

Deep within ourselves, locked in our genetic code, we carry the memories of unifying inner rhythms that reduce ego differences, petty grievances, and the desire to destroy another's life; they have the power to fill us with the desire and ability to resolve difficult issues. We must reduce our compulsion to destroy or devour that which we feel threatens us because the threat is us and we stand too close now. We can no longer do it to them without doing it to ourselves.

Tried-and-True Tools for Building a New World

We need tools to rebuild our cave, the place that protects us all from the outer uncertainty while we live together according to our inner rhythms.

This process is a process of rebuilding connections, and we can work on it through each interaction we have, hundreds of times each day.

We need the tools to understand ourselves better, to grasp our compatibility with each person, to seek to understand the other and find and elevate our quality as we lead our lives as ordinary people, people very busily engaged in the texture of daily life.

Each One of Us Is Unique

The universe is subject to the law of nonrepetition, and humans are no exception. You are completely unique and can never be duplicated. You and you alone can say what you know and feel and question. To withhold your uniqueness denies a component of the full rhythm to the tribe. The rainbow of humanity will still radiate, but it will be paler for your lack of full engagement.

In order to engage with the universe in a nondestructive, nondevouring way, we must know ourselves, our strengths and weaknesses, our positive and less-than-positive qualities and even those that are truly negative. This self-knowledge will help you create and recreate the wonderful boundary of self that allows the full uniqueness of you, cast from the creator and not repeatable, to resonate out and join in this next step for human evolution. To gain this kind of self-knowledge, you will need great and powerful tools.

The path is wide, and we are all on it, going in the same direction, but each step is ours and ours alone. Numbers light the way. Interested? Read on. It gets better!

ALERT

Today, each number has retained its uniquely defined, complex, and singular meaning. They still communicate exactly as before. In addition, numbers have the power to combine and to create, and they are still continuing to evolve in much more involved combinations and formats than before.

CHAPTER 2

The Ancient Powers of Math and Numerology

Numbers are the most perfect and pure form of communication. Numbers gave us the tool to expand our universal understanding of what had always been, and to impart that knowledge on to the future generations. As numbers have become the journey of creation both in the physical and metaphysical world, they have never lost their earliest values.

Duality Is a Party of Numbers

This book is about the energy of numbers, which show themselves in two basic ways: physical mathematics and metaphysical numerology. Mathematics and numerology both use numbers—accurately, effectively, and creatively—in a process of learning about and manipulating the environment. We can use both in our continual struggle to improve and enhance human life, making it richer, fuller, easier, and safer. However, the similarities end here.

FACTS

The difference between mathematics and numerology is like the difference between oil and water. They occupy the same space, they touch on all surfaces, they can exist side by side, but they never mix. In math, the numbers are stationary and physical, while in numerology they are lively and movable. However, both mathematics and numerology build and change reality, whether that means helping to build a new bridge or a new attitude toward life.

Mathematics is the construction of physical systems for understanding Earth's physical laws. The purpose of this kind of understanding is to figure out how to get numbers to serve us better through education and application. Numerology is the science of understanding the interaction of energies as they join together into a single unit, a metaphysical system for understanding the universe's bounty of wisdom. By using numerology, we can relate to numbers as living forces, flowing throughout all of life.

Both systems have served us spiritually. Since this is a book about numerology, let's take a look at where in the forest of evolution the paths of mathematics and numerology diverged.

Combinations, Coordinates, and Equations

Nothing that is now, that has happened in the past, or that will happen in the future will ever be repeated in exactly the same way ever again. In order to work effectively with this law in mind, the early architects of civilization had to use numbers to be able to mimic nature successfully. These attempts could only succeed with the intelligent use of numbers.

Here is an example. A river in its natural course was observed to make six bends before narrowing to become a natural dam, from which animals and humans could drink more easily. Because water became predictably plentiful, herds of animals became regular, making hunting easier. Such observations might be recorded mathematically: the number of bends, the distance between the bends, the varying depth of the river as it progressed to the natural dam, and the accurate measurement of the dam itself. The numbers combined, coordinated, and organized into a system, which could then be duplicated. Trial and error provided the refining of the numbers until accuracy in the duplication was achieved.

Voilà, water as needed, far and wide. That water is quickly put to good use: Drinking water is now in good supply, and it will attract grazing animals that may be hunted. Furthermore, a reliable water source is key to agriculture, one of the earliest signs of settlement and civilization.

Nature Is a Great Teacher

Nature is the great author of life and a consistently wise teacher of how to live and survive successfully. Have you ever had the following experience? You have a problem that is really troubling you. You have turned it this way and that and can't get a handle on the right way to proceed, so you decide to take a walk, just to get some relief and space.

ESSENTIALS

Seek your answers from Nature—it worked in the times of the ancients, and it still works now. Keep your problem close to you as you take the time to walk, sit, observe, and reflect, and the answer will come to you. Sometimes, it will seem as if it had been waiting for you to sit down and pay attention, as if Nature had enacted it specifically for your benefit.

There you are, walking along, obsessing about the problem, and your eye catches a bird soaring on the wind-flows overhead. You watch, fascinated with the slight adjustments the bird makes with its wings to stay afloat. Just a little adjustment, and this wonderful soaring continues.

Suddenly, your mind fills with questions. "Am I making this problem too big? Am I overlooking a slight behavior adjustment that could easily solve this problem? Is the problem not in this life event but in my lack of creativity in adjusting to it?"

Suddenly, a whole series of insights opens to you. You have an idea of what you can do. You can use the image and inspiration of the bird to improve your life. Now you can hardly wait to get back into the problem to see if your new inspiration works as well as you think it might.

Draw Wisdom from Nature

Here is another scenario to consider. You sit on a bluff, gazing at the majestic view, trying to get the freedom of a good perspective on things. Then you catch yourself watching an ant struggling to crawl up and over a rock. To you, this rock is something you can easily jump over. To the little ant, it's a steep hill that it's trying valiantly to scale. To make matters worse, it is carrying a crumb that looks heavier than its own body weight.

The situation looks impossible. The rock is too crumbly and steep, and it looks like the ant isn't strong enough to get on top together with the load. Yet the poor creature just keeps struggling up the same route, doing the same thing, not letting go of the load. And then, before you know it, quick as a flash, a wolf spider appears out of nowhere, and the ant and its load are lunch.

You can't help but see meaning in this scene. It's like a metaphor of our lives. It teaches us, "I have to completely let go of this load I am so worried about. I have to find a new way to go, or else it will devour me."

Ancient Problem Solving

This is precisely the way early humans solved their problems—both physical problems, like how to survive, and metaphysical ones, like how to find one's place in life. Both systems approached and solved problems through observation; people looked to the Earth for the physical and to the heavenly bodies of the universe for the metaphysical. In both cases, numbers played an essential role.

A Solution Leads to a New Problem

However, as problems were solved, new problems were created. When mankind conquered nature, we unwittingly caused a breakdown in the system. Our environment, on which we rely for survival, faced destruction. People realized that their knowledge was incomplete. They saw that they had trouble coordinating numbers in a positive, nonharmful manner. People had to learn and accept the concepts of supply and demand. (Although we do understand this concept today, we are still having difficulties accepting it in the way we live our lives.)

This ongoing problem changed the picture again, making it clear that mathematical formulas needed to be formed (and utilized) to enable us to determine when to stop hunting so the herds could build up again, and then, of course, to be able to use mathematical correlations to accurately decide when hunting could be safely resumed.

Chance, Luck, and Spiritual Development

In the distant past, the turning points of life were determined primarily by luck, chance, and the environment. Luck was the blessing of being in the right place at the right time to catch that rabbit. Chance was happening on the lake when thirst really became unbearable, or, conversely, slipping and falling over the cliff because a rock that had always been secure rolled from under your foot and caused your fall. And of course, the weather played a huge role in life and exerted tremendous control over what could be accomplished.

Spirituality appeared as moments of profound spiritual connection, experienced by early humans when they had temporarily satisfied the conditions of survival and felt the relief of safety. Knowing six antelope would feed the tribe well created rejoicing throughout the tribe, and bringing those six antelope home from the hunt created a source of pride for the hunters. These feelings probably led to a spiritual celebration at the feet of several statues.

People did not know how to control these forces, so they built statues and prayed to them in the devout hope that they would minimize the uncertainty of their lives. They did not yet have a mathematical format to show them the way to create systems that would help them ease their survival issues.

Rejection of Chance

Humans underwent another spiritual leap when they rejected the power of chance in forming their relationships. When they went from mating like animals to forming long-lasting relationships based on personal choice, they came one step closer to being human and to having power over their lives.

It could be argued that as a result of taking charge over intimate relationships, mankind began to learn how to take charge in other areas of human life and lifestyle. Humans built villages, connected them with networks of roads, developed commerce, and continued to roam farther, settling in far-flung areas.

Men now had the ability to build their families, to pick their wives, and to better protect their children. The most successful were able to dominate the gene pool by conquering other tribes and taking their women.

As survival on a daily basis became less and less critical, human relationships became more complex, and, as a result, they developed the potential of being more personally rewarding. Increased safety allowed free time to emerge in the day, and as a result civilization began to develop.

This development of creating and living within civilization was the next spiritual step. Spiritual moments continued to occur as they did before, and they were still tied into survival issues, but now they occurred with the opening compatibility of relationship and family in safer circumstances. Spirituality had the opportunity to grow and expand further through the emergence of the arts, which flourished as people no longer had to spend their every waking moment in the struggle for survival.

The sweet reveling in the gifts of safety led to further spiritual development. Safety and spiritual development are deeply intertwined throughout human evolution, and this is as it should be. Working together, these twinned concepts enact an evolution that will eventually lead to the safety of all humanity: peace on Earth. Clearly, we are still in the process of evolving.

The Power of the Magi

The next important step in humanity's spiritual evolution was the understanding of numbers standing independently as the energy of infinite communication. Humans began to realize that 1 no longer stood only for a lion, a single person, an inventive thinker, or a cosmic person. It also carried aspects of universal energy. When used singly, this energy created 1—communication and universal understanding—and when combined into formulas, it could be shifted and correlated to create states of being we describe even now as magic.

The magi's skills in numerology were highly developed. Over the ages, however, enormous amounts of information were lost, confiscated, and even destroyed. There is reason to believe the records are still stored somewhere, but they are still very much unavailable.

The magi, the genius originators of numerology, led very simple lives. Originally their use of numbers was very simple as well; they did nothing more complex than using numbers in their singular form for mystical insight. When they learned that combining numbers in numerological formulas created metaphysical energetic architecture that they could employ for their own reasons, numerology changed from the freedom of numbers to the confinement and placement of numbers (the mystical architecture) to affect outcome. The progress was the same as mathematics. The evolution was the same. The path that was singular became plural.

In the magi's skilled hands, numbers emerged as infinite life, movement, creativity, and communication with and from the universe. The power behind the numbers from 1 to 9 were understood as infinite energy flows that could be combined by orchestrating the numbers/flows in particular spells. The magi manipulated the numbers' energy currents just as easily as you might solve a simple mathematical equation, such as 2+2 = 4. Numbers and the tribe were never separate, but now they could be harnessed for the good of all.

The numerology developed by the magi had the power to lead the way to understanding the communications of the universe. The magi understood that each number had a different effect in the greater universal context and that the placement of the numbers changes the outcome. They could figure out how to guide people in life using numerology as a tool, just as architects could figure out how to guide the building of safer homes using math. The same numbers now appeared in two diverging roads. Like oil and water, the paths were completely close and completely separate.

The Chinese Art of Feng Shui

Probably the best example of the art of magi numerology is feng shui, the Chinese art of placement. Chinese numerologists developed feng shui based on their interpretation of the living forces that combine into a single unit. Shifting the placement of certain objects alters these forces, which thereby changes the whole environment. Imagine the ability to make such changes not just in terms of physical spaces but in human affairs, in individuals, and in Earth's events. We have lost such powers of numerology through confiscation of records and an overemphasis on mathematics.

The Education of the Magi

The magi training took place in a relationship between a master and a student. The student would attend the master almost as a servant, and the master magi would train his student in the arts of numerology and magic. After enough information was passed on for the student to have a good foundation and a degree of competence, he went into the world. He was expected to lead a very simple life and have limited earthly needs so the focus of his experience would be on the energies of life and manifestation. He was expected to guide others for their own benefit, not his own. This meant empowering others with tools to find their own true inner nature, then providing them with the tools to discipline the negative for the enhancement of the positive, the God within.

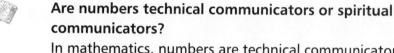

QUESTIONS?

Are numbers technical communicators or spiritual communicators?
In mathematics, numbers are technical communicators.
In numerology, they are spiritual communicators.

Of course, the forces of good and evil are always doing battle with each other in all ways. This conflict took its inevitable toll in the creation of beneficial magi and evil magi. In numerology, numbers are infinite energies with both positive and negative characteristics. This means that good and evil are found in the way the numbers are applied. With the information and knowledge of numbers came the power to help others on their way or to control them for the magi's own pleasure and power. These were very real considerations. Over time, the magi created energy architectures of great power. In so doing, they were able to alter metaphysical reality, just as architecture altered physical reality. By taking the numbers and the values of the numbers, they were able to construct a much larger force and a much larger meaning—the architecture of energy flows.

Numbers as Spiritual Communicators

It was the magi who discovered that the language of the numbers exists in nature and is manifested through the numbers' forms, or their geometric format. The square, the triangle, the cone, and the star are the most common forms.

Spiritual Numbers

These geometric shapes were complete mathematical formats. They are easy to see, easy to duplicate, and they are open to specific interpretations. Here's an example: In Africa, powerful men wore (and may still wear) a lion's tooth, which is triangular or conical in shape. Both triangle and cone, when examined from a numerological perspective, have enormous energy and power. The power of the lion, the power of the symbol of the tooth, the power of the triangle or cone, the power of the number 3, and the power of 1 and 2 making 3 all lend their energy, becoming the same language.

FACTS

The trilogy, the triune, and the triangle have been very important for millennia. This goes back into 3s, into the basic trilogy of the Earth, the Sun, and the Moon. This original 3, when viewed at certain times, has points that are positioned to make a perfect triangle. This is easily translated into the power of and completeness of 3.

CHAPTER 3

Ancient Rulers, Ancient Riches: Numerology in Egypt

Egypt played an essential role in the evolution of numerology. There is probably no culture that used math and numerology more effectively and with greater success than ancient Egypt. Pyramids, golden tombs, and mummies still fascinate us. How did they do it? And why did they do it?

A Tremendously Successful Culture

The culture of ancient Egypt has been heralded for centuries. Ancient Egyptians were master artisans, architects, and philosophers, and the accomplishments of their civilization are still respected. Even today, we still cannot duplicate all of their achievements.

The Egyptians harnessed the Nile and stabilized food production. They created fabulous art and music, and their culture supported a fascinating succession of rulers. They excelled in architecture—their most impressive works are the pyramids, which still remain standing after thousands of years, and the mysterious Great Sphinx of Giza.

Great Architects

We still don't know exactly how the Egyptians were able to construct the pyramids and the Sphinx. It is assumed that the bottom rung of their society, the slaves, did enormous amounts of work, and the architects created inventive devices to move and place blocks of rocks where they were required. Unfortunately, we no longer have the information regarding the power of placement, the energetic coordinations that the architects of the pyramids used to enhance movement.

With the use of energetic formulas, heavy rocks were lighter and easier to move. Physical laws could be adjusted to alter predictable physical outcomes. We are puzzled by the manner of construction of these edifices because in our culture, we leave out the magi/priest role in the development of these great wonders. Priests who were able to manipulate numbers as living systems of energies worked hand in hand with the architects to lighten the laws of gravity. The force of numbers and the force of numerology, working in completely compatible and completely distinct union, provided the tools to defy physical understanding and create marvels. Majestic and stunning in their achievement, these marvels are only part of the whole story.

Mummification

Egyptian doctors also learned the techniques of mummification, which allowed them to preserve the bodies of the rulers of Egypt and other important people in preparation for the afterworld. Scientists who study mummies today are still amazed at how well the mummification process worked. When they unwrap the mummies, they find that the body is completely dehydrated and well-preserved—thousands of years after death. No one in our day and age knows exactly how this was accomplished or, for certain, why. Was it done for spiritual reasons?

The deliberate mummification process was probably perfected for two reasons. The first reason was to preserve the ruler's remains while the tomb was being completed. Second, it is important for us to remember that to the Egyptians, the body represented the physical power that person had amassed in the life. It was the power from the body that had to be transported to the disincarnate world. There could be no physical power unless the body was preserved.

After death and mummification, the body was placed in a tomb along with all the treasures and belongings of the mummy. These wonders and riches represented the physical achievements of the deceased. They would be essential for the journey of the soul, now free from the body, over the River Styx to the afterlife.

FACTS

Much of numerology's history comes from oral tradition passed in secret from teacher to student, and sometimes it varies slightly from the traditional history. The variations are an interesting new view on history as we have traditionally accepted it; this is particularly true with regard to the River Styx. It is traditionally taught that this is a part of Greek mythology, but in the oral traditions of numerology it is a part of Egyptian mythology as well.

To protect these treasures and the mummy itself, the tombs were well hidden in the dangerous shifting sands of the Valley of the Kings in the desert, so completely cloaked in secrecy that we still don't know how to find them all! Many have been unearthed over time, but many more remain exquisitely hidden.

The Pharaoh and His Eternal Journey

The pharaoh's journey over the Styx was a very sensitive and difficult passage, and everything had to be done just right in order for it to be made. So important was this journey, it is not an exaggeration to say that a substantial portion of the ruler's life was devoted to its preparations. The Egyptians believed that each person had arrived to this life from the other world, and that the return to the other side, or the afterlife, needed to be carefully attended to.

Think of it this way. When you plan a trip, you always book a return flight. And while you are away, you are already thinking about the flight back home and making preparations. As the time to depart gets closer, you prepare your luggage, gathering up everything you have acquired on your trip so you can take it back with you. You worry about missing your flight, and you generally arrive at the airport with plenty of spare time.

This is just a small, everyday glimpse of life and behavior that mirrors the pharaoh's ever-present awareness of the journey back to the discarnate realm. The journey over the River Styx created the need for intelligent preparation with a lot of help from trained experts—spiritual travel agents, the priests.

ALERT

The magi had now become the priests of Egypt who guided the rulers in making all their decisions, and, to a lesser degree, who also guided the common people. Alongside the priests, the architects created great architectural creations for the rulers, as well as public and private buildings for the common people.

From the moment of the pharaoh's birth, the priests and priestesses advised him in matters of dress, adornments, education, and even in his choice of wives, in order to keep him in harmony with the astrological birth coordinates. Life would be filled with good decisions—a life well lived—so the return flight would go without a hitch. This was the greatest, richest, most valuable possession of the pharaoh's existence: a life well lived, thus ensuring a journey completed successfully.

Architects and Priests Join Forces

All the preparations for the afterlife were coordinated by a head priest, who worked with the mathematician (as architect) and the numerologist (as mystic priest), who joined forces with priest astrologers. These four extremely adept experts in their fields of endeavor guided the pharaoh's life and death journey. In addition, they were responsible for giving advice and guidance that influenced the daily life and decisions made by the Egyptians.

The Caste System

Remember how the pyramids have all those levels? One builds upon the next until one arrives at the top—a pinnacle—supported by each previous layer. The Egyptian civilization was a very stratified and rigid culture, just like a pyramid. Each layer of the pyramid represented a class of people, and where you were born was where you stayed. The slaves were represented by the huge bottom layer of the pyramid. The ruler, or the pharaoh, was represented by the top, or pinnacle, rock. Since the society had a very closed class system, there was hardly ever any chance of changing one's circumstance in life.

SSENTIALS

There was a great distance between the pharaoh and the Egyptian public. Just as the peak of the pyramid has no direct relationship to almost all the other levels below it, except to be supported by them, so the rulers had no contact with the people directly except to be supported by them and their work. The secrecy surrounding the rulers was great, but the secrecy surrounding their death and passage was phenomenal!

Where you were born was where you stayed. Accountants birthed more accountants. Rulers birthed rulers. Priests and priestesses were a closed society. Each layer of the pyramid represented a group of the culture.

An Unlikely Benefit

Of course, the strict social system meant that there was no personal freedom to change one's life and to move up in the world. However, the sense of absolute, uncompromised, and complete adherence to one's place provided a great opportunity to become very skilled at the family profession.

In the artisan families, children grew up living and breathing art, so when their time came to create art they exceeded the parents' abilities. Farmers got better at farming. Accountants become more skilled with math. Architecture improved with every generation. Slaves stayed slaves. The best they could hope for was finding ways to be a better and therefore more valued slave and passing those skills on to their children.

The same improvements were realized in the ranks of priests and priestesses. Members of this class studied numerology and astrology, in which they developed tremendous skills and knowledge. Again, the pervasive social stability allowed (or imposed upon the people) the learning and passing on of the skill and knowledge. Certainly, the priests were on a more comfortable level of the social pyramid than the poor guys in the lower levels. But they were still bound by the same limitations of birth.

Despite personal limitations, the caste system allowed the development of an extremely high level of quality and excellence throughout the Egyptian culture. As it became more developed and complex, this type of cultural class system produced increasingly high levels of excellence in all areas of cultural pursuit. So the magi, the mystical number practitioners, together with the architects, the physical number masters, got better and better too.

Constructing the Pharaoh's Tomb

The architects were valued for their ability to create magnificent buildings, but the magi/priests were valued more, for they were responsible for the spiritual task of setting the coordinates for the pharaoh's return trip across the River Styx. Let's say that the priests were supervising construction of a temple in honor of a great pharaoh or to become his final resting place. The first consideration would be the astrological aspects of the pharaoh's birth. The astrological progression of the celestial bodies, as compared to the celestial placement at the time of birth, determined the direction the temple would face. The priests would also determine the location of the building based on the movement of the heavenly bodies and their magnetic effect on the structure, as well as on the geological aspects of the space.

Next, the mystical interior designers, the numerologists, would get busy working with the rooms inside the building. They considered the right room locations, sizes, and orientations for the entries, halls, and the inner rooms. For instance, they examined the height, width, and depth of each room, and the relationship each room had to every other was considered in minute detail. Particularly, the numerologists worked with the interior design and placement.

These rooms were priceless gems of placement. Energetically, and sometimes physically, they were constructed as a space within a space within a space. The spaces moved toward the center, with sacred space held within them, a bit like nesting dolls. One within the other, the purest energies were distilled in perfect harmony with the person for whom the space was being created. Not only would the sacred energies intensify from the numerological coordinates, they would also purify.

FACTS

These rooms were valued more than gold, more than gems, and more than temporal human power. These were the rooms in which one could converse with the wise forces of the universe, the masterfully created golden death rooms of the pharaohs. These rooms were always hidden. Their creators kept them a complete secret from everyone except for the few involved in creating the space.

All of these chambers, halls, and rooms were designed toward one eventual goal—empowering the golden room with such powerful and clear coordinates that the ruler's journey would have ultimate success and his power and respect would be undiminished by the rigors of the journey.

It is interesting that the Egyptians weren't in any huge hurry to complete these tombs and temples. Even if the pharaoh died before the completion of his burial place, the construction schedule did not change. The Egyptians really took the time to build the temple or sacred burial cave so that it would be done right. No expense was spared. Nothing was rushed or sacrificed to speed. Step by step the golden room was given its rightful place.

A Dangerous Honor

To have the honor of being involved with the creation, placement, and sealing of the death room was a mixed bag. The work itself, a contribution to the creation of the golden death room, fulfilled one's highest purpose, a great service to the pharaoh, who was to be obeyed completely. The task of computing and coordinating the numerology to preserve the absolute secrecy of the pharaoh's pure vibrational room carried great importance. However, precisely because of the importance and the great secrecy connected to this task, all those who worked on it were killed upon the completion of the project.

Upon the Pharaoh's Death

When the pharaoh died and was buried in the tomb as a mummy, his astrologer, numerologist, slaves, artists, and even his wives were all put to death along with him. And once the passage over the River Styx had been launched, *no one* was allowed to influence this journey—each burial chamber was to be "hidden for all time."

SSENTIALS

The only exception to this rule of death was the architect, who would have both hands removed so he could never repeat the design. It was then arranged that he too would have a far shorter life. Such was the tremendous emphasis on the spiritually driven need for secrecy in the death room.

To have another person find and enter the tomb room—whether that person was malicious in intent or just a bungling do-gooder—could cause chaos and confusion in this highly specific energetic state that compromised the larger spiritual plan and way of death.

For this reason, these temples, often hidden in desert caves, were never meant to be open or accessible for the public to view. It was not like our modern conception of the tomb of a beloved leader that is visited by thousands daily. It was designed to be absolutely secret forever!

The Importance of Numbers

Numbers are alive. They can remain in place, in which case they show how to develop a reality that is obvious and agreed upon by many. Or they can be shifted to create an outcome that is guided by the mystic numerologist to produce a change in perceived reality.

By shifting the coordinates of numerology, distortions of time and space would occur, creating a reality that contains secret pockets of illusion. A sacred space could be hidden in the illusion, where no ordinary person would be able to see what was really there. In the case of the secret burial caves in the desert, the numerologist would be expected to guide the workers to an area where, through careful measuring of the geography and by graphing the coordinates with the stars, two goals would be assured. The space would remain hidden forever, and, more importantly, the passage to the afterlife would begin with the correct coordinates.

The fact that the tomb was piled with things of great value gives a false sense of the priorities of the ancient riches of the ancient rulers. Sure they had gold and other treasures, but their most treasured possession, the one they entrusted to the mystic/numerologist, was the ultimate goal of their entire lives—a safe journey of the soul over the Styx. During this journey, the physical resting place remained undisturbed, allowing safe movement from the death room to the discarnate world without losing any of the accumulated powers or significance gained during the course of life.

CHAPTER 4

The History of Numerology Continues

Although the civilization of ancient Egypt gradually waned, other cultures picked up numerology as part of their spiritual quest. In particular, numerology flourished among the Celts. It also saw an interesting rebirth at the hands of Pythagoras, a Greek scholar and magi who set numerology on a new path toward greatness.

The Celts' Secret Language of Numbers

Brittany and the British Isles were the birthing grounds for a faith ripe with Earth, ritual, astrology, magic, and numerology—very different from Egypt's rigid, systematized, philosophical moorings. Filled with woods, hills, green plants, and flowers, Britain was a place where animal life flourished and the beauty of nature served as spiritual inspiration. This was the world of the Celts, the next flowering place of numerology.

The Celts passed down the tradition of numerology from master to student, through a lineage held in utmost secrecy. The elderly numerologist, or astrologer, was a welcomed and treasured member of the Celtic culture, and many young men sought his instruction. After rigorous testing to prove one's ability to stay focused, to endure, and to have firm desire, the chosen one would begin his training in the language of numbers and symbols. As the student learned, he developed the ability to understand the language of the symbols and to make energetic equations with the numbers. This must have required intense long-term commitment, and it is really no wonder that these wizards are always depicted as old men.

ESSENTIALS

These wonders of energetic skill traveled throughout the known world. Each ancient culture has its oral traditions, woodcuts, or written symbols remarking on their presence, from China to India to the British Isles, and their presence was felt in each place. They had their day in the sun, and then they were felled by what has become eventual inevitable persecution. Only China has retained a long-term history of embracing the science of energy.

The Winter Solstice

There is a place that shows today the same amazing potential that can be achieved by the combination of energy and physical architecture. Of course, this place is Stonehenge. A fine example of the art of placement as defined by astrology and numerology, it still stands, engaging the alignment of celestial bodies, most especially at winter solstice, each year.

As the solstice starts, the streams of light from the sun enter the temple structure in their assigned place, recreating their previously understood effect. The astrologers and numerologists of those days are gone, but the structure that reconstructs their beliefs remains.

The Advent of the Winter Solstice

The winter solstice was the day of celebration, for it marked the Earth's birthday. According to the Celtic faith, each person's birthday was embraced as an embarking point for a new cycle of personal learning. On winter solstice, the Earth, as a living female planet, was embarking on her new cycle of learning as well. It was the most auspicious of times to harmonize one's personal process with the larger process of the Earth and coordinate it to all the universe. It was a day of ritual, celebration, wearing the finest clothes, feasting, and rejoicing in the wonder of life and love.

FACTS

The ritual of winter solstice, which started when the first rays streamed through the Stonehenge pillars, was designed to clear and cleanse from the soul the shadows of trials of the previous year. The energetically engaging ritual facilitated preparation for a new year. There was a deep desire to embrace with a receptive heart the new learning the coming year would bring.

Ritual Was the Tool for Energetic Clearing

The winter solstice ritual was done in profound reverence and gratitude for the Earth, the universe, and our place in it all. This was not ritual as we generally know it today—a series of meaningful steps repeated as touchstones, or memory markers whose purpose is to enrich and anchor our personal lives. No. Each element had its pure energetic contribution, given a place of predetermined mystical placement to enhance its quality of contribution.

Elements, goblets, and musical tones didn't represent something else in a metaphoric way. The elements of ritual *were* the language of the ritual. Where the people stood, the colors of their clothes, the movement of their dance, the music, aromas, and smoke were part of the energy of the ritual. Each one was used with skill, intent, and knowledge of the energetic properties it would bring to the solstice.

Ritual was not used to remember or reassure. It was divined to enhance energetic alignment and liveliness between the people, the Earth, and the universe. Placement and correct astrological timing energetically coordinated each element and each person for an event of majesty, simplicity, and great spiritual enhancement.

Rituals of Today

We still have wonderful rituals that carry with them a strong feeling of magic that enfolds the event. Marriages, christenings, funerals, celebrations of victory, and sharing the grief of loss are just a few. In the past, people called upon the numerologist to coordinate the numbers of the bride, groom, place, day, time, and year. Through this coordination, the numerologist's goal was to create a placement in time that would bring the best possible life situations, viewpoints on those situations, and harmonious resolution to the embarking couple. This is one way numerologists still serve the people in this day and age.

Designing the Ritual Space

The ritual space was created by the architect, the astrologer, and the numerologist. The astrologer would choose the location of the ritual based on celestial movements. The architect would make the physical adjustments to the exterior required to increase the beauty of the setting; for instance, he might place the perimeter stones of the assigned space as directed.

The astrologer would orient the place for the entry and exit points. The numerologist would place all the elements required for the worship within the wooded temple, pointed out exactly from where the elements of earth should be taken, and finally, set the living equation of numbers to create an energetic environment, or an energetic architectural unit inside of which an environment of masterful spiritual attunement could be experienced by all participants.

In this faith that sought to know and live the balance of earthly and universal energies, the numerologist priest provided the energetic unit in which all the other tools that were incorporated into the ritual became more effective in their energetic action and interaction.

ESSENTIALS

Sometimes the architect would also help choose the location so that it was sure to meet the architectural requirements for worshipping. The woods of the British Isles were vast and filled with nature spirits. These beautiful natural spaces, crafted by our greatest architect of all, Earth, were then chosen with great care.

Today, ancient numerology is most commonly seen in the art of placement. Some call it magi numerology, while others see it as energy placement. In the case of the Celtic numerologist, the actions and purpose are the same—altering energies to create a unification that changes outcome, a miraculously changed harmony, and beauty in the world.

The Role of Men and Women

In the ritual experiences of the Celtic times, both priests and priestesses created and conducted the rituals. Earth was seen as a female planet. Women provided the connection to the Earth and her wisdom, while men were seen as guides to the ways of the universe. Men and women worked together to retain the harmony with each other as they each learned their own particular life lessons.

The numerologist and astrologer were of profound importance in clarifying and guiding these understandings as they helped to establish times of smooth passage from one human experience or role to another, from boyhood to adolescence, from single to married life, and so on. They also offered guidance and counseling, helping people resolve the questions and dilemmas of creative interaction with life events.

This metaphysical one-to-one counseling was done with the rulers, as in the case of King Arthur and Merlin, but it was also done with the common people as well. In this way, the secret skills of numerology and astrology began, thankfully, to become more of a mainstream element in the Celtic world.

The Numerologist's Unique Function

It was this interaction with daily life in more mundane ways that afforded a different approach to the skill of numerology. With their understandings of living number coordinates and energy systems, numerologists created places of worship, meditation, and self-reflection that were able to transport the practitioners to higher and higher levels of self-understanding. The principles were the same as those applied in ancient Egypt—creation of architectural space within a space within a space, with each new interior reaching higher levels of energetic intensity. These highly refined energetic units were coupled with the energies of Earth and a system of faith that combined universal guidance with Earth's wisdom abounded.

FACTS

This Celtic faith took the guidance of the universe as it had been gained from astrologers and from the energetic systems constructed by the numerologists. These were then balanced into the nature of Earth for the benefit of both. The faith did not suppress the Earth's nature—instead, it learned from nature the ways necessary to conduct life in such a way as to stay in harmony with nature.

Numerologists, all trained in the utmost secrecy, helped to create an energetic environment where people could elevate their understanding of their personal potential and how to best direct the ongoing harmony between Earth's forces and universal directives.

Fabulous and Threatening Skills

Numerologists/magi were skilled in a variety of powers and magical abilities we now designate to the world of fanciful lore, including these:

- Distortions in expected reality. This power is often portrayed in movies, as when the air shimmers and an opening to another reality or a spirit emerges.
- Temporary defiance of physical laws, such as gravity. This was when sticks would fly through the air. Huge rocks were moved quite effortlessly. A person could walk above the ground or on water.
- Seeing the past, the present, and the future. These powers might include divination, clairvoyance, seeing into the past, and so forth.
- Enhancing the energetic balance and harmony of life. This set of skills, which might have included energy healing, slowing down the aging process, and making wise decisions that reduced the unhappy stress and strains of life, diminished the wear and tear of life on people, buildings, and nature.
- The art of placement, which created environments of grace, inspiration, and healing.

It's almost certain that this list should be much longer, but we have lost so much knowledge of the skills of these finely trained men. We can only know the whole picture by learning more today about what numerology can create.

The Decline of the Celtic Civilization

Unfortunately, the Celtic civilization faced great peril at the hands of the Roman army. The Romans had a firm grip on numbers, which they used in the art of warfare. It's ironic that without the survival demands of war and warring, humanity may never have developed such a complex and vast system of number management, which became the science of logistics.

The Romans took on a huge task with the science of logistics. The calculation of distance to be traveled to the country slated for conquering, combined with the number of warriors making the journey and the length of time it would take, was huge. Now let's factor in how many oxen, wagons, horses, stirrups, leather straps, horseshoes, baskets . . . even if we stop there, we can see that the list must have been enormous. Everything needed to be reduced to a system of numbers. The numbers needed then to be compiled, compared, and finally, put into action.

When the Romans lost a battle or when they finally lost the war, it was as a result of mistakes in their mathematical formulas. Food ran out, swords ran short, the tour ran too long, men got weak and sick, or the numbers of the enemy were miscalculated. The list goes on and on.

The Romans built statues to gods and goddesses to help them out with their various concerns, but more often than not it was accurate number calculation that helped out the gods and goddesses. A successful battle may have created a banquet celebrating the god of war, but it was the little guy in the back of the tent adding up his figures who really made it all happen.

After the Roman Conquest

When the Romans conquered Britain, a serious suppression of the holistic arts started. The exception was in Ireland; the Irish had such a highly cohesive and structured social system that even the invincible Roman army knew they could never conquer them, so they left them alone.

FACTS

The faith of the Celts lives on to some degree in Ireland. Elves and fairies are a regular part of life. Women are born with *faigh,* or the ability to see earthly events psychically. There is great cultural unity around the love, beauty, and faith that nature inspires.

Despite the greater safety provided in Ireland, the more dramatic works of astrology and numerology still faded away. An enclave of men and women continued to pass along what they knew, but the safe, accepting, and open environment had changed dramatically. The magic arts could not be learned and controlled as easily as a sword. Certainly, the sensitive arts of magic and numerology were too subtle to be interesting to or even learnable by the battle-hardened, brutish Roman troops. So the forces of power and authority shifted.

Numerologists could adjust the energies between the incarnate and discarnate world. They could slow down and speed up the relationship to time. They could alter the perceived outcome of events. They could create what we would call magic in being able to adjust realities. They were the priests and priestesses in charge of teaching and showing the spiritual truths of life. But against the overwhelming brutality of Roman swords, they could not protect the population and their faith from suppression.

As the old Celtic ways became practiced by fewer and fewer people, the arts were passed from teacher to student, from father to son, from son to grandmother, from grandmother to daughter as best they were able. Tarot cards and playing cards again became a form of passing on the language of the symbols—circles, triangles, cones, lines, clubs, spades, diamonds, hearts, and so on, together with their meanings, many of which we are now trying to retrieve. These tools became the vehicle for focusing one's intent and coordinating one's own energies, with the goal of shifting perception to see the past, the present, and the future.

The Lost History

Although much has been lost in written, recorded skills, in many cases the oral reports and teachings have been preserved. But the oral history has fallen into the category of lore, of not-to-be-believed magic, with very little concrete knowledge of how these energy conditions were created. In today's mathematical, scientific world, the oral heritage no longer seems real, and it does not get the credit it deserves. As we uncover what has been lost through our in-depth exploration of the vast potential of numbers, present-day and future numerologists will continue to reconstruct what has been lost and also to move forward into uncharted living formulas. At that time, numerology will take its place with mathematics as the co-language of the universe. Mathematics speaks of the physical universal laws. Numerology speaks of the metaphysical, mystical universal laws.

Thanks to the Gypsies

After millennia of suppression and violence in Europe, is it any surprise that the ways of energy wisdom went underground across the European continent? Luckily, there was a connecting bridge between those times of old, when this wisdom of numerology was woven into the fabric of everyday life, and today, when math rules and we see signs of numerology slowly returning. Only a private, protected, and secretive group of people could provide safety for the information and for themselves. This would have to be a group that was not powerful politically but that could use the wisdom constructively, a group that was nomadic and could keep out of harm's way. This group is known to us as the Gypsies.

FACTS

We still have the wisdom of the old ways, thanks to the Gypsies. Emerging originally from India's mystical culture, the Gypsies became the students of all the various skills that emerge from combining energies to create and alter outcome, especially in areas like astrology and crystal-ball gazing.

Keepers of the Magic

The Gypsies excelled in the world of magic, which they honed and used to serve as a tool for personal growth. They took the tools of the magi's trade out of suppression, slipped quietly past the military, and began to do sessions with locals as they passed through the area; they practiced healing, divination, astrology, and numerology. As their skills grew, they became known; eventually, specific identifications, such as "the fortune-telling Gypsy," were formed among the people.

Over time, the Gypsies have suffered for their use of these skills. But they did produce a stable heritage of knowledge that has been passed down through their fascinating lineage. Anyone who now picks up a book to study numerology owes a nod of thanks to these mystical European nomads and their durable, loyal commitment to energetic skills and the mystical metaphysical arts.

Pythagoras, the Conceptual Father

Pythagoras is the member of the lineage of numerologists whose memory, story, and inspiration has survived over time. He is an example of a man who knew both of the sides of numbers—math and numerology. During the span of his adult years, Pythagoras produced an environment in which his enlightening knowledge could be taught, recorded, and passed on.

Stories about Pythagoras vary somewhat, but here is what you need to know about this man. Pythagoras' parents lived on the island of Samos at the time when Delphi was an oracle for all of Greece. When they visited Delphi, the Oracle told them that the mother was pregnant with a boy, and that this child of theirs would grow into a man whose work would be useful to all of mankind throughout all of time. The oracle further advised them to take a leave from the island of Samos and instead go to Phoenicia, where the child would be born.

Samos was in a state of political confusion at the time, and the Oracle wanted the child to be born in a place like Phoenicia, which was filled with the culture, arts, and harmony. The parents followed the Oracle's will, and Pythagoras was born in Phoenicia.

When Pythagoras was one year of age, his parents took him to be blessed by the high priest who resided in Lebanon. Upon their return, the family resumed their life in Samos.

A Time of Learning

Pythagoras was said to be a lovely child, with a natural talent for unearthing wisdom from the events of life. His parents, committed to educating him to his greatest capacities, hired private tutors and sent him to the best schools. By the end of his teen years, it was clear he would need to leave Greece and seek further knowledge in foreign lands. His teachers recommended that he should travel to Egypt, for it was in Egypt that the astrologers' and numerologists' teachings flourished in the mystery schools.

Egypt was, as we have seen, a culture committed to keeping valuable information secret. When Pythagoras arrived, he was not greeted with great welcome. Instead, he had to pass many tests of endurance and disciplines of mind and emotion to prove his mettle and talents. After he succeeded in meeting all the challenges set before him, Pythagoras was finally admitted into the study of the mysteries, a school otherwise available only to Egyptians born to that role. He was a natural and studied in the Egyptian schools for about twenty years.

A Well-Trained Practitioner

When Egypt was captured by Babylon, the Egyptian priests were sent to Babylon, and Pythagoras went with them. In this odd twist, the exile actually allowed him to enhance his studies by learning from the Chaldean priests.

As a result of working with and learning from priests, magi, and rabbis of great belief and skill, Pythagoras learned from many different voices of faith. He found that each philosophy was based on basic truths adapted to different social conditions and locations.

Pythagoras' training brought him to a deep understanding and acceptance that all of creation is harmony and that numbers are the language that teaches how to relate these harmonies into their potential rhythm with one another. Pythagoras also learned techniques of altering awareness. In these states of meditative connection, he observed many realities moving through time and space in a marvelous spacious harmony and rhythm. Tapping into what he had learned and adding to it his own brilliance, he constructed a method of teaching the science of numbers we now know as numerology. This was during a twelve-year period, after which he gained freedom to depart from Persia.

Pythagoras Begins Teaching

When Pythagoras finally returned to Samos, he found the island in chaos of war. Because of this, he departed again, this time taking his mother with him—presumably, his father was deceased. His first dedicated task for humanity was to return to the Delphi temple and restore it from the ruins of greed and bribery to its earlier glory, acclaimed as a source for truth and prophetic wisdom.

Deeply committed to teaching what he had learned to eager and talented learners, he sought a safe environment in which to establish the school of his dreams. Certain that to do so in Greece would create time-consuming and perhaps life-threatening controversy, he traveled to Crotone, on Italy's southern coast. In this peaceful and sunny environment he founded and directed his school.

Ready to Really Teach

By this time, Pythagoras was in his late fifties, and he was ready to teach his deeply held beliefs in care for the spirit, soul, and body. His school taught a wide and vital range of subjects, including philosophy; moral and social forms; music and art; hygiene and nutrition; energy medicine and herbs; leadership skills and duties; the spiritual need for assuming responsibilities in life; and self-perfection as spirit and soul embodied. Pythagoras longed to provide an enlightened format, and he succeeded in training people for a culture where science, education, and all areas of social and economic development would be applied with practical physical and metaphysical wisdom to enhance the physical, emotional, mental, and spiritual development of each citizen.

Pythagoras taught, as all magi always have, that God is within and that the task of a life well lived is to continually seek self-awareness. Self-awareness comes both through education and through the acceptance of responsibility in directing one's life to attain a higher and higher quality as a great human being.

Running Afoul of the Establishment

As Pythagoras' power increased and the love of the people for him and his ideas grew, it scared those folks who were in inherited or snatched positions of power. He promoted the idea that societies should be governed by mystical sages and scientists; meanwhile, the forces in power, who had none of these talents, plotted against him. Crotone was able to give him thirty years in which to teach before the tides of abuse of power turned against him. Everything was burned. The books, the charts, the philosophy, the hopes and dreams . . . even the students and Pythagoras himself.

His Wise Teachings Prevail

Pythagoras organized the sciences of numerology, mathematics, astrology, and astronomy. He created the word "philosophy" and gave it its meaning. He blessed vegetarianism, nutrition, and personal hygiene. Equality between men and women and among people of all races, social reform, informed biology, and eugenics were cornerstones of his school and hoped-for culture. He taught physical knowledge and metaphysical wisdom as equals. Honored over time, he is referred to as one of the most truly learned men of history. The Oracle was right.

Although Pythagoras and his school were consumed in the fire, his ideas lived on through the students who survived. They adhered to Pythagoras' teachings and applied them in their daily lives. It is through these students and their written records of numbers that numerology was recorded, passed on, and eventually appeared in the mainstream.

Pythagoras had some basic themes that seem to emanate from his teaching. These can, of course, be understood through the outline of his beloved numbers:

1. Seek singularly ideas with curiosity.
2. Hook up with these ideas.
3. Learn to use ideas to live the life you choose.
4. Be willing to plan and structure in order to achieve.
5. Always stay alive to excitement.

6. Love is the force of family and friends.
7. Seek to live according to your own personal standards.
8. Personal success, achieved in a good way, brings a better life to all.
9. Devote oneself to service.
10. A life well lived includes compassion and equality for all.

It was always through the wisdom of his numbers that the beloved teacher Pythagoras expressed his deepest and most heartfelt beliefs.

Pythagoras didn't hide the sciences behind closed doors in order to make them available to only a few. Nor did he limit his knowledge and wisdom to verbal sharing. He opened up the long-held, wise secrets to anyone who was accepted to his school and the culture that grew up around it. From this point, it became easier—though not less risky—to share the ideas and practice of numerology.

CHAPTER 5

Seeing Beyond the Numbers

The numeral values of numerology have been noticed throughout time by many talented people. What they noticed and how they developed systems to teach their observations is everyday numerology. But there is greater potential here for you. Instead of just reading and copying a system, how about understanding the bottom line of how the system was defined? Which came first—the system or the numerals?

Learning How to Be Your Own Magi

Now that you know the history behind numerology, you can go on to master the tools you will need to be a numerologist or magi in your own life. By understanding numbers as representatives or individual conduits of the flows of vital, lively energy, you will be able, like the magicians of old, to create the art of placement in your own personal inner world. You will be able to predetermine outcome, and as a result, you will become luckier, happier, healthier, sexier, and more spiritually developed.

You will learn how the numbers are combining within you, right now, as you read these words, in this moment. You can identify with numbers, these flows of liveliness, as they blend and unify within you. Your thoughts, perceptions, and actions are the unit—you yourself—that these lively interactive flows create. By coming to understand the unit, or pattern, and how it animates you, you can begin to understand how to strengthen weaker areas of your flow energies and reduce excessive energy, thus creating balance and harmony within. That is the first and often the only step needed to find and then relate to balance and harmony in life.

QUESTIONS?

Is it harder to learn math or numerology?
To learn the basics of math *and* numerology is easy; to really learn these sciences in depth gets harder as the level of needed skill increases. Furthermore, both math and numerology contain power: Math has the powers of technology; numerology has the power of generating energy to create a predetermined outcome.

As you continue to read on, you will get your own tools. You will be able to follow steps to see your life through the eyes of a numerologist. You will understand how to shift your reality to change your outcome, for numerology is personal growth.

You're the Magi

You come home from a *very* busy day. You have a headache and your mind is racing toward a flat-line state. You want one thing—to sit down, or better yet, to lie down. "Don't speak to me, I'm just lying here breathing, and that's the most I can handle right now." However, you have two kids and their associated needs—homework and bedtimes—ahead of you. You think of the numbers.

You take a look at the "Numbers Are Personalities" chart and confirm that 6 is the numerological equivalent of home and hearth. You think of 6. You draw it in the air, you doodle it. You take 6 breaths. You tap your leg 6 times. You gnash your teeth 6 times. You shrug your shoulders 6 times and stamp your feet 6 times. And finally, you say "Six" 6 times.

Numbers Are Personalities			
1	singular	6	home and hearth
2	relationship	7	the intellectual seeker
3	balanced fun-lover	8	expect success
4	the solid one, structure	9	humanitarian
5	the doer	10	all-seeing whole 1

What you have done is shifted the effect of the vibration we identify as 6, which expresses home and hearth and harmony. You have strengthened it, raised it closer to your emotional responses and physical actions, and created an environment where you have rearranged the numbers or aspects of vitality to create an outcome of your choice. Amazingly, you will feel more in harmony with the demands of your home. The kids now seem more precious, the dog so dear. The energy flow of 6 has shared with you a bit more liveliness with which to engage with your home. You will have less irritation, more gratitude, and an increase in soul-satisfying receptivity.

The Magi Approach Is Unique

The numbers are like friends that can assist you, different friends in different ways. It's like putting on a color that is flattering one day, but on the next day you need another color vibration to balance you. Think of numbers like this, and change your life!

Does it sound odd? Try it. Numbers are alive. They carry their presence, their personalities, their unique aspect of life, within them. We need only to think of them, or of one in particular, to engage numerology and create an altered mix of the energy flows that are us.

Numbers Bring Us the Vibrational Opportunity

Numerologists, ancient and modern, see time as a huge energetic vortex flowing from the universe throughout the Earth, spiraling counterclockwise. This is the flow of light or color, the yin and yang, aura, qui, chi, bio-energy, sparkles, or whatever other term you might use to describe it. In numerology, this energy is time, and the movement of time is, of course, made up of energetic flows creating a unit. We are fed, connected, and nourished energetically by this universal flow, which is identified through *numbers*.

Number vibrations are brought into the physical through sound, and sound is the first step in manifestation. That is, numbers are vibrations that create the world for us all. Vibration is communication.

We are all made up of skin, bones, chemicals, and spirit (or soul, or universal personality). Spirit is vibration. Vibration is the essence of spirit. Numbers are the expression or identification of vibration. They *are* vibration. Numbers are the language of the universe. It is for this reason Pythagoras said, "Everything is disposed according to the numbers."

Thought and sound generate the movement or action in our physical life, for all action is born in thought. In turn, thought is affected 100 percent by energetic vibration. Because numbers are vibration, it follows that we can alter our vibration through our knowledge of numbers and their individual essence.

Vibration carries on the rays of light the messages and information from the universe on what potential is available for us to create today. Each day is different from any other. The types of opportunities to engage in each day vary according to the information coming in an energetic vibration or light from the universe. One day might bring extra challenges; another day will flow more harmoniously than usual. These interactions between us and our surrounding life, and how we choose to engage these life experiences, show us synchronicity in the most intimate way.

SSENTIALS

Synchronicity is the signature of the gods—as when the parking place opens up when you need it, the question comes when you know the answer, or the opportunity opens when you are ready to step into it. Synchronicity is what all great spiritual teachers show their students—how to live one's life in harmony with the whole, within time.

The Symbols and Energies of Nature

When life emerged on Earth, the energies were filled with potential for human development. But not much had been created. The energies were a lively void of raw potential. Even though much more has been developed, we still have ongoing universal support for our continued evolution. We activate this potential continually through intent and action.

As you remember, early humans saw symbols in the nature of the Earth and the heavens, and adapted them. From these forms, they eventually derived the pure language of singular numbers. How did it ever happen that these symbols of numbers became both math, a scientific language, and numerology, an energetic language? And how could it ever be that numbers could provide a language of understanding, a pure and consistent tool for thousands of years in hundreds of thousands of lives?

We do know that numbers have been assigned their mathematical values, but what about their numerological values? Have they been assigned too, or are they inherent in the numbers? Was the language of numerology created by the human need to assemble ambiguous systems that we can project our own beliefs onto, or are numbers truly communicators between people and the universe? Is numerology a tool for self-knowledge, a skill that enables relationships to improve, luck to increase, and more efficient spiritual development to occur, or is it hogwash, a tool for self-deceit and escapism, with virtually no true value?

You will find the answers for yourself as you continue to explore the world of numerology. For now, you should progress forward with an open mind and make the following assumption: Hundreds of thousands of people over thousands of years can't be flat-out wrong.

A Symbolic Language

As early humans developed the need to have numbers in their lives, it was natural for them to convert the most common symbols of nature, and the heavens that surrounded them, into the needed symbols. Straight lines, circles, semicircles, and triangles were forms found in life. Derived from them, ancient folks realized, the geometric forms could serve as a numerical language.

Circles. This symbol is a line with no end and no beginning. It can be started anywhere from a point of contact, and it completes itself. The circle is a constant flow line of wholeness and completion, simultaneously flowing and completing. Also, the circle reminds us of the shape of our Earth.

Semicircles. A semicircle is exactly one-half of a complete circle. The one-half that is enclosed gives the symbol form. The other half is openly receiving to the energy of life and experience. This symbol is inspired by the form of the moon as it waxes and wanes and its changing form during eclipses.

Triangles. A triangle is made up of three straight, intersecting lines, replicated in the formation of the moon-Earth-sun triad, constellations, and aspects of nature.

A straight line is not really common in nature. It is a singular oddity in the otherwise rounded world of nature, so its special character marked it as a singular occurrence. A straight line had no center and could extend up and down limitlessly. Actually, to go up and down forever or to have the potential to go either way as limitlessly as one chooses is an apt description of the numerological 1.

These forms were there in nature for all to see, pure forms of communication that needed no further description to clarify the form. Furthermore, they were commonly understood among various cultures; in written form, they were common to all despite language barriers. Simple, consistent, easily replicated, they varied in size, but their meanings remained the same.

Humans needed a form of communication that transcended speech, and they found that using these symbols opened the doors to a new way of communicating that encouraged intuition, inspiration, creativity, ingenuity, and imagination for useful, happier lives. Gradually, as people developed the ability to move from symbols to numbers, each number took on a specific meaning, and numerology was born.

FACTS

Communication between people has always been a challenge, and they have always looked for a form of communication that does not lose its meaning in translation. Simple symbols and numbers provide the needed common ground. A woman in Africa and a man in Alaska will both agree on the form of the symbol they are both seeing, as well as on the numbers, whether they use them mathematically or numerologically.

True Intuition

To interpret symbols and numbers, you need intuition. True intuition is not a guessing process. It is a deep inner conviction that something is right. Although what you intuit may make no logical sense, and you may not be able to prove it with facts and logic, it can nonetheless serve you as a guiding light, especially at the turning points of your life.

In fact, the greatest thinkers are those who have been able to use an exquisite combination of intuition and logic to further their ideas and life. Think of it this way: Just as you need logic to manipulate numbers in math, you need intuition to manipulate numbers in numerology.

Working with the Nine Pure Numbers

The numbers 1 through 9 are considered pure numbers. That's because they each represent a pure quality or, in other words, a characteristic that is pure (not in the sense of being perfect, but unaffected by any other quality). All the other numbers come from a combination of pure numbers. Just as red, blue, and yellow are the primary colors, and all other colors are a combination of the primary ones, so are 1, 2, 3, 4, 5, 6, 7, 8, and 9 the primary numbers, with all other numbers being formed from them.

QUESTIONS?

Why do single numbers stop at 9?
According to ancient numerologists, Earth is school, and its vibe number is 10. Everything on Earth happens in groups of 10, which is a compound number made up of all the numbers that precede it. In fact, many ancient calendars had 10 months, which makes more sense according to numerology.

In numerology, these other numbers are known as compound numbers, which may be converted back into their pure numbers by adding up their digits together. Hence, the number 10, a compound number, may be expressed as 1+0 = 1.

However, the number 10 is different from the other compound numbers; it contains all the qualities of 1 through 9 and becomes all of them. The difference between a 10-derived 1 and a pure 1 is that a pure 1 is like a beautiful tree in your backyard, complete in itself, while a 10-derived 1 is like the backyard. The number 10 expands the singular in 1 as it absorbs all of life's experiences.

In general, each number has three qualities:

• The constructive quality, which is the positive evolving use of the vitality of the number.
• The quality of avoidance, as when one turns toward behaviors that deny true contact from occurring.
• The third quality is when one turns into the destructive (masculine) or the devouring (feminine).

Moreover, with every number there is the following choice of how to interact with the options the energies bring:

• To improve your quality as a person.
• To compromise your quality as a person.
• To wound beyond easy repair your quality as a person.

Yet we still have not yet answered one important, fundamental question. How can numbers be math on one side of the coin and, on the other side, be messengers or carriers of wisdom that bring understanding of our place in the fabric of life on Earth and our place in the universal family?

Flow Line Energies

Math is mental and physical energy; numerology is mental and spiritual energy. When you mentally decide to draw a line, any line, you are also leaving a "flow line"—a line of energy that flows along the shape of the line you are drawing. Therefore, the shape of the flow line is its essence. This flow line is a stream of energy that is drawn from the force of life, infinity, energy, wu chi, the collective, time, love, the source, the void—it is known by so many names because each culture or belief has a different way of calling it.

Flow Lines Are Numerology

As you make a line, its flow pattern is drawn forth through your intent to create the symbol and distinguish it from infinity. As the flow line expresses itself as a symbol, it separates, or flows into distinction from infinity. The flow line expresses its nature through form as it expresses its unique attributes, separate from and yet part of the whole.

ESSENTIALS

In numerology, the energy of the flow line may be called infinity. It is a vast, limitless, spacious energetic force. It is the embodiment of potential, the focus of meditation, prayer, spiritual dance, faith, the arts, great sex, deep trust, and so much more.

It follows, then, that the energetic nature of the flow line of 1 is different from the flow line that creates $2, 3$, and so on. The individual personality expression of each number comes to know itself through the process of its moving out from infinity into its own existence and its own right. In other words, when you are writing a flow pattern, out of necessity it excludes all other options afforded in infinity. By the nature of its exclusion, then, the pattern comes to know itself. Each pattern becomes a singularity in its form and in its content—and then it returns to infinity!

We make a O, and a circular flow line is created with the pen, pencil, or brush mark. As the flow line completes, the circle is the living vitality of completeness. Create another flow line, the flow line 1, and you have followed exactly the same process. Only now what you have created is singular. It has no center, and it reaches up and down.

If you attach the vertical line to the circle, you create a center at that juncture, and, at the same time, you redirect the vertical flow line into the circle. Now the two flow into each other, and what has emerged as a result is a heavenly sphere grounded into Earth, 9. This symbol then becomes the language and expression of the spiritual humanitarian who draws from spiritual awareness and shares it with humanity.

The flow lines relate to the Earth and the universe. "Up" is upward and universal. "Down" is downward, in contact with Earth. The left side is the intake side. The right side is the outflow side. Roundness is feminine, flexible, open—as in a semicircle, or complete, as in a circle. Straight lines are masculine, direct, and focused.

FACTS

"Feminine" and "masculine" flow lines are not designated exclusively for men or women; instead, those terms describe certain aspects. Numbers 1, 4, and 7 are said to be masculine because they carry aspects of focus, action, singularity. Numbers 3 and 6 are said to be feminine because they carry aspects of receptivity, balance, connectedness, and comfort. Numbers 2, 5, 8, and 9 carry both feminine and masculine characteristics.

The Flow Line of ◯

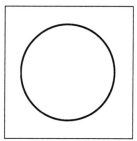

- **Form:** A perfect circle and its own center.
- **Gender:** Feminine.
- **Energetic flow:** Starts at any point in its circumference, finishes precisely at the same point, creating a continuous flow line.
- **Characteristics:** Wholeness, completeness, filled with endless life of the Earth.

The Flow Line of |

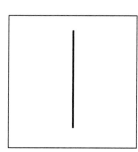

- **Form:** A straight line, no top, no bottom, no center.
- **Gender:** Masculine; describes the mental.
- **Energetic flow:** The flow line goes up and down limitlessly because it has no center.
- **Characteristics:** Singular, contained, seeking, reaching, exploring.

The Flow Line of 2

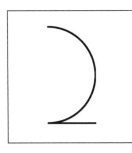

- **Form:** A perfect semicircle in connection at its base with a single horizontal line; its center is where the semicircle and the horizontal line meet.
- **Gender:** Feminine and masculine; intuitive.
- **Energetic flow:** The left side of the flow line gives form and protection to the open, receptive, curved container it forms on its right. The semicircle flow line connects to the strong, grounded, horizontal contact with Earth. Two very different symbols in firm alliance and balance.
- **Characteristics:** Cooperation, understanding, relationship, balance.

The Flow Line of 3

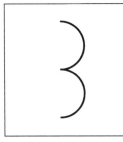

- **Form:** Two connecting semicircles, one above the other; the center is in the middle, where they touch.
- **Gender:** Feminine; emotional.
- **Energetic flow:** Rounding to its left, forming two receptive containers on its right, rocking connection to both the universe and the Earth.
- **Characteristics:** Self-expression, creativity, fun.

The Flow Line of 4

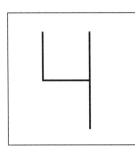

- **Form:** A number made up of four connecting straight lines at right angles to one another; the center is where the square meets the line.
- **Gender:** Masculine; physical.
- **Energetic flow:** Receives from the universe, structures it, and grounds it.
- **Characteristics:** Structure, discipline, reliability, stability.

The Flow Line of 5

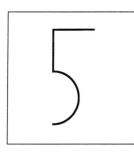

- **Form:** Two straight lines and a semicircle. One straight line reaches into the mental plane, supporting heaven, the other connects the mental and the semicircle, which rounds on its left and forms a container on its right. The center is where the vertical line meets the semicircle.
- **Gender:** Feminine and masculine; physical.
- **Energetic flow:** A reaching for and a focusing of mental energies; drawing direct, focused movement down to connect the rounded, protecting container rocking on Earth.
- **Characteristics:** Curiosity, adventure, shaker-mover.

The Flow Line of 6

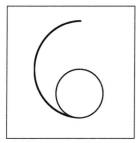

- **Form:** A larger semicircle with a smaller circle curled into it at its base; its center is where the line touches itself.
- **Gender:** Feminine; emotional.
- **Energetic flow:** The flow line curves to the left, containing and securing the smaller circle on its left.
- **Characteristics:** Nurturing, comforting, a number that represents the home and hearth.

The Flow Line of 7

- **Form:** Two straight lines joining on the top at an angle; the upper line is one-half the length of the lower line and horizontal, connecting into the diagonal flow line. The center is where the two lines meet.
- **Gender:** Masculine; intuitive.
- **Energetic flow:** The flow line connects into the mental energies and after taking a sharp turn, runs a downward diagonal course to no apparent end . . . to the devil, if not restrained.
- **Characteristics:** Spiritual, analytical, stillness.

The Flow Line of 8

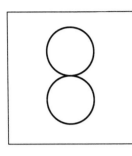

- **Form:** Two complete circles, one on top of the other; the center is in the middle, where they join.
- **Gender:** Feminine and masculine; mental.
- **Energetic flow:** The flow line is two flows moving in two complete circles, joining in a flow of unification (notice that an 8 flipped on its side forms the infinity symbol ∞).
- **Characteristics:** Complete, unified, it represents the giver and receiver, expects success.

The Flow Line of 9

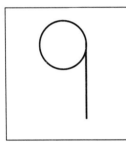

- **Form:** A full circle on top, connected to a line going straight down; the center is where the circle and the line meet.
- **Gender:** Feminine and masculine; a blend of emotional and intuitive.
- **Energetic flow:** A sphere in heaven connects to Earth through a downward-focused flow.
- **Characteristics:** Universal, humanitarian, intuitive.

The Flow Line of 10

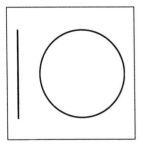

- Ten is a compound number.
- Ten is made up of each of the preceding numbers—1, 2, 3, 4, 5, 6, 7, 8, and 9—and their characteristics.

The Flow Line of ||

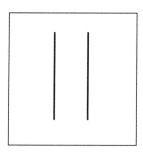

- **Form:** Two single parallel, straight lines; no center.
- **Gender:** None.
- **Energetic flow:** Flow lines are extending up to infinity and down (to the core of the Earth, or to the devil). But because the balance of reaching up and down is maintained, imbalance with the dark doesn't happen like it does with the 7.
- **Characteristics:** Spiritual mastery.

The Flow Line of ⊃⊃

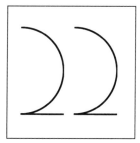

- **Form:** Two semicircles connected to horizontal baselines; the center is where each symbol connects the semicircle to the base and the synergy that is created.
- **Gender:** None.
- **Energetic flow:** Two very different symbols in a perfect reflective match.
- **Characteristics:** Relationship mastery on Earth, where everything is in relationship; spiritual mastery.

In addition to pure numbers, numerology also singles out the compound number 10 and the mastery numbers 11 and 22. The qualities of mastery numbers supercede their compound qualities—that is, they are not added up to a pure number. Instead, they remain double-digit numbers with their own meanings.

Every number is equal. Every number is compatible with every other number. Every number has its own path to all the following qualities: compassion, love, equanimity, unity, and acceptance. Every number is completely distinct and in harmonic balance with the others. This ability to be distinct and remain in symphony with the group is called *syntony*.

The Potentials of Completion

It's fun to follow this path one more step and see what the flow lines would be expressing if the pure symbols were completed, like this:

1	would remain the same flow line—singular, limitless potential in either direction.
2	would become a sphere on a horizontal line—grounded completeness.
3	would become the 8, the power of life found through a light and open heart.
4	becomes a square with a single line connecting to the earth—stability is still the expression and the challenge is to not get closed and rigid like a poorly grounded square.
5	would become a triangle on a circle, a representation of great strength and special gifts—the triune resting on a circle of completion.
6	would become a circle containing a smaller circle—that which is complete, protecting, nurturing.
7	would become an isosceles triangle—perfect strength, perfect form.
8	stays complete.
9	stays complete.

So with the flow lines extended, the possible full personal growth that each symbol represents becomes clearer. The numbers 1, 8, and 9 start complete and work on expressing this completeness in harmony and balance with their life experiences. They're experiencing rest within the structure of the form; much of the experience is spent keeping the flow structure strong, so containment of the pattern is possible.

The others—2, 3, 4, 5, 6, and 7—are evoking more through experimentation in life to discover aspects of completion. With these numbers comes more movement, more seeking from without, an engagement with life on various levels.

Flow Lines Are Guides

Flow lines are indicators, markers, and our guides in life. They existed before we existed, and we harnessed their powers in the numbers we use, both in mathematics and in numerology. Numbers have the power of the flow line energy to help you know yourself—physically, mentally, emotionally, and spiritually.

As we have grown, changed, and evolved as humans, the Universal is always guiding us. As creatures of complete free will, we can develop our potential and in this way expand the self-knowing of the numbers. They guide us, and, in turn, we continue to work on and develop them.

CHAPTER 6

The Relationship Between Letters and Numbers

Numerology has been used for thousands of years, since ancient times, when lives were so different from ours. We need modern tools to help stabilize a modern life, and we also need the practical and modern skills to handle its stresses. Is numerology up to the task?

Bringing Numerology into Your Life

We have filled up a lot of pages here talking about the Egyptian, Celtic, and various other ancient numerologists. It is all well and good to talk about how great everything was back in those creative, life-affirming times. It is easy to extol the virtues of magic and its everyday occurrence, and we find it very natural to love the creation of wonders from the ancient world. But the real issue is more specific and a little bit different. How will numerology help now, right now in your life, and where can you use it? What does numerology have to offer you, today?

Life is filled with many pressures. You have worries and concerns that you might like to put to rest; there might be personal qualities you would like to alter in order to be more comfortable within yourself and in the life you are creating. To do these things, you need to get a handle on the tools of numerology. At this point, you already know something about basic numerology, including its history and symbolism. Now you need to learn the details. Specifically, what you need is information that you can put to use. The relationship between letters and numbers seems like a good place to start.

Where the Alphabet Fits

Each letter of the Latin alphabet (the alphabet we use when reading and writing the English language) has its own numerological value, based on its order. This system is very straightforward: A has the value of 1, B has the value of 2, and so forth, all the way down to Z, which has the value of 26 (which is converted into 8 by adding 2 and 6).

ALERT

Note that 10 becomes 1, but even though it is converted, it does not lose its 10 value. It takes the value of the 10—all the numbers combined—and becomes a special sort of 1. This special value is endowed with a vibratory combination of all the 10 qualities, though now in a singular form. So when 10 changes to 1, there is a vibratory expansion that occurs.

Number Values of the Alphabet			
A	1	N	14 = 5
B	2	O	15 = 6
C	3	P	16 = 7
D	4	Q	17 = 8
E	5	R	18 = 9
F	6	S	19 = 10 = 1
G	7	T	20 = 2
H	8	U	21 = 3
I	9	V	22
J	10 = 1	W	23 = 5
K	11	X	24 = 6
L	12 = 3	Y	25 = 7
M	13 = 4	Z	26 = 8

In this way, letters A through I correspond to the pure numbers 1 through 9, so they are also pure. Their characteristics are identical to its particular number's. For the rest of the alphabet, the corresponding numbers are compound numbers that are converted to their pure roots. In numerology, the art of energy, this conversion process creates a greater complexity within the root number, but it also adds greater variety, a quality we recognize as the basis of humanity.

For instance, if a man's name is Bill (which begins with a B), he will have a firm vibration of 2, which signifies relationship. The more Bs in a name (for instance, if his name were Bob), the more the quality of the pure 2 is carried. Now, let's say your name is Ursula. It begins with a U, a letter that correlates to 21, and you know that 2+1 = 3, so the interpretation might be that you are a relationship-oriented singular person who loves fun, which is the true expression of balance.

Other examples: A G is a 7, which as we have already seen creates the flow pattern of seeking and of stillness. A P is also a 7—its corresponding number is 16, and 1+6 = 7—but in the case of Pamelas and Pauls, the combination of 1 and 6 brings to the 7 a flow line of the G singularity and comfort that are components of the G and 7 seeker.

ESSENTIALS

Each letter becomes a pure root number, but the path they travel to get to the root—the flowing, for instance, made by the 2 and 4 to create the 6—is different. The magi understood this, and used the energy flow lines of various number combinations to redefine the pure number.

The letter X, which is number 24 in the sequence of the alphabet, has the root number 6. The 2 brings an interest in relatedness. The 4 invests X with the power to structure. When these join in flow lines with the 6, you have a person who is stable, enjoys relationships, and is a comfort to be with.

Numerical Values of Letters							
A	1		singular	N	14 = 5		bringer of creation to action
B	2		balancer	O	15 = 6		self-trusting adventurer
C	3		creator	P	16 = 7		a force for creative analysis
D	4		structurer	Q	17 = 8		powerful and autonomous
E	5		person of action	R	18 = 9		struggle with use of power
F	6		comforter	S	19 = 10 = 1		great spiritual vision
G	7		seeker	T	20 = 2		necessity of making a choice
H	8		stable power	U	21 = 3		receptive creativity
I	9		humanitarian	V	22		transformation of mental ideas to physical manifestation
J	10 = 1		justice	W	23 = 5		defined and creative action
K	11		spiritual contributor	X	24 = 6		standing strong and protecting
L	12 = 3		creative force for self and other	Y	25 = 7		decision-maker
M	13 = 4		strong, creative structure	Z	26 = 8		great intuitive power

The Flow Lines of Letters

Flow lines are everywhere. They are created through the incessant interaction between form and space, both of which are necessary for enacting outcome. The letters' flow lines follow exactly the same laws as those of the numbers.

Remember, the first nine letters of the alphabet (from A to I) are pure. The rest of the letters, from J to Z, are compound letters. In them, the flow lines combine to create more and more variety and profusion. Their units of energy are ever-growing, creating life as we know it.

The Flow Line of A

This letter is a well-grounded symbol that stands on two legs. The top half is a pyramid pointing up. The bottom half is a container for the Earth's energy.

A pyramid is the most efficient way to draw universal energy to Earth. The base receives this energy and stabilizes it. The symbol is further grounded by the container made for Earth's energies in the lower half. The center is the horizontal line, which provides further grounding.

The letter A is singular, grounded, and contained. It represents one's own counsel as well as those who are able to get intuitive knowledge and draw it into action.

The Flow Line of B

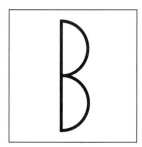

The letter B is made up of two same-sized semicircles that are perfectly balanced. They are connected by a vertical line on the left, which meets precisely with the connection to the semicircles.

The semicircles form two same-sized energy containers. The upper one contains the spiritual and mental type of energy. The lower contains energy of the emotional and physical realms.

The letter B represents balance and inward stability. It is steady, the letter of a builder.

The Flow Line of C

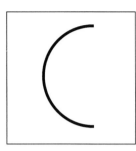

The letter C forms a single line that extends into but does not complete a circle. It curves to its left, and the symbol has a rounded base and top.

It is a protected container, rounded, receptive, one that is mingling energies within. It has a rocking, self-righting relationship to the ground.

This letter is durable, comforting, creative, and resilient.

The Flow Line of D

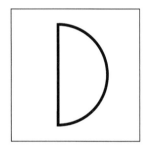

The letter D forms a large semicircle that curves to the right, which is coupled with a vertical line that precisely meets the tips of the semicircle.

Its strong vertical flow line anchoring a semicircle creates a contained energetic space.

This letter finds own gateway by providing the gate for others. It is strong and comforting, structuring and grounding.

The Flow Line of E

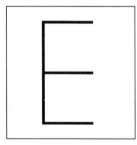

The letter E is made up of four straight lines. Three are horizontal, and each one is half the length of the anchoring vertical straight line. The horizontal lines connect top, center, and bottom, creating two balanced, structured spaces on its right.

The flow line of E is a strong vertical grounding line on its right with three horizontal flow lines that direct the vertical, extending flows to the mental, emotional, and physical. Energies of the mental and emotional commingle in the upper space. The emotional and physical commingle in the lower space.

This letter represents great analytical skill and the ability to understand and structure. It is very stable when engaged with life, comprised in equal parts of the spiritual and mental, emotional and physical.

The Flow Line of F

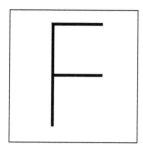

The letter F is formed by three straight lines. One is a strong vertical line between heaven and Earth; the other two are horizontal lines, each one-half the length of the vertical line. One forms a top; the other meets the vertical at the middle. The vertical line forms the base.

The strong vertical flow line on its right draws down the mental energy from the top line and the emotional energy from the middle line. These join and ground on a single spot, where it makes a strong connection to Earth. The energies commingle in the structured upper area.

This letter represents forceful beliefs and rigid or fixed opinions. It relies on mental clarity, but it may need support.

The Flow Line of G

The letter G forms an almost fully contained circle, with a rounded base and a horizontal line that is connected to the lower end of the incomplete circle.

The incomplete circle creates a container on the left, as it curves to the right and ends with a supporting line as a resting place for the energies it contains. The base is kept from the freedom of rocking by the internal platform of support.

This letter is a comforter, receiver, and strong supporter. It will take on burdens and stabilize itself through them.

The Flow Line of H

The letter H is formed by two strong vertical lines extending up and down on either side of a horizontal line, which creates a bridge that is the exact center point of the two vertical lines.

The two points of contact with the heavens flow directly into Earth. They are stabilized by the middle line, and they create two structured openings.

This letter is very strong. It represents those who walk with confidence, stay strong under outside pressure, and have powerful insight.

The Flow Line of I

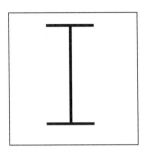

The letter I is formed by a central vertical line, topped and bottomed by two horizontal lines that are each one-third the length of the center line.

The upper horizontal line stabilizes and supports the spiritual energy that is drawn down by the vertical center line. The horizontal lines also reach out to the mental energies both to the right and to the left, drawing the mental in to support the spiritual energies.

This letter is delicate but stable. It represents a private inner world, mental understanding of spiritual wisdom, and a clear adjustment of one's life in order to live what is felt intuitively.

The Flow Line of J

The letter J is formed by an upper horizontal line connecting to a central vertical line, which joins a semicircle on the bottom.

Its flow line extends both ways into the mental while it supports the spiritual. The strong central line flows into a semicircle at the base. This creates a rocking relationship to Earth, with some balance problems.

This letter represents weights and measures, spiritual insight, and looking for the balanced approach. It can be self-absorbed because of balance issues, but generates rebirth when balance occurs.

The Flow Line of K

The letter K is formed by a strong vertical line that reaches up and down as well as by another line that is bent at the midpoint, creating a diagonal line to join the strong vertical.

The flow line of the vertical is directed to heaven and Earth, as is the single diagonal line meeting at midpoint. The internal space created is a V, open to receiving heaven and receiving Earth.

This letter is a self-directed spiritual teacher. It is spiritually uplifting and stable, balanced between heaven and Earth.

The Flow Line of L

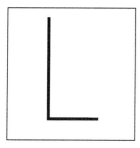

The letter L is formed by a strong vertical line that joins a base horizontal line half its length.

The flow line pulls from the heavens and from the ground, and it directs the flow line out the left side.

This letter is a force to reckon with. It is filled with direct action. Often spiritually motivated, it drives the self as hard as it drives others.

The Flow Line of M

The letter M is made up of two parallel vertical lines joined by two diagonal lines meeting at their midpoint on the ground.

The energy of its flow line comes from its strong relationship to the Earth, which is seen in the bases of its upward-pointing triangles. However, this letter also manifests downward-pointing triangles that harness the energies from heaven.

This letter carries the qualities of very grounded femininity, earthy and nurturing. It is like a wise mother bear—it knows when to give a kiss and when to give a kick.

The Flow Line of N

The letter N is formed by three straight lines of the same length—two single verticals connected by a diagonal that intersects the top of its right vertical and the bottom of its left vertical.

N's flow lines ascend from the Earth to touch the heavens. The flow of the diagonal draws the force of heaven and Earth to touch points. The empty spaces are receptive triangles.

This letter is a seed sower, and it can bring the ability to increase.

The Flow Line of O

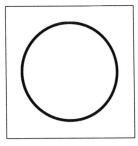

The letter O is a complete circle that can be started at any point. It has neither a beginning nor an end, and it contains within itself a fully enclosed empty space.

This letter represents vast sight. It is visionary and intuitive. It controls deep quiet inner rhythms, and it contains great wisdom.

The Flow Line of P

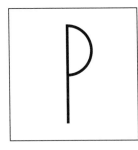

The letter P is formed by a straight vertical line with a semicircle connecting on its right from midline to its upper point.

Its vertical line is supported by Earth. In its semicircle, P contains the space of heavens and emotions.

This letter is gracious and well-meaning. It is a powerful builder and represents spiritual structuring.

The Flow Line of Q

The letter Q is a perfect, complete circle with a root extending below the line.

Its flow line is a circle balanced between heaven and Earth, with a root going down to the energies of the Earth. The Q circle forms a contained space for all the energies to mingle.

This letter is complete and individualistic. It is female in power, and it carries great authority.

The Flow Line of R

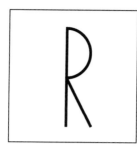

The letter R is formed by a straight vertical line with a semi-circle on its upper left side and a diagonal that intersects where the lower semicircle joins the vertical and then goes straight to Earth.

Its flow line energy feeds on the direct connection from heaven to Earth and its semicircle contains a commingling of mental and spiritual energies. A lower leg of the R represents the energy that runs through the physical.

This letter represents self-acceptance and genuine contact with another. It comes to elevate karma.

The Flow Line of S

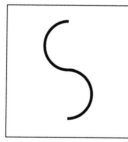

S is formed by two semicircles facing opposite directions—the upper semicircle opens to the right, and the lower semi-circle opens to the left.

The curves of S join heaven and Earth and rise up much like a serpent to the heavens, ambling through the energy fields.

This letter represents mystical and intellectual wisdom, earthly charisma, the movement of life, and serpentine force.

The Flow Line of T

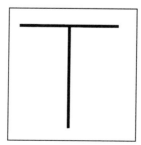

The letter T is formed by a vertical line that begins in Earth and ends at the top, where it is covered by an intersecting horizontal line.

The horizontal line supports the heavenly energies with a mental analysis. Vertical draws this force to the Earth.

This letter is about seeing your options or being caught between two choices. It may be pinioned or surrendering.

The Flow Line of U

The letter U is formed by a single, flowing line that draws the heavens to the Earth.

Its flow line connects the spiritual to Earth with a rounded base, creating a space of great receptivity.

This letter is about receptive strength, warmth, and a promise that heaven knows the way, but Earth gives the tools to progress. In English, Q is always paired with U—great female empowerment.

The Flow Line of V

The letter V is formed by two diagonal lines that meet at the base. Its flow lines create a drawing-down from heaven and a seeding into Earth. V represents an image of arms reaching upward. It transforms ideas into physical reality, and it creates ideas and follows through as a builder. It is a majestic letter.

The Flow Line of W

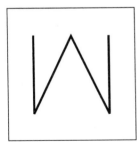

The letter W is formed by four even diagonal lines that create three open-ended triangles. Two of the lines receive the heavens, grounding into two focused points to the Earth. The third, in the middle, provides a center and receives the Earth.

This letter is a blender of ideas, a mediator. It understands heaven's way and Earth's centeredness.

The Flow Line of X

The letter X is made up of two straight lines crossed at the midpoint. Its flow lines cross from right to left on a diagonal flow, receiving from Earth and heaven and centering it at the midpoint.

This letter is all about endurance and the balanced perspective. It is courageous, here to benefit self and others.

The Flow Line of Y

The letter Y is formed by three straight lines intersecting at the midpoint, two on the upper half and one supporting on the lower half.

Its energy flow joins at a midline center, where the upper flow joins into the mingled flow to Earth.

This letter represents the decision-maker. It is balanced and carries the wisdom from the spiritual.

The Flow Line of Z

The letter Z is made up of two horizontal lines connected by a diagonal line that crosses the center area. Its flow lines are well-connected and supportive of heaven and Earth. Its cross line provides additional connection and strong support.

This letter represents prophetic vision, good will, benevolence, and impact. It is intuitive in matters of human affairs.

In numerology, the shaping of each letter is critical. A well-shaped letter will provide the maximum vibration. (The same is true for numbers.) If you have messy handwriting, it might do you good to practice your letters—just like you used to do in grade school.

QUESTIONS?

Are you beginning to get your own understanding of the energies and their creating?
Learn about these energies. Let this concept of life give you a new dimension in your understanding of what it's possible to experience. What the ancient numerologists achieved and conceived is still possible. The tools and skills need to be uncovered again.

CHAPTER 7

In Tune with Numerology and Life

A ncient and current-day numerologists teach that we are here in our lives for the purpose of seeking to know ourselves as we elevate our quality as an individual person within the continual challenges life presents us. But to what end? Will this attitude help us build a happier life? And who determines what is high quality?

You Are Free to Fail

Numerology states that each one of us has free will. We have the complete right to respond as we choose to any situation, and then we have the opportunity to learn from those choices. We get to see if we ended up with the outcome we wanted to create or not. If we didn't get what we wanted, then we can use hindsight to re-evaluate the way we used our power of choice.

Many philosophers as well as numerologists have taught that there is no failure in life. It's all about learning. As Erich Fromm, a psychoanalyst and writer, said, "Man's main task in life is to give birth to himself." When we chastise ourselves for our so-called failures, we are reacting to being measured by the yardstick of our culture.

FACTS

Failure in one culture can mean success in another, depending on any particular society's standards. When we judge ourselves, we often feel overwhelmed by our own shame rather than seeing that, if we feel we have failed, we are not through the learning experience yet. The feeling of failure comes over us when we have not gotten the outcome we were hoping for, and we feel shame at our disappointment.

It's Nothing to Be Ashamed Of

Pure shame is interesting, from a scholarly point of view. It is the feeling we get as children when we respond to the world in innocence only to have the world respond to us in an unexpectedly negative way: with criticism, demeaning remarks, abuse, or humiliation. However, there is something important that you should keep in mind. Shame is really a reminder that we acted originally in pure innocence!

True shame is a sign of an act done in innocence that is poorly received or even received in a way that is mean-spirited. We have hindsight to examine our chosen response at a certain turning point—a point that is now past. There is no point in returning to the past and endlessly criticizing anything—whether it's yourself, others, or life in general—for it is only over time that the actions of that particular moment in the past could have developed into this experience that now disappoints you.

ESSENTIALS — Hindsight is a tool that allows us to objectively evaluate our past choices in certain critical events. Hindsight lets us say, "Okay, what was I trying to create?" "What way of directing the situation did I choose?" "Knowing what I know now, which actions would I have taken?"

However, we can never really know what the outcome would have been if we had done something differently. That is why beating yourself up with hindsight makes no sense.

Take Risks and Experiment!

Numerology teaches that our lives truly are the way we make them by experimenting with the truth and then finding out what truth is. Because cultural values and spiritual values can be quite different, it can take a while—years, or even decades—to get enough perspective on life and events to be able to see your own truths.

We can drive ourselves crazy trying to control our response to certain events and their outcome. There are people all over the world, good people, who have had horrible things happen to them. It helps at those times to recognize that for the people who experience them, the bad times come through no fault of their own. Still, those people are going through a tough time, and it is easy for them or us to lose heart, become discouraged, and feel shame.

People often complain, "If I was only . . . life would be better, and I would be happier, more loving, etc." The fill-in may be "thinner," "more loving," "smarter," or "wiser"—or thousands of other options. People come to believe that these things are keys to happiness. But the key to true, stable happiness is through only one doorway—self-knowledge.

The numbers in numerology bring us choices for responding to life situations. Building constructive action is the best way to get maximum growth or truth from any situation.

In Control of Yourself

We have to admit one simple basic truth in life. We cannot truly control outcomes—and that includes events, other people, and so on. We can only have complete control over our own responses, and we refine our reactions through what we learned from this life event.

Life is difficult—that is another bottom line—and it is very easy to get lost and very far away from your soul's reason for being in this life. Then, the big issue is this: What exactly is it that I am learning here?

If we can't control outcome or events, and we don't have the influence to make people do what we believe is right, then how do we live in acceptance of life as it is? How do we let well enough alone? How do we go placidly amongst the chaos and haste with the deep inner peace that comes from having that boundary in place that lets us know when to step in and engage to try to affect a situation and when to let it slide past? When do we respond in concern for what is happening without trying to get it to go somewhere we want it to go? These are daily and challenging questions, and it is these dilemmas that give us that negative feeling of being lost, or out of sync, or rushing so fast that life has little true pleasure.

Choosing Personal Reactions Wisely

We all need guidelines that we can trust, flexible guidelines that give us parameters with the room within to be truly ourselves. No one benefits from doing exactly what they believe another has told them or is telling them to do. We all must choose our own reactions so we can feel 100 percent responsible in responding to the outcome of our choices. If we follow another blindly, then we give the outcome to them and disengage from our own learning and growth. What we are looking for is responses in the great classroom of life that are ours. We want to create responses that keep us engaged with the parts of ourselves that react to life as worthy, that are worth the effort and capable of reaping true satisfaction.

Three Ways of Behaving

Essentially, you have three choices: constructive behavior, nonengaging behavior, and destructive behavior. The following descriptions of these three types of behavior may help to clear up for you what your best reaction might be:

1. **Constructive behavior.** You can react to an event in a way that is constructive to your own spiritual, emotional, mental, or physical development.

2. **Nonengaging behavior.** You can choose not to engage—to react, but in a way that actually hides you from the world. This type of behavior creates a personality that hides one's true nature from the world—sort of abandoning the ship while still riding on it. If you choose this type of behavior, you won't interact in a way that allows equality to exist.

    This style of relating always brings great frustration, because the eventual outcome is that your life is directed by something other than your self. When you feel like a victim, rejected, unfulfilled, out of control, like you aren't getting back as good as you gave, then you have most likely been interacting with life without engaging it in your true nature.

3. **Destructive behavior.** People who choose this way of behaving are destructive or devouring.

What Does This Mean?

Constructive behavior allows you to engage the aspects of the number that is you in a way that your self-knowledge and positive interacting with the world increases. Nonengaging behavior is behavior that seems interactive. Actually, however, it creates situations in which you aren't really giving anything of substance to life. It is therefore impossible for anything of true value to be coming from the experience for you. Destructive behavior is what happens when the drive of interaction is to take from others or direct others according to one's will.

This type of interaction does truly create, and personal self-knowledge can be gained, but it violates one of the most basic laws of life. We have all been sent here to have free will to maximize our own personal growth. To take away another's free will through destructive or devouring behavior is to go against this most basic law. This behavior creates a deep soul wound. The power and control can feel good for a while because it can feel like the basic truth of impermanence doesn't apply— "We have control!"—but eventually it all falls apart. The person is left controlled completely by what he or she was using to be destructive or devouring. The complete lack of personal freedom that this eventually brings creates a true downward turn of the soul.

FACTS

Numbers carry within them the potential for wisdom or for the waste of time or for destructive behavior. We get to choose which of these potentials to activate, and that's a responsibility! Which response will you have? What part of your potential for expression will you choose? What do you now know about yourself? That is where wisdom lies.

Each number carries its own characteristics in each of the three possible behavior patterns. It is up to you to choose the behavior on your own. This ability to choose responses, to have that moment where the choice is available and then you decide which way to go, is the ability at the heart of the value numerology offers to you. It can be much easier to decide how to create the outcomes you want if you have ancient wisdom giving you the tools to better understand your strengths and your weaknesses.

Your Full Range of Choices

This is why it is so very important to have the full range of potential behaviors in each flow line. Here is an outline of the three choices for each number.

Behaviors of Flow Line Number 1

Constructive Behavior:

- Being original.
- Acting with creative independence.
- Acting courageously.
- Matching commitment to willpower.
- Leading.
- Acting from inner force and selfhood.
- Pioneering with courage.

Nonengaging Behavior:

- Acting with positional stubbornness.
- Showing true selfishness.
- Unwilling to accept support.
- Performing actions that lead to lack of stability.
- Bragging with no substance.
- Arguing for the sake of arguing.
- Being unmoving, inert; blustering.

Destructive Behavior:

- Grandstanding: Me, me, me, me, and now, let's talk about . . . me!
- Domineering, denying others an equal voice.
- Bullying with highhanded, browbeating dictatorship; true tyranny.

Behaviors of Flow Line Number 2

Constructive Behavior:

- Making close and deep contacts.
- Bonding in a deep inner rhythm.
- Acting in a loving and tactful manner, with equanimity.
- Displaying a moderate, gentle, harmonious nature.
- Exhibiting service without martyrdom.
- Acting friendly, being cooperative.

Nonengaging Behavior:

- Acting with ambivalence and self-doubt.
- Showing a low belief in personal power, being extra-sensitive.
- Behaving in a way that leads to apathy and kowtowing.
- Being self-absorbed.

Destructive Behavior:

- Manipulating through sulkiness, bad temper, and lying.
- Acting in a truly cruel, sadomasochistic, devious manner.
- Playing tyrant, victim, and then tyrant again.
- Being sly like a fox.

Behaviors of Flow Line Number 3

Constructive Behavior:

- Being truly carefree, with optimism that is based in reality.
- Applying personal creativity to all life, like a natural artist.
- Being an aesthete, with creative imagination.
- Loving social interaction, being a kind friend.
- Being embarrassed of one's own talent.

Nonengaging Behavior:

- Showing silly, superficial behavior; no depth.
- Whining and complaining.
- Gossiping; no attention to personal growth; no sense of class.

Destructive Behavior:

- Promoting intolerance and bigotry.
- Filling others with envy and suspicion.
- Creating distrust and being a coward.
- Being sanctimonious.

Behaviors of Flow Line Number 4

Constructive Behavior:

- Getting organized, having the ability to apply ideas.
- Providing practical and patient service.
- Being able to endure.
- Being filled with devotion and loyalty.
- Being trustworthy, economic.

Nonengaging Behavior:

- Acting dull and plodding.
- Not willing to take risks.
- Being tight with money.
- Thinking in dogmatic ways, being rigid and severe.
- Being restrictive of self.
- Showing a stubborn refusal to budge.

Destructive Behavior

- Loving to destroy with violence.
- Breeding inhuman behavior.
- Lacking empathy.
- Generating jealousy, cruelty, violence through true hatred.

Behaviors of Flow Line Number 5

Constructive Behavior:

- Having an active, clever mind; displaying mental curiosity.
- Living an active life filled with versatility and variety.
- Loving progress and personal freedom.
- Embracing life's activities with a sense of adventure.
- Being a great companion and fellow traveler.

Nonengaging Behavior:

- Being completely irresponsible to anyone other than the self.
- Indulging the self, which leads to carelessness, thoughtless behavior, and inconsistency.
- Having base values.
- Pursuing sensation.

Destructive Behavior:

- Becoming corrupt.
- Engaging in substance abuse.
- Being an uncontrolled free thinker.
- Enjoying a complete indulgence of sensation.

Behaviors of Flow Line Number 6

Constructive Behavior:

- Having a protective, loving nature.
- Creating a harmonious home, within and without.
- Being compassionate and empathetic.
- Believing in balanced, firm justice.
- Giving comfort by bearing burdens willingly.

Nonengaging Behavior:

- Acting in a flurry of nonproductive activity.
- Worrying, meddling, interfering.
- Being a true martyr.
- Giving sympathy filled with pity.

Destructive Behavior:

- Being a constant spoilsport.
- Undercutting relationship with suspicion and jealousy.
- Behaving tyrannically with loved ones.
- Expecting slavelike devotion from loved ones.

Behaviors of Flow Line Number 7

Constructive Behavior:

- Having a peaceful nature.
- Being spiritually motivated.
- Loving analysis, science, medicine, and research.
- Having refinement, being elegant, poised
- Being enigmatic; still, silent.
- Having wisdom.

Nonengaging Behavior:

- Being cold and aloof.
- Exhibiting high-strung nervousness.
- Showing irritability.
- Self-doubting.
- Undercutting sarcasm.
- Acting confused and erratic.

Destructive Behavior:

- Creating turbulence and confusion.
- Showing great weakness to sensation.
- Cheating others.
- Expressing true malice.
- Being devoured by the darkness.

Behaviors of Flow Line Number 8

Constructive Behavior:

- Having power, trustable authority.
- Enjoying the kind of success born from a just, discriminating drive to preserve.
- Enjoying self-reliance that thwarts dependency issues.
- Showing self-control.

Nonengaging Behavior:

- Being driven by the desire for money, recognition, and power.
- Exhibiting a low level of compassion, tolerance, and caring empathy.
- Creating isolating stress, strain, and anxiety, leading to poor judgment and inefficient use of energy.

Destructive Behavior:

- Being a true tyrannical bully.
- Acting abusive and vengeful.
- Lacking justice and justifying unscrupulous behavior.
- Seeking revenge for imagined wrongs.

Behaviors of Flow Line Number 9

Constructive Behavior:

- Making an expression of Universal Love.
- Attending to a higher law; serving humanity selflessly.
- Being a magnetic humanitarian who is filled with compassion, equanimity, and understanding.
- Showing a breadth of vision and empathy.

Nonengaging Behavior:

- Acting highly emotional.
- Showing soppy sentimentalism.
- Proving an inability to concentrate and focus all the forces of the 9.
- Being a loose cannon.
- Behaving like a dreamer, no true accomplishment.
- Sitting up in a cloud and deciding to join life when life suits them.

Destructive Behavior:

- Living a life of pathetic dissipation.
- Exhibiting a permissive, immoral character that degenerates to obscenity, total lack of civility, and glowering.
- Acting embittered with life.

Behaviors of Flow Line Number 10

- The 10 will carry the qualities of the preceding numbers, now integrated in a single 1.

Behaviors of Flow Line Number 11

Constructive Behavior:

- Spiritual teaching and leadership fueled by intuition, brilliant revelation, inspired invention, and charismatic fire.
- Exhibiting a solid spiritual foundation.
- Understanding that the material world is seen as only the tool for creating options.

Nonengaging Behavior:

- Having no clear, focused direction.
- Being unreliable; uninterested in deep human issues.
- Acting contained, self-superior.
- Imposing beliefs without sensitivity.

Destructive Behavior:

All the crummy qualities of someone who feels they deserve what they want because people are undeserving and imperfect, but the 11 is so much better. These include:

- Dishonesty
- Cruel manipulation
- Degrading debauchery
- Miserly greed

Behaviors of Flow Line Number 22

Constructive Behavior:

- Living with material mastery and accomplishment on all levels of reality.
- Exhibiting empowerment.
- Being a practical idealist.
- Having an uplifting presence.
- Living with the stillness of inner peace.

Nonengaging Behavior:

- Demonstrating over-aggrandizing, unrealistic behavior.
- Being unable to find a solid sense of self-worth.
- Acting with scornful indifference.

Destructive Behavior:

- Making power-driven, vicious attacks on others.
- Being scornful, degrading of others.
- Being capable of all aspects of crime.

Two Focuses

This book concentrates primarily on two ideas. The first may be represented by the 1 (singular): the idea of beginning to really understand numerology, the art of placement, and your place in it, within yourself and within your life. This is because you have something important to offer here. The very fact of your having picked up this book and reading it shows you have an affinity for numerology. If you understand what is going on, that this is an energetic language, you can make your own contributions.

ESSENTIALS

If you really begin to expand into the life view numerology offers you, you may use its wisdom to take another step. You may have the skill developing to use it as it is used now, but you may also expand your interaction with these energies of life to create the art of placement in your life and in your world.

The other idea behind this book focuses on 2, relationship: the idea is to teach you a system that will help you personalize the wisdom of numerology in your own life. Learn more deeply about your own gifts, obvious and dormant. Use the numbers to help gain insight into others in your life. Find the resources within the formulas to improve your loving nature and, therefore, your love life as well. You can find your lucky number and learn how to use it. You can use these ancient numerological formulas to accelerate your own vibration in order to help you keep up with these fast-moving times.

CHAPTER 8

Your Soul Essence Number

Numerological formulas have guided thousands of people before you, and now it is your turn to receive that guidance. You can use these formulas as tools to help you expand your awareness of your most basic, most reliable characteristics. What is your deepest characteristic? Your soul essence. This is the very center of you, and numerology gives you an ancient formula to determine how best to get more settled into the person you are here to be!

You Are the Center of Your Life

You are the spark that illuminates your life. You carry within yourself all that is required to move your life in exactly the direction that is perfect for you and your learning. There is just this one little issue standing in your way, and it has to do with choice. There are so many choices, choices every day, from what toothpaste you should use to what job you want, choices that can help you improve your relationships, be successful, and define your spiritual path. Such important aspects of life are created and affected by each choice we make. In a very real sense, the life we have right now sits at the top of every decision we have ever made. If you have areas of your life you want to change, you have to change the way you make your decisions.

Numerology can give you the tools to guide those decisions. With numerology, you will be better prepared to make decisions that are in keeping with your deepest nature. Decisions of this type can very naturally help you create a life that reflects you and all that you would like to manifest and create in your own wonderful life.

The following should be your premise for approaching the science of numerology:

You are the center of your life.
You are the creative spark that illuminates your own life.
You carry within your nature all that you require
to create the life you want.
Life is a banquet.
You don't need anything from anyone anywhere
to start enjoying the banquet now!
You are, right now, at this moment, fully self-empowered!
You don't need more money, a better relationship, a better childhood,
an easier boss, kinder parents/kids/friends, or more understanding
to be able to create what you want.

You are exactly right. You can be living in your life right now as the person you dearly want to be. Just get going, each day, and give it your best, with the numbers as your loyal and wise guides.

What Is Totally and Completely You?

What is so deeply your nature that when you are aligned with it, you fill with harmony and self-love? You, and only you, are able to bring forth this great part of yourself and to craft your life to be perfectly suited to your soul's expression.

Numerology teaches that we are all cast from the creator as a spark of personal essence. We travel the universe learning about the nature of ourselves as this spark, always learning through a variety of experiences that are available. We speed through time and space in a micro millisecond of time that is our own space. Our personal quality is our most sacred commitment to the Universe and the Creator. *It is this constant elevation of our own qualities within the experience of life that is at the heart of the reason for life itself.*

Wherever we are, this essence is the centerpiece of our nature. If you think of a pebble dropped into calm, deep water, you can envision that first you have the initial impact. Next, there are the progressive concentric circles that develop as a result of the touchdown of the pebble. According to numerology, you are constructed in a very similar way.

First, you bring your nature into your life. Your birth time and date become the entry point that sets the coordinates for your life journey. You have a preplanned life-lesson focus, and you immediately relate to this commitment. Next, your soul nature and life lesson coordinate with your birth year. After that comes the best manifestation of your talents. All of this is comforted and centered by your reconstructor of self-love. Finally, all of these qualities coordinate with your name. Then, from these concentric circles—which you can also understand as patterns of yourself—you interact with life.

Your Soul Essence Is the Core of You

The first order of your life's business is to determine your soul essence vibration. This is your most important mission because until you have your own energy packaging together, it isn't really possible to bring harmony to your connections to life. In this harmony, you must also be able to have synchronicity, a good rhythm of learning, and balancing support throughout the remainder of your life experience.

Here is the ancient formula:

1. Write out your full name (first, middle, and last) in capital letters. Shape your letters according to the flow line patterns you have learned!

2. Write the correct root number above each vowel. Again, shape your numbers in the old numerological way! To refresh your memory, here are the numerical equivalents for each vowel:

   A = 1
   E = 5
   I = 9
   O = 15 = 6
   U = 21 = 3

3. Add up the vowel root numbers of your first name, middle name, and last name.

4. Finally, add up the final vowel root numbers for each name.

As you write out the letters of your name, remember that you are working with flow lines, which means you are working with energy. To get the essence of the flow line vitality, you need to make sure each step is done in keeping with the wise authority of the ancients. Letters must be written out as you have seen them, with circles, semicircles, and straight lines.

The following is an example of how to calculate your soul essence number.

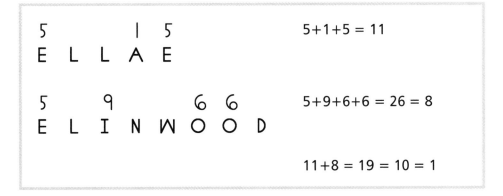

It is very important that you use your true name as you calculate your soul essence number. If you are addressed differently by different people, please consider which name resonates with you most deeply. For more information on the importance of names, see Chapter 12.

First name: _____   Total: _____

Middle name: _____   Total: _____

Last name: _____   Total: _____

Final total: _____

Soul essence root number: _____

The soul essence number that emerges from this formula can remind and confirm to you the nature of your deepest, most meaningful essence. This is what you came into this lifetime to express, in all the affairs of your life. It is the part of yourself that you long to know about and that you were made to share fully with others. To live life from this center core of yourself is to live from your soul.

Numerology Is the Art of Placement

These carefully constructed placement charts set the coordinates for the energetic aspects of your numerological formula. This will help to increase your insight and intuition into what the units of combining energy are expressing. Don't make the mistake of assuming that these steps hold no value. Bad things aren't going to happen if you skip them, of course, but the best things won't happen either.

As you work on your numerology formulas, always remember to write out the letters and numbers in the simplified, numerological way, as you have seen them appear in this book. Moreover, remember that when you work with words, you write the numbers *over* the vowels and *under* the consonants.

Looking with an Ancient Eye

But what does your soul essence number represent? You have two ways of finding out. First, you can consult the ancient masters of numerology, who have compiled this information over thousands of years. Second, you have the power of intuition to look inside yourself and find your own interpretations.

ESSENTIALS

Numerology is common to all, but at the same time it can be very personal. Numbers are living energies, and they are everywhere, even as a part of you. That means that you have within you an exact understanding of what they are.

Meditate and look inside yourself to find the meanings of the numbers, and then see what the masters have left for us as their interpretations and experiences (as the following sections describe).

Soul Essence

This is the essence of one who is here to claim the qualities of learning and giving that are associated with singular contributions.

Achievement, creation, invention, family, and friends are expressions of the 1's ability to achieve and create success. The 1 is loyal, a leader who is fair and given to spurts of amazing generosity. The 1 shows and inspires others by personally demonstrating what they are capable of doing as individuals.

Symbol	Possible Behavior
Straight vertical line	Stands alone
Connected up and down	Draws from heaven and Earth alone
Narrow line	Keeps self very singular

The soul learning is to see life as a self-reflector and not as a theater to perform in. In doing that, the balance of appreciating the equality of all things—including the 1—becomes the treasured drop of wisdom gained from the life.

Soul Essence 2

Soul essence 2 is filled with the capacity and desire for contact with others. This personality loves individuals, groups, communities, nations, and the world as a whole. The 2 essence is a tireless worker for others, who wants to create environments in which people thrive, in which the focus is usually comfort, security, peace, and harmony. The desire to create a better world promotes the ability of the 2 to be diplomatic, empathic, emotionally sensitive to the unsaid words of others. This in turn creates an astounding ability to welcome in all and then more: "Always room for one more."

Symbol	Possible Behavior
Rounded top	Receptive
Straight horizontal line	Very steady
Large container	Lots of space for life and others

There is a natural humility that goes with the 2. This creates a quiet, sometimes obscure life and an amazing ability to be blessed in the small wonders of life. The only rigidity is in the support of others, which 2 will do with a quiet force few will go against.

The learning is to gain the golden drop of wisdom through developing a commitment to a sense of purpose and direction that gives direct benefit to the 2.

Soul Essence 3

This soul essence is pure light and fun. This is an essence that loves to share and inspire joy and happiness. This tends to automatically draw friends and admirers by the droves. The 3 soul essence draws fun from everyone and everything. Like a happy puppy, the 3 goes through life with ears flapping, tail wagging, engaging, with a pure joy of being alive.

The 3 essence doesn't recognize tragedy and loss as a reason for depression or self-doubt. It is not really true that the 3 essence is a specialist in escapist behaviors; instead, it is more that every situation has a silver lining, and it is this element that the 3 essence sees and relates to.

You will never find a 3 essence holding onto any memory that makes them dour. The victim view is simply not part of their character or how they approach life. This essence is joy of living, and life is indeed a pleasure. The cup is not only always half-full, but that half is bubbling over the top.

Symbol	Possible Behavior
Very rounded	Relaxed and flexible
Balanced, but looks like rocking comes often	Likes to move around two spaces for life, can't get enough of life

The lesson that 3 essence can derive from life is to settle down, focus, concentrate, and enjoy life. That means enjoying not just the ripe fruit but the whole process—and that includes planting, tending, pruning, nurturing, and finally eating the fruits of life. This means learning to use patience as a tool for keeping interested in the process. The 3 essence has virtually no concentrated patience.

Soul Essence 4

The 4 soul essence is the pure soul of dependability, structure, loyalty, and trust. In other words, this essence is everything you would associate with a firm, solid expression of the best of values, morals, and traditions. Because of the amount of structure that is creating the space, you have a person who is very disciplined—for a cause.

This is a soul essence who upholds the most basic structures or morals of the culture. In the Western world's case, this would be partnership loyalty, family care, a respectable job, and true national support. This soul essence is traditional, not particularly inventive, but very loving. The 4 essence is invested in both needing and giving a consistent and constant support. The 4 soul essence is inclined to see others' needs before his or her own and is therefore capable of putting others first when making decisions.

Symbol	Possible Behavior
A strong structure	Very structured person
Sharp angles	Likes things to be clear and direct
Base much smaller than the top	Receives much from heaven and takes the time to turn this bounty into action

The 4 soul essence will learn the value of always adding to and updating self-knowledge to avoid a limited point of view and holding onto the past. The 4 essence will also gain wisdom on having the scope of self-knowledge to withhold that which cannot be freely given.

Soul Essence 5

The 5 soul essence is the mental seeker and emotional explorer who is constantly on the move. This essence is restless and freedom-oriented, the shaker-mover energy personified. The constant curiosity makes the 5 essence very adaptable to life but not often really changed by it. Something of a dilettante, this essence adds a special liveliness to any situation it finds itself in.

They are usually ready to move on to the next experience whenever the present one no longer holds the attention or interest of their vastly experiential nature. This natural way of expanding into the full panoply of life's banquet embraces most dearly the arts, music, great food, travel, and fine clothes and jewels. To this soul essence, all these things mean the good life that has been sought, embraced, and fulfilled.

Symbol	Possible Behavior
Strong upper mental reach	Curious mental energies
Strong, structured emotional space	Emotions and drive to success are one
Very rounded, grounded base	Constantly on the move

The learning that the 5 essence will have as life naturally unfolds includes loyalty, consistency, fascination with the process, and a patient acceptance that everything opens, but only in its own time. You can't get a bush to bloom by telling it to.

Soul Essence 6

The 6 soul essence is the nurturer. It embodies a powerful essence of protective friendship, loyal love, a comfy home, and a deep, steady root that gives endless support to others. So deeply connected to the physical and emotional rootedness, the 6 essence carries a deeply comforting, calming, and reassuring quality that speaks of life as a challenge at times but one that remains eminently trustable. The 6 essence demonstrates to others how to hold back the fear of life's unexpected twists and turns and believe in the power of comfort and sustaining love as an ever-present force to balance the impermanence of change.

Symbol	Possible Behavior
Soft and rounded	Feminine and nurturing
Returns to itself	Keeps loved ones safe
Protected space	Protects

The 6 essence is inclined to work out of the home or in a very homey refuge, a protecting environment, counseling or conducting laws that protect. The 6 essence expresses all the qualities one associates with home in all aspects of life.

Everyone is greeted as a guest/friend and is given stable, loving, parental support. The 6 essence has a great natural compassion and empathy for others. The 6 essence will give tremendous love and support to others. That's because deep within, the 6 essence knows he or she is fully protected and nurtured by spirit. This deep acceptance of protection as a birthright brings comfort and acceptance to anyone in times of well-being as well as in struggle and even in times of peril.

The lesson that the 6 essence will draw from life is to be able to develop a flexible boundary between themselves and others. This boundary will enable them to have a more objective and firm, assertive response to people and life events.

Soul Essence 7

The 7 soul essence is the most enigmatic or least knowable of the numbers. This essence is always alone, with an involved and evolved relationship to his/her inner world of science, philosophy, and other pursuits of the intellect. It is this relationship that is the 7 soul essence's primary relationship. Because this inner world is the 7 soul essence, he or she is inclined to perform his or her life becoming a living example of the scientist, the philosopher, or the doctor, instead of just being a human being.

The soul essence of 7 is so deeply engaged with the world possibilities conceived in the mental that it is easy to become the embodiment of them. Filled with wisdom, but too inner-related to be easily skilled socially, the 7 essence can give to others vast, intrinsic, and valuable wisdom and be more aligned with the wisdom than the people.

Symbol	Possible Behavior
Strong mental line	Is moved by intellectual inquiry
Diagonal line going down	Goes for the bottom line
Very defined	Loner

The 7 essence loves to examine from every angle. It analyzes everything and hates to be drawn into messy human stuff—fighting, dirty hand work, chaotic environments. With a talent for order, containing a deep and private well of self and an odd combination of spiritual with survival fears, the 7 essence can only be loved if the other person takes the time to know him or her.

The 7 essence will automatically be learning how to be alone and, at the same time, fully content and never lonely. Also, empathy and compassion for the challenge of true life events will create a more personal attitude with life in general. As the 7 essence becomes more comfortable with life, much of the fear and longing transforms to courage and the ability to find beauty in the wee moments of life.

Soul Essence 8

The 8 soul essence can be summed up very simply in these two words: expects success. Imbued with talents for organization and systems of any kind, and further blessed with an affinity for large affairs and events and the personal power to conceive, organize, and direct them, the 8 essence has the love of and ability to achieve on a great scale.

The 8 essence will never ask another to work harder, give more, or strive more than 8 essence does. But others should watch out, because they are tireless workers, imbued with their visions, energized by their imagination and projects, and filled with love when they are creating great things. This essence is a power source of hard work to create good.

Symbol	Possible Behavior
Two complete, connected circles	Very complete power
Two circles connected in the center	Balanced
Rounded on all sides	Doesn't collapse under pressure

As life rolls along, the 8 essence will learn tolerance and the balanced hand of justice for those that are endowed with other, very different qualities. They will develop patience with the process, recognizing the goal can only be achieved when the process is well supported.

Soul Essence 9

The 9 soul essence is the expression of universal awareness and all that universal wisdom expresses. This becomes extraordinary generosity because the 9 essence always feels completely cared for by the universe. The 9 essence's great faith in universal abundance enables the 9 to express a very high order of love. This has to do with sacrifice, but without victimization; sympathy, but without pity for another; understanding without arrogance; and service without treating the person served as a needy, lesser being.

Symbol	Possible Behavior
Upper circle	A higher look at things
Straight line to Earth	Self-directed
Upper circle is complete	Complete universal wisdom

The 9 essence longs to have deep personal love, but this essence emanates such a deeply universal impersonal quality of love that the deep human love is often hard for the 9 essence to really achieve.

The 9 essence, who is beautiful inside and out and beloved by most, is often moved to share his or her wisdom in the media to connect with the most people, not for his or her ego but to get the wisdom out.

As the 9 essence goes through life, there will be the inevitable lessons, and these generally have to do with clarity in regard to the abilities and nature of others. Emotional steadiness can become illusive as the 9 encounters earthly challenges. Like Jesus throwing over the money changers' tables in the temple, the 9 essence can struggle for emotional steadiness.

Soul Essence 11

The 11 essence is filled within. This essence carries as a daily teaching and, if evolved at being human, it includes a daily everyday expression of what a spiritual teacher is. In the old definition of spiritual teacher, the teacher stood on the podium and lectured, encouraged, and enlightened the "masses." This is the 11 of yesterday. The 11 essence still has this love of God before its love of humanity, but it tends to express ideals without being accessible as a human being. But the 11 essence is more and more evolving into a deeply human person who glows with amazing spiritual dimension in the blessed, ordinary muck and mire of human life. The 11 essence is a treasure of spiritual teaching and deeply personal human love that ignites the best in all it meets.

Symbol	Possible Behavior
Two parallel lines	Balanced
Goes up and down endlessly	Wisdom from knowing the best and worst
A road between two straight lines	Knowledge fills it up

As the 11 essence lives his/her life, more and more appreciation will develop for the amazing, even miraculous ways people lead their lives and how the glow of human love empowered by spiritual truths emerges somewhere in every situation.

Soul Essence))

The 22 soul essence embodies the characteristics of all the other numbers, including the qualities of the 11 essence, combined. As a result, you have someone who understands the laws of the universe and knows that these laws are only useful if they are applied in harmony with nature's laws. So you have a powerful, practical builder. He or she does not build for personal power, ego needs, experimentation, or from personal insecurities. The 22 essence builds to improve existence on the physical level so all else can grow and thrive. This essence is a true believer in the maxim that in order for human growth and potential to ignite, create, and be grand, the practical, physical aspects of life must be in place. "Care for the body, and the creativity and true nature of the soul will be released."

Symbol	Possible Behavior
Two very firm bases	Very, very grounded
Fits together perfectly	Easily find compatible common ground with others
Two different types of containers	Retains much knowledge and wisdom regarding life

The soul essence, the center of your nature, then expands through other number patterns, each sculpting your energetic flow into life. The first area to have this influence is your touchdown moment, or the moment of your birth.

CHAPTER 9

The Numerology of Your Birth Time

Your birth time is the beginning of all the numerology formulas. It is with the exact time of birth that you can build a formula that shows you the person you are constructing and expressing through the course of your life. It is this person that is expressed through your soul essence.

Touchdown Time

When we are born, we have what is called our touchdown time. Your touchdown time is the moment when you came into your life. In ancient numerology, this moment is found in the numbers 1 through 9 and their essences.

Remember, we are a part of a universal family, and we travel the universe seeking self-knowledge, the purpose for our life here. We travel the universe in our soul essence, which is constant, gaining wisdom through our experiences.

It is important to realize that the soul essence is affected by a person's birth time, for it is our birth time that hones and focuses us as well as defines our reason for life. The birth time defines the area of focus we have decided we want to learn about.

What Are You Learning?

Earth is a 10-essence planet, and you now know your essence number too (see Chapter 8). The birth time, date, and year will give you a close-up look at what is your life focus for your learning.

The soul essence comes up to the vibrational boundary of life's focused lesson, and then the essence and the lesson harmonize as best they can. (Since it is a lesson, the essence hasn't learned it yet.) The two form a blended unit of expanding aliveness that sees life with certain perceptions or distortions, and therein lies the lesson. To learn, over time, the difference between what is truth and what is perception that is based on illusion.

This essence blend is a unique, never-to-be-repeated blending of you—essence and learning. The more you learn and experience how the blending works and what is created from it, the more tools you will have to guide yourself, and perhaps others, to a happier, more satisfying life outcome.

Life's Focus Formula

The ancient numerological formula provided here will use your birth date to derive one of eleven possible root numbers (1 to 9, 11, and 22), which will help you figure out your reason for being here. As before, the sequence and placement of the flow lines is important.

To get your life focus number, you need to add up the digits of the month, date, and year of your birth. For instance, if you were born on January 23, 1967, your formula would be calculated as follows: 1+2+3+1+9+6+7 = 29 = 11. That is, your reason for being in this life can be described through the number 11. (For a more specific life task reading based on your specific year of birth, see Appendix A, which contains a list of all years, from 1920 to 2010.)

Essence Numbers by Month			
January	1	July	7
February	2	August	8
March	3	September	9
April	4	October	10
May	5	November	11
June	6	December	12 = 3

Let's say that your soul essence is a 6. The interpretation would go as follows: You would be bringing to your life an essence of home and hearth, and through this nurturing quality you will learn spiritual mastery.

How Your Birth Year Affects You

You can gain further insight by examining the year of your birth separately. To stay with our example, let's see what vibrational orientation 1967 carries. The numbers 1967 add up to a 5 essence, so the interpretation that you make might run something like this. This person is a nurturer who is here to learn and express spiritual mastery and who must use their variety of experience and direct involvement to engage life. No laziness or dilettante behavior would satisfy the quest for growth.

Here is another example. The birth date is October 2, 1955. That makes the soul essence number 2. The life purpose number is 5. The year, 1955, brings a 2 essence along with its associated challenges about how to keep yourself intact while you are with those you love, working so hard to create a better world. The key is not doing it all but to let others carry their own weight.

Each year brings with it a task, and everyone in the world who was born during that year has a shared commitment to learning the year's task. From the couple of test years we've already examined, we can understand that the year 1922, for instance, brought in people who were defining their relationship to being shaker-movers. This doesn't mean they all needed to learn to shake and move or that everyone already knew how to do it. What it does means is that for each person born that year, the way they created in the world and their exploration of thoughts, places, and ideals were of fundamental importance to their ongoing personal spiritual evolution.

ESSENTIALS

The life task isn't something we impose on life. It is a lens we look through. With every life experience we have, from the simplest to the most complex, this is the tool we apply to the task. Whatever your number for your life task, you should apply the appropriate tools to develop the potential of the number in everything you do. You should also remember that in so doing, you enable yourself to perceive the life experience in a way that is harmonious to your ultimate life purpose or learning.

Life is filled with such amazing profusion that applying any lesson—let's say, the lesson of 4 structure, for example—to every experience allows you to recognize how profuse and filled with opportunity life is. In every experience the structuring, appropriately applied, joins with the experience, and in the union of the two what emerges from that blend or union is your assured growth.

For instance, to put it simply, say you want a good toothpaste. You can just run out and grab one. But if you are a 4 task, you gather information on the best toothpaste for your needs, and then you make your decision. The type you buy blends with your oral well-being and your lesson in life is enhanced by the pleasure of healthy, clean, white teeth. By using the 4 appropriately you have now, in the simplest of ways, made an enhancement to your personal life in a small but very meaningful way.

What Your Life Focus Number Represents

You can use life focus numbers to learn what your life's task is, as the following list explains:

1 You are here to take 1 to the highest point of development, with no excuses.

2 You are here to develop your ability to become deeply involved in a union with others to achieve the desired outcome.

3 Your job is to give up reservation, self-absorption, or holding back. Immerse yourself in the joy of life, and be like a happy, tail-wagging puppy.

4 Your attention to structure and responsibility and to giving your own personal stamp will achieve your life purpose.

5 You must learn to be adaptable in the midst of life. Allow freedom and variety to be grist for your mill of personal wisdom, profiting from every experience.

6 You enjoy a readiness to be of service to family, community, nation with loving trust that each experience that demands from you new levels of loyalty and nurturing is only for your highest good.

7 You are walking the path of the wise, solitary one. This is a life for you to seek the highest of truths, increasing your knowledge and wisdom, and using your increasing wisdom to offset a curiosity about the darker side of life.

chart continues on next page

8   You are here to come forward, to move into business, finance, and organization. Hone your power and prestige abilities.

9   You are here to learn service to others in the most humanitarian spirit. No undue regard of self, for you are always connected to the eternal flow of life. Now just give it to others.

11   You are here to elevate, elevate, elevate. Bring all of the experiences of life to the highest, wisest level of the mystic who glows quietly in the rush of life.

22   This is the learning of serving where you use every skill, every talent you possess, to construct on a large scale for society's betterment.

Your Birth Time Worksheet

● Your essence number: _____

What it means: _____

_____

_____

● Your life focus number: _____ = _____

                                      month   day   year

What it means: _____

_____

_____

● Your birth year: _____

What it means: _____ (see "Life Task Calendar," Appendix A)

_____

_____

Think about how your soul essence number blends with your life focus number and how your birth year number clarifies your life's task. If you feel you need to do so, add your own interpretations to these numbers.

_____

_____

_____

_____

_____

_____

_____

_____

_____

Your birth year's flow line number is your very basic first step to uncovering your life's task. Refer to the Life Task Calendar in Appendix A to learn about the vibrations of your particular birth year.

Numerology is a wonderful combination of consistent meaning of the numbers and the intuitive interpretation of their blending. The energy blends exactly like concentric circles that expand across the surface of smooth water as a result of the impact that a stone makes in hitting and sinking into the surface. Your soul essence is the center. It's the dot on the chart, the center of you now expanding to your life experience.

CHAPTER 10

Success and Self-Love

There are lots of formulas for success. Books are written regularly about the beliefs, habits, and disciplines of highly successful people. Numerology has formulas to contribute to your success in all areas of your life. This is success as you define it, success that gives you a deep sense of personal satisfaction within the context of your life, as it is crafted by your hand.

What's the Meaning of Success?

Success means very different things to each one of us. Its definition can change over time, depending on the circumstances of our lives and our current goals. Success may be defined in terms of one's career, personal relationships, or it could mean triumph over hardships, such as illness.

The ingredient common to all success experiences is the ability to center and recover in the privacy of your own inner world. That means knowing how to design a space of nourishing retreat from the rush, the crazy pressures, and the disappointments of daily life.

Your Sacred Space

Numerology and its formulas provide the tool to define a sacred space for you that is yours alone. In a sense, it is like your inner garden of self-love. You can share what you have gained from this private garden with others, but you can never invite them there. Nor can you deeply tend and nurture this part of yourself while with another. This is your most private, personal, and sacred place. It is where you recover from life, reconnect to your soul, and refurbish yourself for yet another day.

FACTS

The reconstructor of self-love draws you to an internal memory that fills you with self-belief and inner joy. Perhaps this memory is a fantasy, another life experience, a treasured dream or heartfelt soul longing. It may be all or none of these. What it is for sure is your inner ticket to grace, self-love, and acceptance.

Reconstructor of Self-Love

The number that identifies your sacred space is the reconstructor of self-love. To calculate this number, follow these steps.

1. Write out your full name (first, middle, and last) in capital letters. Shape your letters in the old numerological way, as you have seen it done in this book!
2. Write the correct root number below each consonant. Again, shape your numbers in the old numerological way!
3. Then, add up all the consonant root numbers together. The result is your reconstructor of self-love.

For example, here is how to calculate the reconstructor of self-love for Jane Smith. (Note that Jane was given two names at birth; if she had a middle name, you would have also used it in calculating her reconstructor of self-love.)

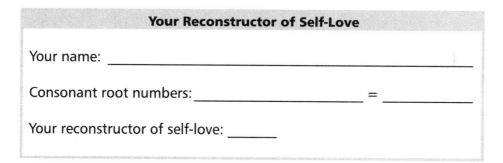

$$1+5+1+4+2+8 = 21 = 3$$

According to these calculations, Jane Smith's private path to self-love and recentering is 3. In her inner world, she reconstructs her path to self-love by thinking and imagining friends, fun, and popularity. People are adoring, and they provide a loving and responsive audience wherever she goes.

Your Reconstructor of Self-Love

Your name: _____

Consonant root numbers: _____ = _____

Your reconstructor of self-love: _____

To see what your reconstructor of self-love represents, refer to the following list of numbers:

1 You imagine yourself as a slayer of dragons, a leader of people. You are creative, inventive, undaunted by challenges.

2 You dream of creating a safe and protected environment for all whom you love. You are gently in the background, making sure it is all complete and loving.

3 You fill your mind with popularity, fun, and appreciative audiences who love the humor, artistic beauty, and elegance that flow from you.

4 You become within yourself the stability that all depend on. You are ceaselessly serving family, community, and nation with loyal, unswerving devotion. You are upheld by all as the hero and patriot.

5 All thoughts have to do with personal freedom. Unbounded, unrestrained, you travel wherever you desire, unhampered by anything.

6 You see yourself as the great comforter of all. Your home is a wonderful expression of art, welcoming to all and nourishing to each and every one, filled with love, hearts, flowers, and doves.

7 Your inner world is filled with the aged beauty of accumulated wisdom and intelligence. Your house is aged wood, elegant comfort, rich and blooming gardens. You walk in the inner grace of the ancient wise and valued mystic—silent and all-knowing.

8 You are the center of the business community; on every committee and in charge of great successful organizations. Everything you do is conducted on a worldwide basis.

9 Always the observer, you long for personal love, but you have the deep complete recognition that yours is a path of complete giving, selfless service, and humanitarian grace personified.

11 You are the messenger of the universe who brings the words, actions, and standards so needed by a struggling world. Universal love pours from you, and you are blessed by all you see.

22 Yours are the dreams of worldwide business, science, medicine that draw together in activities that construct an Earth-friendly atmosphere where systems and Earth both benefit from each other.

The only caution in finding and using the reconstructor of self-love is that you not use it as a route to escapism. It is important that you not use your wonderful gift to create such a strength in your fantasy world that you pull away from contact with others and reality. Instead, you are reminded of the importance of using this most lovely part of your inner world to refresh and reconstruct your burdened self!

The act of returning to the reconstructor of self-love provides a protective quality within the soul, and in this way, it provides a protective quality to the whole experience of life. The pattern for the reconstructor of self-love is as follows:

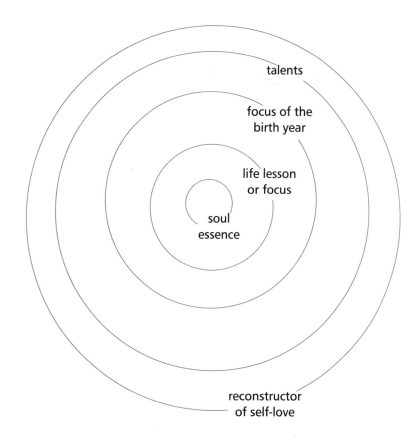

Spiritual Recentering

Spiritual recentering can be accomplished to some degree through many well-known activities. These are only a few of all that's available:

- **T'ai Chi:** Balances the energies within the body.
- **Qigong:** Opens the body to more breath and balance.
- **Yoga:** Creates an inner environment in which the spiritual nature and the human nature are yoked together.
- **Meditation:** Lessens the tension between the universal personality's desire to grow from experience and the body's obsession with safety and survival, reproduction, and inclusion.

Other quiet creative activities include gardening, exercising, cooking, reading, gazing at clouds, zoning out, getting a massage or body work, and many more. These are the few times when you can nourish the emergence of your reconstructor of self-love.

FACTS

One important fact is that this most precious, delicate, and rejuvenating part of yourself knows itself in solitude. Create a life of balance so you have time to let yourself nourish yourself.

Reflection Time

Take a realistic look at your day, your life, and your commitments. List a few times each day where you meet the requirement of solitude for your reconstructor of self-love to activate. Also put down anything that appeals to you. It's your list of things that are meant to increase your balance and self-awareness in your own life.

For Greater Balance and Self-Awareness

- Times for solitude:

_____

_____

_____

_____

_____

_____

_____

- Ways to reconstruct:

_____

_____

_____

_____

_____

_____

_____

_____

CHAPTER 11

Expanding the Energy to Your Talents

This chapter will continue to examine your life's energies and to explore how numerology can help you understand your energies and then make modifications that are for your good and the good of all. One of the areas that you will examine is your natural talent and how you can be applying it in your life's work and your career.

You Are a Unit of Energies

We have focused on how numerology is defined by understanding the interaction of energies as they join together in a single unit. Units of moving, alive, intelligent energy are hard to diagram; the diagrams here are the images as we might imagine them to look.

In the center is the 0. The 0, we remember, is the everything, the emerging of your essential center—your soul essence, a constant fountain of your essential essence spilling into you. The soul essence is drawn from your connection to the Creator. It is like an umbilical cord to the Creator. It is this part of you that travels the universe seeking self-knowledge and wisdom.

Soul essence

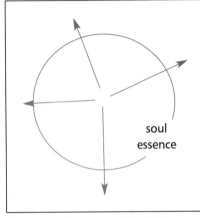

soul
essence

We now have the first interaction that the soul essence encounters as it flows into life. This first interaction is the union of the soul essence with the life commitment of the life focus or the life lesson. As the interaction occurs, the essence of the soul meets its first challenge. Since we are learning something that we have no idea how to do, there is a challenge with this mingling. By understanding the strengths in your essence and the strengths in your lesson, you can begin to change how the lesson is controlling your perception of life.

ESSENTIALS

Self-essence is what we experience when we feel our soul, or when we have a soul love, or soul work, that we want to develop in a unit of interacting energies. This is what allows us to experience soul love, soul work, and soul life as an everyday reality—the magic in living.

For instance, if you are a 3 essence with a 5 life focus or lesson, there would be a problem for you that concerned how to have genuine personal freedom and also be able to create a stable, contributing life.

The 3 and the 5 would commingle in a way that your constant on-the-go nature would make it hard to develop meaningful long-term friendships/relationships and jobs that really tapped the essential creativity of the 3. You can visualize the interaction between the soul essence and the life lesson with the image on the left.

Life lesson or focus

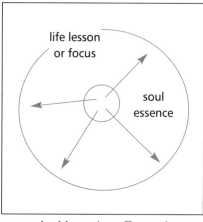

From here, the flow continues into the life expression by commingling next with the year of birth. This puts the person in harmony with all the other people born that year. That's because all these people have a similar common ground of learning. From that common ground, each person enters that yearly orientation with his or her own personal and unique slant on the issue for the year.

Talent focus

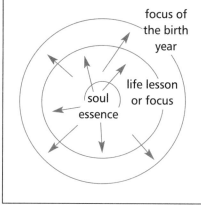

Now, you can extend your energy unit into your talents. Your talents is where you get to plant the seed of yourself, engage life, and begin to prove what you are capable of. It is through your talents that you engage life by assuming your responsibilities.

As you, an interacting unit of universal and earthly energies, continue to flow into experience, the next commingling is your reconstructor of self-love. This marvelous gift occurs only in very private, solitary moments. It is with this force you rekindle yourself as it nourishes you to the root of your soul.

This complete unit of energy now flows through your name. The vibration of your name determines how you are able to access this amazing potential of you and how you can share it with the world. The name is tremendously important. As you have seen, both your soul essence number and your reconstructor of self-love depend on it.

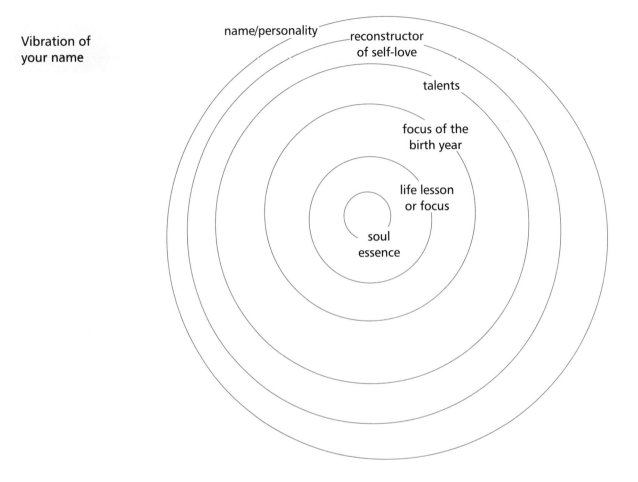

Vibration of
your name

name/personality

reconstructor
of self-love

talents

focus of the
birth year

life lesson
or focus

soul
essence

ALERT

You can have a name that allows the finest qualities you possess to bridge to the world, and you can also have a name that makes it impossible for you to get even one point across clearly. To really change your name, it is best to work with a master numerologist. They have a breadth of experience that can avoid pitfalls.

Magic Begins to Happen

The unit of energy we are diagramming shows the way the energies flow from you into your life experience and then the way you meet other energy units. As the energies unite, relatedness is born. Smooth, deep, and easy connections are usually experienced as some degree of love. Bumpy, shallow, and difficult connections are usually experienced as problems, and we tend to steer clear of those.

The potential is for each connection with another person to be as harmonious as the connections allow it to be. All numbers are compatible, so when we run into the incompatible, there is an adjustment that both need to do to change the outcome. It requires work, and as we know, most people do tend to belong to the lazy end of the spectrum!

It also requires knowledge on how to create this new harmony. Numerology is a great tool for this. Once you have the knowledge, you will find that it makes the process of changing outcomes fun. *Presto magico,* we are less lazy about doing the required work! Now we are starting to understand the interaction of the flows.

How You Set Up Your Life

The flow of your soul essence, tagged and identified through a number, gushes forth joyfully into your life experience. The first part of your unit that your soul essence connects with is your soul's life path or life's lesson. Ancient numerology teaches that we choose our family and early life from birth and that we use the time from birth to eighteen years of age to set up the life lesson.

It works like this. Say your life path number is 2. What you are learning in this life is essentially to fit in, find your place, and make great, long-lasting relationships. Well, the ancient ones taught that you would pick a family or life situation that would not easily allow you to acquire these skills. As a matter of fact, ancient teachings tell us that we tend to choose a family that sets up our childhood in a way that makes the life path a real lesson. So you may be born into a family where you are given very little guidance or support, where the 2 life path has to become very self-reliant. So the 2 life path grows. Then, after eighteen, the relationship problems become a real challenge. The choice is yours: You can either learn how to get along with other people, or you can remain lonely your whole life. That's a real lesson.

Or maybe you are on the 9 life path. You were born into a home where a parent required a lot of service. You, as the child, did what was required, but you didn't get love and appreciation back. So the child served, but there was no true circle of human love in it. This is a different point of view on the lesson. The home set an environment for service. But it was service of the tyrant, and part of the 9 life path is to learn love and service together. So adult life comes, and the learning process has to do with learning the difference between enforced service and service that creates a full circle of love between server and receiver.

The lesson is love and service, but the tool for learning the lesson isn't just more service. The lesson actually comes from self-care and self-nurturing. When the interior flow of self-love and self-nurturing (the 6 essence) is built up, then the understanding of how to serve—that is, to give continuously while effectively inspiring others to be loving—is learned. When the lesson starts being absorbed and moving along, you then have a serving humanitarian filled with the warmth of human love and self-nurturing.

FACTS

We all have a lesson that is set up in childhood. We are all learning how to do something, our lesson in this life, but it is really easy to lose focus on what we are learning. This is where the numerological formulas are so valuable. They point the way to your most essential statements of yourself—your soul essence—and your focus for the life—your life task.

How about a 5 life path? This 5 life path could come into a home where everything is done for them. Or it could be a home where both parents were very poor at interacting with a child that had potential. The home could also have been a place where the 5 life path's creative unique spark was consistently diminished by a well-meaning but very controlling parent. Any of these scenarios can turn the 5 life path into a life lesson, where trusting personal freedom, knowing how to use potential, or just getting activated enough to make a good living becomes a "lesson."

Learning the Lesson

Your life task will come to you in many different ways. There are so many different ways it may seem like a bunch of different lessons, but it isn't. It is the one lesson you have dedicated this life to learning. The lesson doesn't change—your life experience does, however. So changeable and challenging are these experiences that they begin to take charge of us. We forget we are learning a specific lesson, and that's the way we lose our focus.

This loss of focus happens to everyone. But when you lose that focus, the challenge begins to take you over. Take a step back, regroup, review your life path again, remind yourself of your essence, and take some solitude with your reconstructor of self-love. Then, when your focus is regained, go at it again.

Life is a huge classroom. Take your place with grace, acceptance, and wisdom. And give thanks to numerology and all who preceded you who brought it to this point in time.

What Is the Purpose of Work?

Our personal work defines the way we engage life. Responsibility is the tool we have been given to engage us with life, and love is the key that opens us to the world of responsibility. We fall in love and take on marriage. We love deeply and have children. We want to share our gift, or maybe we are driven to have things. And that's why we work.

Each engagement with responsibility is our ticket to life, to learning, to knowledge, and to wisdom. This is the reason we are here. To get involved, each in our own unique way. Large involvement or small involvement—it's our choice. In order to engage life in a way that lets you flow continuously from essence, you must commit to your life task. You have your return to self-love and your soul talent. When you achieve your task, you will have added another tool to your toolbox in the process of becoming the quality human you long to be and that you came here to be.

Making Yourself Effective

You need to know how to manifest your talents in a way that means you are harnessing your soul essence and engaging your life path. You will be happily focused on your commitment to the universe as you learn this lesson. You have a human form, a role, a job, and a task that enable you to converge your soul essence. Your life path is the next needed step.

You need a way to express your soul and learn your lessons at the same time. In this way, one expression is not sacrificed for another. You don't want the life task at hand to so subsume the soul essence that life loses its joy. On the other side, if the soul essence doesn't have anything "real" that it can ground, no responsibilities, then the person becomes so deeply ungrounded that very little human growth or learning is really accomplished.

The concern here is your place in life—the niche that fits you and that you fit in. Into this niche you tuck your soul essence, flowing with the joy of being alive and the pleasure of having your life well served so you are filled with soul satisfaction.

ESSENTIALS Even in the roughest of times—and life does get very rough—numerology will be steady within you. No matter how deep the challenge, you will have the deep joy that you are on track, your timing is right. It's hard work. That's because we do get our lessons through real-life events, but in some deep and odd way, it also feels right.

Another Purpose for Work

There's another great gift that comes from having a niche in which to manifest your talents. When the lesson gets hard, if you return to your niche and delve into the task at hand with all your heart and soul, you will have found a wonderful way to rebalance. With both your reconstructor of self-love and your niche in which you can express your talent, you have two wonderful tools with which you will be better prepared to persevere through the challenges. It is the harmonizing of the soul essence and the life lesson that creates your rebalance. It's not the same as escapism. That has its place too, occasionally.

Escapism contributes nothing to the world, so it should be done for vacations. Your rebalance occurs in the midst of a deep life challenge. The reason for that is simple: Your soul essence and your life lesson rebalance during the time you meet the challenge, and that feels wonderful. It grounds, strengthens, and—most importantly—it creates a renewed sense of purpose and vigor.

Your Natural Talent Number

So, what is this next formula that completes the initial unit you have to work with? It's the numerology formula you use to determine your natural talents. To calculate your talent number, follow these steps:

1. Write out your full name (first, middle, and last) in capital letters. Shape your letters in the old numerological way, as you have seen it done in this book!
2. Write the correct root number below each letter. Again, shape your numbers in the old numerological way!
3. Then, add up all the root numbers together. The result is your talent number.

For example, here is how to calculate the natural talent number for Janet Taylor:

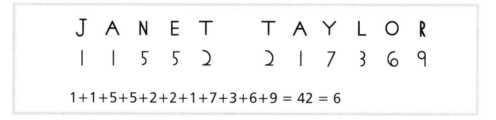

$$1+1+5+5+2+2+1+7+3+6+9 = 42 = 6$$

Now, it's your turn:

Your Natural Talent Number

Your name: _____

Root numbers:_____ = _____

Your natural talent number: _____

What Your Talent Number Means

The Natural Talent for 1

You are the one who goes forth undaunted. You go where others fear to tread to light the path and show the way. You are the first to be there. This puts you into the ranks of leadership, like this:

- Pioneer
- Inventor
- Originator
- Chief executive officer (of corporation)
- Head of the house
- Self-employed

You spur others to action. You create movement. The force of your pioneering enthusiasm creates the cutting edge for the rest of us.

The Natural Talent for 2

You are a graceful fit. You make another's companion beautifully. You can understand where another is coming from. You love being in friendship and relationship. Being alone for too long is like walking with one high-heeled shoe on. You excel at people-oriented things and the serving professions, like these:

- Teaching
- Psychic/medium
- Counselor
- Secretary
- Nurse

- Child-care or elder-care provider
- Diplomat
- Networker

Any form of art that has several people in it, like dancing, singing, or writing, is an excellent area of pursuit for you. You would do well as a group leader of personal growth experiences, a massage therapist, or a body worker. You provide the environment that is the gentle glue that helps others feel more loved, understood, settled down, and comfy.

The Natural Talent for 3

You are the spark of fun. You bring the pure joy of being alive to life itself. You are the butterfly who reminds the tiller of the soil to look up and see all the beauty that surrounds him. You are the happy networker for fun. You are the light at the end of the tunnel. You are the breath of fresh air in a stale life. You make a wonderful teacher if you like what you are teaching. The following areas of pursuit are made for you:

- Singer
- Spiritual teacher
- Couture designer
- Creator of breathtaking jewelry
- Counselor who finds better employment for people
- Fund-raiser
- Hostess par excellence

- Esthetician/nail and hair care
- Energy worker

You have great personal charisma. Even if you are having a rare bad day, you nourish and refresh the people around you.

The Natural Talent for 4

You are the solid one, but you're not a bit boring. You bring order into chaos. You make sense out of the crazy aspects of life. You encourage people to have belief in themselves that is practical. You are the glue that binds. You are the teacher of tradition and wise truths. You are the practical contributor to humans. You can be any of the following things:

- Technician
- Accountant
- Professor
- Doctor
- Law-and-order official
- Farmer
- Teacher of older children
- Architect/builder

You're a great organizer and counselor, a gentle leader, and the type of person who understands trends. You provide the foundation, and what's more, you show others how to create one for themselves.

The Natural Talent for 5

You are the zippy electricity of action. You are the traveler and connoisseur. You are the one who shakes them up and then moves them along. You are action, the Energizer Bunny in life. You like challenge, prominence, and the limelight. You excel at moving things along. The following pursuits are made for you:

- Travel agent
- Lawyer
- Politician
- Actor
- Master of ceremonies
- Inventor
- Travel agent, travel writer, any travel-associated work
- Great mayor/civic leader
- CIA agent
- Researcher in electricity, science, and aspects of medicine
- Computer whiz
- Athlete
- Winner!

The Natural Talent for 6

You are the nurturer. You are filled with compassion. You are overflowing with understanding and the desire to have more. You comfort, and in doing so, you create security. You nurture and calm the weary. You are the embodiment of gentleness and a firm hand. You excel at things like the following:

- Alternative and holistic medicine
- Hospital administrator
- Social/welfare worker
- Teacher, especially of younger kids

- Chef or restaurateur
- Bed and breakfast proprietor
- Hotel owner/manager/maid
- Vacation planner
- Musician
- Writer

The Natural Talent for 7

You are the mysterious one. You hold the keys to the intelligent way. You are the restless seeker. You can withstand public pressure and unpopularity. You march to the beat of your own drum. You are excellent at seeking out the underside of the issue. You excel at doing the job well and taking the heat if need be. You shine at pursuits like the following:

- Judge
- Lawmaker
- Policy planner
- Lawyer
- Mystery writer
- Banking/financial management
- FBI agent
- Highly skilled accountant
- Artist who works with detail and excellence
- Teacher of anything philosophical

The Natural Talent for 8

You are the essence of your own personal motto: Love everyone, trust few, and paddle your own canoe! You are the big boss. You are the one who makes the plans. You expect success. You think big, and you think the complete picture. You rely on your own decision-making skill. You inspire others with the overview that leads to success. You excel at things like these:

- Chief executive officer (of corporation)
- Chief information officer (of corporation)
- Financial manager
- Big business owner
- Owner of your own business
- Organizer
- Art promoter or patron
- Designer of dramatic clothing
- Career counselor
- Fund-raiser
- School principal
- Community leader

The Natural Talent for 9

You are the teacher of spiritual essence as a part of life. You are the natural healer. You are the lover of animals. You are the humanitarian concerned for all. You are the extender of life and faith. You excel at things like the following:

- Minister, rabbi, or spiritual guru
- Spiritual reformer
- Mystic counselor
- Psychic
- Doctor of medicine
- Practitioner of holistic arts
- Energy worker/acupuncturist
- Composer/writer

- Charity fund-raiser
- Motivational speaker
- Veterinarian

The Natural Talent for ||

You have been given the task of expressing spiritual qualities well! You are sustained by the universe. You have a vision for humanity. You have a reformer's hopes and dreams. You are blessed with understanding. You always see a way it can be better. You are the spiritual teacher's spiritual teacher. You excel at pursuits like these:

- Spiritual worker
- Writer/poet
- Minister
- Artist (drawing/painting)
- Chorale leader/musician/choir director
- Charity provider in any role
- Motivational speaker
- Professional advisor

The Natural Talent for))

You are the builder's builder. You are the practical mover who gets others to produce. You are the heart and soul of stability. You are the manifester. You have a very strong will. You excel at pursuits like these:

- Reformer of a culture
- Business executive who makes it better and bigger
- The unifier of the family

- Teacher of how to do it bigger and better
- President/governor
- Leader in world affairs
- Benefactor
- Organizer of community programs

Get the idea? There are lists and lists of potential jobs for any essence. Read the lists here, get the feel of yours, and explore for the essential talents that might be just the right one for you! Read the ones that directly apply to you, then get a job reference book at the library. Look up categories and see all that is offered in these fairly general categories.

CHAPTER 12

What's in a Name?

In *Romeo and Juliet,* Juliet tells herself that "a rose by any other name would smell as sweet." However, numerology doesn't completely agree. Names and what they mean numerologically offer a complete and dramatic perspective. They have a profound effect on how we relate to and experience others.

Seeing Your Life

One way to understand how this works energetically is to try this image. Say you are going to strain some pasta from the water it's been cooking in. When you pour the water and the pasta into the strainer, if it is strong, water goes right through the screen and the pasta is prevented from further movement and stays behind the screen. Energetic units and the way they interact are like this. Some things flow through or flow together easily, and others don't even make it through to interact with anything but the strainer.

There is one main difference between pasta and vibration. In the case of vibration, the lack or abundance of full flow-through with energy isn't caused when one element is heavy or another flowing. The flow or lack of it is governed by the vibrational compatibility or the diminishment of interaction. Without meaning to, we create dams. We dam up our ability to flow fully into life with the vibrational qualities of our name.

QUESTIONS?

What are the elements of your unit?
You are made of a soul essence, life task, year of birth, natural talents, and a reconstructor of self-love. This is a package, a bit like a computer program now ready to go. The first job is to get the bugs out. The second job is to learn how to use the program. And finally, when the hard work is done, we get to apply the useful qualities the program brings us to improve our life and upgrade our skills.

Each Step Is Progress

Life is a big adjustment. When we are born, we need to get used to our family and our surroundings. Along with the pleasant and the enjoyable, there is also the difficult and uncomfortable—things like noise, smog, foods that don't go down too well, teething, and illness. And most importantly, we have to find ways to interact with our surroundings that enable us to get our needs met.

Over time, we get the bugs out. We handle discomfort with more stoicism. We adjust our senses to accommodate all the various intense sensory qualities of our world. We adjust to food sensitivities, and we learn how to get what we want. We change or alter our behavior. Like putting a strainer around our behavior, we give some things and hold other parts back.

We Go One Step Further

The next step is to get a handle on how to use life. This is the highly experimental time. Usually from about two to twenty years of age on, we are experiencing. Each experience can be seen like a strainer that accepts parts of us and disallows other parts to flow through. If we feel accepted and comfortable being ourselves, then we engage with life more fully. If we are ignored, controlled, put down, or treated as too much bother, then we control or monitor how we engage with life.

We become cautious with a critical or abusive person. We become relaxed and open with an accepting person. When we become cautious, we are engaged in the act of sieving what we give to life. We change our behaviors based on the response we are getting. We sieve back more of ourselves in some situations and with some people than we do with others.

ESSENTIALS

Something similar happens with your name and how it interrelates with your universal unit. The vibrational combination of soul essence, life task, year vibration, manifestation of talents, and reconstructor of self-love all come together to create the basic unit of vibrational qualities you have brought with you. They were all in you when you were born. This is God's gift to you. What you do with these gifts is your gift back to God.

The Life Journey

The moment you entered your body was and is considered to be the most sacred of moments. This moment of passage imprints into your unit of energy a pattern of vibrational coordinates that mark your path in life.

Numerology teaches that this does not cast your life in stone in the sense that all you need to do is get on the bus and ride a predestined journey. Not at all. Numerology teaches that this moment of touchdown and the imprint it leaves on us bonds our unique quest for learning into the vibration of Earth. We would call these coordinates strengths and weaknesses, talents and defects, or views on life—such as pessimist or optimist, taker or giver, a powerhouse of energy or a passive follower. Now, with your birth time perfectly coordinated by the universe to give your own unique unit the best possible welcome into life, you are here. We come here to prove what we are capable of doing.

This is a hard school because we are learning to respond appropriately to every situation life brings us. "Appropriately" means knowing when to respond physically, or emotionally, or mentally, or spiritually. By having the development in each one of these areas absolutely equal to the others so we can actually *choose* our responses.

FACTS

We all know people who respond emotionally when what is needed is a mental reaction. We all know people who do the opposite. There are people who respond spiritually when a physical response would be more in keeping with the situation, and vice versa. No one can tell another how they should be responding for their own highest good, but we can watch others and learn about ourselves and choose our own responses better.

The process of learning to show what we are capable of as contributing people who use every situation in life as a gift to raise our personal quality is *very hard*. This is a difficult school, but we are here, which means we want to be here, mean to be here, and are allowed to be here. But the bottom line is that it's hard. It's hard because we get our experiences for learning in real-life events, events that can be tremendously painful and demanding. One could say this universal school is equivalent to MIT or Harvey Mudd. It requires everything we have within to make it through and be happy and satisfied with our quality improvement over the span of our years.

And then because we are all essentially on loan to one another, the universe calls back the loan at its own timing. We have many, many hellos and good-byes in our life until we reach the coordinate for our own journey back to where we came from. At a time that is meant to be controlled by the universe, not us, that coordinate appears in the energetic or vibrational pattern of life, and in much the same way that we matched coordinates to be born, we now match coordinates to die. Our body returns to the Earth, and we continue our journey through time and space on our micro millisecond of time.

This is a *huge* experience . . . this life. Would you go to Harvey Mudd without the right books? Or would you enter MIT with no computer skills? That would be unthinkable, but this is exactly what we do when we enter this school and get a name that doesn't suit our learning and our purpose for being in life.

Names Mean Many Things

Some Native American tribes named their children twice—after birth, they gave a baby a name that suited its early development and their apparent personality, and then again in early adolescence, being influenced at that time by the child's personality.

We do not have this orientation in our culture. We create the name basically based on parental preference or family lineage. The importance of the name is acknowledged because much is built around it both metaphysically and physically. People are known by their names, declared by their names, compared by their names. Names are used to make blanket statements: "I have liked every Nancy I have ever met"; "Never met a Jeff who was fully grown up"; "Bet there are no Pauls in prison." We comment on names: "That is such a pretty name"; "What an odd name." Some people do runs on names: "Every Jane I have met becomes a friend"; "All the men I meet now are named Jim." Some names resonate deeply within us and others seem to jar when they are said. What we are responding to is the vibrational way the name coordinates with us.

Names Change

Although we think of names as permanent, sometimes people do change their names, as the following demonstrates:

- People who have a name that "isn't me" might change it in the course of their life.
- A child headed for adoption will often be given one name by the birth mother. The adopted parents will then give the child another name.
- When a woman marries, she will sometimes take on the last name of her husband.
- When a child is named after some other member of the family, the child is often called by a nickname to prevent confusion.
- People will often shorten a person's name, particularly a child's name, to a nickname because they just don't want to take the time to say the full name. We have names that become routinely altered to another, quite different name, like Richard to Dick, Robert to Bob, and Elizabeth to Lizzy.
- Sometimes people are addressed by a term of endearment instead of their given name.
- We have a series of names—first, middle (sometimes many middles), and then last, and sometimes we switch them around to get another first name.

There are a lot of times when name change becomes a part of a person's natural life evolution.

Names Make a Difference

Each one of these given names, name changes, name alterations, and names that are slapped up close against us in a flow line pattern has an effect upon how we insert ourselves into life and love. What we want in numerology is one name that has been picked with skill at the time of birth, one name that the person is called throughout his or her life. This provides a consistent and steady engagement with life. The person comes to know him or herself over time. They become filled with self-knowledge as a result of their consistent flow through their name into life. If the name has been skillfully picked with the child's uniqueness as the foremost consideration, this steady and stable development into maturity creates a life that is deeply harmonious with what the person is here to experience.

With each name change, the vibrational unit of the soul needs to readjust to the new terms of engagement now outlined by the new name. There will be an inevitable period of adjustment. This period of adjustment, if the child is lucky, will be adapting to a name that is a better vibrational fit. Or, if the child is not lucky, he or she will be adjusting to a name that makes life, which already in the best of times is demanding, more difficult than it needs to be.

FACTS

The name is the translator of your essential self. It is the tool that lay numerology uses to identify who you are and what you're here to do. You come from another world into this one, and your name is the projector that projects you onto the screen of life. A nonharmonious name creates a murky projection, and a harmonious name creates a clear projection.

The Most Difficult Names

Being named after another person makes it very, very hard to define your own uniqueness. Changing your name to take on your husband's takes on the karma of your husband's family, since the last name is the karma. It may make your life easier, but it might also make it harder. In either case, it isn't your own unique karma.

You could, of course, use a nickname, but that's not always a good idea. Generally, it gives the person less room to move since nicknames are usually shorter than full names. Fewer letters, fewer root numbers, and therefore a smaller palette of vibrations to work with.

Most of the numerology you have learned here has to do with your name. What if you have a name that isn't right for you? This is the problem a lot of people have, whether they're aware of it or not. To investigate this problem further, as well as to find out how you can change your name to best fit your life, see Chapter 13.

Compare Your Names

When you work on your numerology charts, use two different names. When doing a chart, start with the full birth name. Then do a formula on the name used to sign checks, your everyday legal name. The birth name shows what was the initial treasure box of self and challenge that was brought in. The name that is used now shows what is being focused on and accomplished, or what area in the person's whole potential has come to the fore as a result of interfacing with life's events.

ESSENTIALS

The name that you use now may be abbreviated, a married name, a New Age name, or a middle name that has been switched to your first name and written on checks as the first of two names. It can be these and many more.

In casting a chart, it is useful to see what you had to start out with and how that pattern is being directed now into a secondary name. In numerology, the birth name never goes away. It always is the first baseline coordinate. Any adjustment in the name creates an adjustment in the basic pattern. This adjustment can enhance the skills and focus implied in the birth name, or it can complicate and confuse an otherwise clear and set course through life.

Start with the first full birth name, which you can think of as the first floor. Next, do the name you use now, the second floor. When doing a chart on a friend, just the current name is usually enough to get a feel for the person. If, however, this is someone who for whatever reason is important to you, start with the birth name and then do the now-used name.

For instance, let's say that your chart's birth-name soul essence is 8, and your current-name soul essence is 5. You have a chart here with a lot of basic soul power, and the adjusted root number will be directing the 8 to expression. The person will be either a great force to reckon with wherever they go—which will be many places—or a person who has a lot of unfocused restlessness. The general rule of thumb is clear and simple. Stay with your birth name, and sign your checks using the full name.

CHAPTER 13

Consider a Name Change

Your name is you. You are known by it. You are described through it. It is your name that identifies you more than your Social Security number or your driver's license. How many times a day do you suppose someone calls you by name? Look at your name as an energetic pattern that you flow through into the world. Is that name truly your own?

Is Your Name Truly Yours?

How can you tell if your name is the best for you? Well, start with your birth name. You have been building a life with this name up until now. How is your life? On a scale of 1 to 10, how happy are you? This is your key to accessing how well you are progressing on your challenge.

QUESTIONS?

Do you want to be happier?
Then you need to progress more evenly. Perhaps as importantly, you would like to have a greater amount of self-knowledge. Your name alteration might be a key.

Your Name Is Your Ticket to Life

Imagine you had decided to go to a school, a hard school that taught many, many things. Your decision was to learn about an aspect of life that just fascinated you—biology. You were so interested in this subject that you applied to and were accepted into this very hard school. You were thrilled and excited to be able to attend this school. You entered the school filled with the joy of learning biology, and you went immediately to your counselor and guide.

Your counselor thought you looked a lot like another student she had worked with, or perhaps she had just read about a great streamlined program for kids. Or maybe she decided you had a great speaking voice and you would probably be a good singer and that's the education you should have. And you are here, still getting settled into this fabulous school filled with amazing opportunities for you to learn so much about yourself in the field of life on Earth, biology. Your counselor looks at you with great welcome and happiness that you are here, and then without a word draws up a class schedule that has no life science in it. Your passion and total commitment to learn about your chosen subject of life on Earth doesn't actually affect her decisions about what classes to put you in. You look like a perfect singer, mathematician, doctor . . . whatever. But she doesn't take into account the entire nature of you, and most of all *what you are here to learn.*

The Learning Starts

You enter the school programs in the pattern of learning that the counselor has set up. It's not your program, it isn't you, but you can't waver from your great interest in biology because the desire to learn it runs so deep. Your subject of interest *is* your nature; you and your lesson are one. But you are in these classes—art, math, English—that are all useful, but you have to look so much harder for your own love life on Earth.

You have to do a lot on your own. You make more mistakes, and your learning is hampered. You start to get a little bogged down, and the friends you draw are also bogged down. Their classes don't fit their passion for their learning either. You all support one another, *of course.* You knew the school was hard, but this is so much harder because none of you are able to learn about the experiences to which you are naturally suited. You and your friends all begin to doubt yourselves on the one hand—will I make it?—and support one another on the other hand—of course we will make it, and if we don't, well, who cares?

Dreams get compromised, trodden on, and destroyed all the time. So slowly, over time, you and your group of friends, perhaps even your community, find ways to accept the deep sorrow that the most basic reason for being here is getting swamped under everything else. Your lesson, instead of being a positive learning, becomes a struggle to learn. You learn because your lesson is you, but it is very hard and discouraging. And it didn't need to be this way!

What It Means

In this story, the you is you, the counselor is the person who named you, the school is life, and the classes you are in are your name. Names can create either a smooth, rewarding connection to life or an uncertain connection. Many people believe the name is picked by the baby before birth and transmitted to the parents. This may well be true. Who knows for sure? But if your name doesn't seem right, if you are always looking at other names, or if in just the last few years you find it doesn't fit, now may be the time to make a few adjustments to the classroom.

You Get to Pick

It is very, very important for you to choose your new name yourself. This is a very important decision to redirect your life. At every gateway or turning point of life, you always want to collect needed information, but you don't want advice. No one else lives with the outcome of your decisions as directly as you do. You have to be able to look at yourself in the mirror each day and take responsibility for the choices that brought you to this moment in time. Then you can fully reap the bounty of both the expected and unexpected and the outcome in your actions.

After you pick some names, take them to a skilled astrologer/numerologist. Together, you can go back to the moment of your birth and take a close look at your birth energy pattern. Watch your practitioner study the coordinates, and compare the names you have chosen as possible candidates to make the best choice.

The practitioner should discuss with you your potential name. You should learn how it will alter your patterns and therefore how it will change the way you interact with life. He or she will redo the formulas from the new name, and you can talk at length about how this shifts your awareness of your essence and the work you are here to do.

FACTS

When the name change process is done well, the correlating links between touchdown, essence, task, talents, self-love, and name become an effortless flow of mutual partnership and assistance.

There are ways you can link into this information yourself as well. The work is a bit complex, because it includes both planetary movement and numerology, but it is a fun experiment.

Remember, what you are seeking is the right combination of numbers and letters to maximize your ability to be yourself—the person you want to be—*at all times!* Trust your own intuition about what is right for you.

The best, the very best, way to get a new name is to work with a highly skilled, well-trained astrologer/numerologist. But for yourself and your own information, your own fun, and perhaps to get a new name, let's begin understanding how to do it.

What to Consider

These are the areas of concern that should be looked at when changing your name:

1. To achieve good progress with the life lesson, it is critical for you to select a unit of vibrations (your name) that creates an environment for optimum benefit. They must support the life lesson and facilitate the sharing of the great treasures you bring into this life.
2. The first name is your key to unlock your life, while the first letter is the cornerstone on which the entire structure of your unit is built. Of course, you want a name through which the qualities that you want to accentuate can flow freely and well supported. This has to do with the structure of your first name and how it relates to your birth touch-down time and the balance with which it supports the development of other aspects of yourself.
3. The last name is your karma. Karma is not a punishment. It is the effect of an earlier action, which is to say it is your tool for learning. It is that which holds you to the wheel of life and learning. The numerical value of these numbers can show you what you have been given to work with karmically.

ESSENTIALS Each letter of the alphabet has its own very specific quality. When you combine letters into a name, the particular letter-number combination creates a unit of energy through which that person organizes or creates his or her personality. This is why name changing is so powerful. Unless you know what you're doing, it's really better not to meddle with your name.

A Case Study

For instance, the name Sheila Cornell would look like this:

```
      5  9     1              = 15 = 6
  S  H  E  I  L  A
  1  8        3              = 12 = 3

*S is the cornerstone letter
                              6+3 = 9 (KEY)


     6        5              = 11
  C  O  R  N  E  L  L
  3     9  5     3  3        = 23 = 5

                             = 11+5 = 16 = 7 (KARMA)
```

First Name

The name "Sheila" as the key to the life learning and expression is done through a 6/3 = 9 combination. At a soul level, Sheila is based in the family, the maternal, the nurturing, community, and country. Her key to life rests on the S = 19 = 10 = 1. She brings from deep within her soul a knowing of singular expression and spiritual humanitarianism. This can be a deep soul memory of standing alone in a strong belief. The S is the snake, the symbol of great wisdom and full-body connection to the mysterious ways of Earth.

Her reconstructor of self-love—a very important key to a balanced life—is an inner personal life filled with fun, popularity, and variety. All this combines to a total experience of finding and expressing a new type of humanitarian. The S shows she carries in her heart the learning of wisdom she gained in another time and place. This humanitarian loves family and fun, and through this warmth her humanitarian key to life emerges.

So Sheila's key to her life lesson resolution is wise humanitarianism. She is family-oriented. Fun is her dream of what a perfect life would be, and being the humanitarian of warmth and love in matters of home and pleasure are the key to movement in the life lesson.

Last Name

Sheila's last name provides the karma formula. This tells us that her soul's karmic challenge is 11, signifying great spiritual wisdom and knowledge. The inner reconstructor of self-love is a 23 = 5. Karmically, this would indicate that the desire to utilize the wisdom of the soul 11 to be a shaker-mover in the culture had occurred in another time and space. And this now leads to a 7 karma, a karma to look deeply for the truth, to seek pleasure, fun, and people, but with a problem in not using her family and her spiritual wisdom for personal profit, personal selfish knowledge—or, in short, an unsharing personality. This life would be devoted to becoming truly personal with others. Having everyone become an extended family 6/3 = 9 should weaken over time her tendency to look only inwardly for what is real and what is true.

The Full Name

Now, looking at the entire formula would indicate that this person was born with great inner wisdom, a desire to benefit humanity, and a great love of family. She then detaches and may become powerful and very inaccessible. She is here to share with great good will and nurturing her profound spiritual truths and glide as gracefully as a snake through the challenges of life.

Look at this name and see the numbers that might make this journey or learning harder. A 2 in the first name could make her too relationship-oriented to find comfort in the detached aspects of 9. An 8 in the last name could have given her too much hunger for power to be able to overcome the mandate of the karma, which is to get close to others, while still rejecting selfish power.

Birth Time

In this case, "SHEILA" doesn't have a 2 and "CORNELL" doesn't have an 8, but the touchdown time or birth time might. Many people who have changed their names will find within usually one or two years that their lives have changed. Let us say Sheila Cornell was born, or touched down, on August 21, 1964. In numerology, her life path is 8+2+1+1+9+6+4 = 31 = 4.

The blending of her touchdown time vibrations, which include an 8 and a 2, bring her a life path of 31 = 4. She must learn to bring fun and a strong sense of self into a structured, steady approach to life.

Sheila is head librarian of a large library. She works long hours, has a husband, two children, and a long drive to and from work. Her work is filled with silence and books. Her life is structured by her work environment, and even though she likes her work, she feels that every other aspect of her life is chaotic. She can't really enjoy her kids or husband because work and the environment of it (karma) make it so hard to do a successful transition into her home and be as warm, nurturing, and fun-loving as she longs to be. Her touchdown time shows she must create a structure and then restructure to create smooth transition and the movement she longs for.

A Big Change Is Not Needed

Sheila wants a slight name change that would make this transition from the 7 karmic environment to the 6/3 = 9 soul-longing smoother through the flow of the 4. Well, let's see if Sheila can go through an adjustment that would help.

ESSENTIALS

It is best to change the first name, not the last, until you have a good handle on what you are doing. The first name has a lot of vibrational flexibility in it. The last name is mandated (or preset) before birth, and rules over karma, so it also has the promise to the universe on what you will focus on accomplishing while in this life.

Learn a Bit of Astrology

This is where astrology and numerology join. To continue the process, you will need an additional guide, an Ephemeris, like *The American Ephemeris for the Twentieth Century* by Neil F. Michelsen, revised by Rique Pottenger. In this book, the planets that are retrograde are shaded. Look up your birth year, month, and then day. Make a line under the planets that correspond to your day, look at the shaded ones, and write them down.

Retrogrades and Your Name

In our change of Sheila's name we will be working only with the shaded, or retrograde, planets. "Retrograde" means that in the sky the planets appear to be going backwards. They don't actually reverse their direction, but they do alter their movement, and this has a very interesting effect on human beings. Whatever portion of our behavior the retrograde planet affects becomes difficult to access.

For instance, when Mercury, the planet that affects communication, is retrograde, connections and communications of all sorts will become delayed. Or if Jupiter, the planet of comfort, home, hearth, beauty, and health, is retrograde, remodeling, moves from one home to another, beauty treatments, or health treatments can become miserable to experience until the retrograde is over.

In changing your name, you absolutely do not want to make those retrograde positions more difficult. So you do not want to send more vibration into them. If you have a retrograde planet, look up its corresponding number in the chart that follows.

When a person is born with retrograde planets, it is where the person has some completing or finishing-up work from another time and place to do. A retrograde Mercury indicates that the person comes into this life very unfamiliar with speaking out and communication of their inner truths is hard. A person with a retrograde Jupiter can have great difficulty in understanding how to behave in a way that helps home, health, and beauty to be wonderful and harmonious.

Planet Values			
Sun	1	Jupiter	6
Moon	2	Mercury	7
Venus	3	Pluto	8
Saturn	4	Uranus	9
Mars	5	Neptune	10

Sheila Cornell was born on August 21, 1964, when two planets, Mercury (7) and Saturn (4) were in retrograde. This retrograde Mercury is going to make it even harder for her to express her karmic path and express verbally what she knows. And since her soul number is 6/3 = 9, a lot of the 6 and the 3 can also be nonverbal. This ability to nurture and have fun through action and acts instead of by using words will be a big help for her.

The retrograde Saturn, or 4, is also her life path 4. This can make her *very, very, very* serious about everything. The soul essence of 6/3 = 9 is going to be hammered by that very severe and serious retrograde 4 and the diminished verbal skills of the retrograde 7. So what Sheila doesn't want in her first name are more 7s or 4s. They will blend into the already dense 7 and 4 and make it extremely hard for her to get free. We can say that her parents did a good job naming Sheila, because the qualities of "Sheila" can bring such a light and free joy to these heavy hidden aspects of the 7 and the 4. But can she enhance it a bit?

Trying Out Changes

What if Sheila changed her name to Sheilea? Let's take a look:

```
      5  9     5  1      = 20 = 2
  S  H  E  I  L  E  A
  1  8        3           = 12 = 3

                          2+3 = 5
```

If Sheila became Sheilea, she would have a 20 = 2/12 = 3 equation with the result 5. It would enable her to have more fun in a smaller group, one on one, than the 6, which stands for family. It would encourage her still to have fun and it would direct her toward combining these, the 2/3, into a 5. This will execute a desire to have more experiences and not get into ruts.

Her job would be fun, and people would combine perfectly with her 5 and bring her a whole new outlook on the relationship of work and pleasure. It would be easier for her to express a range of feelings nonverbally as well as verbally, and she would be able to take the pressure off that retrograde 7. She can dance, laugh, make faces, and demonstrate her feelings in a number of nonverbal, eloquent expressions. All of this should bring the joy of life to the fear and suppression in that retrograde 4. What we would have here would be a lighter, happier person—in this case, all by adding a single letter to a first name.

Get Help from the Experts

These changes are so complex that most of the best astrologers/ numerologists can't see all the ramifications a change will create. You and you alone will walk this path. So let it be well thought out. Seek a specialist for the final surgery on your name, but in the meantime, have some fun. Play around with your name equations and your birth, or touchdown, equation. Get a name that runs smoothly with your touchdown/ birth time, and you are off.

Make sure you check the retrogrades. Don't pick a name whose numbers have the retrograde numbers. If a single letter has the same number, this doesn't matter so much, but you don't want to have your added numbers, and most especially your root numbers, to have the same number as a retrograde planet on your birth date. If it does—first name only now, since you're leaving changes to the last name to the skilled ones—then work to change it one letter at a time. Then use the names you have always loved. Look around you, everywhere, and apply them all. It can take a while. This is you and your life we are talking about here! Over time, you will find a name that is right.

First name:

VOWELS: = _____

_____

CONSONANTS: = _____

Key: _____

Last name:

VOWELS: = _____

_____

CONSONANTS: = _____

Karma: _____

Full name:

_____

ALL LETTERS: = _____

Talent: _____

Birth time (total of month, date, year): _____

Life focus number: _____

Retrogrades: _____

New first name:

VOWELS: = _____

_____

CONSONANTS: = _____

Key: _____

New first name:

VOWELS: = _____

_____

CONSONANTS: = _____

Key: _____

New first name:

VOWELS: = _____

_____

CONSONANTS: = _____

Key: _____

CHAPTER 14

Naming Your Baby According to Numerology

We have covered names and the effects of names in Chapters 12 and 13. This chapter will help you put that information in perspective as it is your turn to pick out a name for your baby. This is a momentous event that will affect his or her numerological vibrations in life and the perceptions and personality of the child as he or she grows.

Why Naming Is Important

Babies are named very soon after their birth, and sometimes even before they arrive in this world. Names come from many sources. Many parents even experience a dream in which the baby's name is revealed, and some may follow the dream because in the dream it felt so right. Other parents can spend an enormous amount of time choosing a name.

There are fabulous books on the market filled with beautiful names from every country. Friends and family members give many ideas and suggestions. In some cultures, it is customary to name babies after members of the family.

We say both names, first and last, to see how they flow together. By the time the infant has arrived, the name has been chosen and is given to the baby. If the parents haven't yet decided, the county recorder will apply some pressure so there is a name on the birth certificate. Very few babies are unnamed after a few days of life.

From a numerological perspective, with the possible exception of the names that were dreamed, a great step to enhance the personal development of the child is missed here. People name their baby before they really understand the personality of the child and what name seems right based on who they are.

ESSENTIALS

Occasionally you run across someone who renamed their baby a few months after birth because the name just didn't seem right. It is also not too uncommon to have children ask for another name that they "like" better, a name that fits them better, or a name they are more relaxed with.

A Name Establishes Vibrational Identity

Numerology teaches that the name forms the first and most compelling of the energetic forces surrounding us that we have to contend with. Because numbers and letters carry vibrations, and because your unit is ablaze with vibrational interactions, you have to flow with your universal self and the gifts you have been given to express here through your name. It very quickly becomes not just a name but you.

You become saturated with it, subsumed into it. You shape yourself to coordinate with its vibration and in doing so, you are sieved by the name. Now there is wonderful sieving that happens when a child is born with great shyness. A name that carries a vibrational consistency of gentle confidence can change their life from one of self-absorbed inner pain to a gentle journey into life.

A name can help a person who is short on patience move through experience with an intense interest in many diverse things so that the short patience isn't a big problem. The name can also give the child a vibrational timing that makes *everything* move too slowly so the poor kid fills slowly with fury. A name can bring maturity or constant adolescence. A name can alter courage and make it just stubbornness, take fear and create great sensitivity to others, take passivity and turn it into action, or the name can do the opposite in any of those cases. Never underestimate the power of a name or the power that the name has to interact with each one of us to alter and shape our talents to create our destiny.

Now if the truth about names stopped here, there would be certain good names for us all, and, conversely, there would be the troublesome names we should all stay away from. But, of course, it isn't that easy!

FACTS

We are really talking about three sections, or units, that come together when we come into life. The first is our own energetic package that we bring into the world, so uniquely ourselves, to create the potential experience and learning in a life. The second is the birth time. This is the second, minute, hour, day or night, month, and year of your birth. The third is your name. Once these three things have come together, you are wound up and ready to go.

In order to have a name that allows your unit coordinates to line up harmoniously with life, you have to deeply consider the birth time. This is your moment in time. This is your timing for leaving another reality and entering this one. At that moment, the coordinates of vibrations are the point at which Earth opened for you and you passed through into your awaiting body.

Different Approaches to Naming

In Asian countries and in India, the parents of newborns often consult an astrologer/numerologist before they name their children. The birth time is recorded exactly, and the time is taken to an astrologer/numerologist. According to the skill of the person casting the chart, the astrologist/numerologist then envisions the child's inner nature and orientation for the life's journey. The vibrational patterns that are numbers are studied very closely. The strengths that the child brings in are studied. They are clear to a skilled practitioner.

The practitioner also studies the challenges that were brought in until he or she has a good understanding of them. The parents bring in a list of names they have chosen and a name is picked from this list that will coordinate the new baby into life on a vibration of engaging that allows the child maximum access to the gifts and good solid tools for overcoming the portions of self that could create harm to the child or others as adulthood progresses. The practitioner never presents or picks a name. This is karma, and it can only be done by the parents, or later in life, by the person him or herself.

The Ancient Customs

This is also the way of the ancient cultures that had numerology, and its compatible partner, astrology, so well integrated into their culture and life view. It would have been unthinkable for the parent or family to project their will onto the child in the form of the name, with no concern for the nature of the child. Not only was it seen as insensitive to the totally unique qualities of the child, it was seen as shortsighted for the growth of the culture. If you have generations of people all diminished in their capacity to share who they are and what they are here to contribute by their name, how would the culture ever evolve to meet its potential?

Naming Was a Great Event

Naming ceremonies were a cause for great celebration. The highly skilled astrologer/numerologist carefully pored over the parents' pick of names. From the numbers of the birth chart and the obvious life goals of the child, the names were narrowed, and finally a name was chosen. The coordinates were harmonized with the child's purpose, and the name was born. Then from this name, the soul essence, life task, year's effect, talents, and path to self-love could be seen as coordinates that expressed fully the natural intent of the child.

QUESTIONS?

What moment in time carries the greatest importance?
The touchdown, or birth time, carries every single piece of information that is needed to know the person, now just a baby, who has just entered life. The touchdown and the information it carries is considered important for astrologers and numerologists, in their efforts to best assist a person in his or her life's work.

Two Schools of Thought Around Names

There are two basic approaches to how a name should be given. One is that the name is chosen by the person before he or she enters life, and that this choice is communicated to the parent or another adult (for example, a godparent), and that this is the best name because it is what the child wants and therefore should have. The other approach is that the naming is done for the purposes of the namer and not the person being named.

The First School of Thought

Stories abound of how the name for the baby was picked when it came up suddenly and the namer felt, "This is the name! I know it!"

Often, the name is communicated in a dream. Typically, the dream has within it a strong sense of how wonderful and right the name is. This emotional state the namer experiences in the dream creates a wonderful inner feeling of joy and excitement, a wonderful rightness that the giving of the name in this dreamlike form is absolutely right for the baby. Usually the namer also senses the divine aspect of the experience, and this greatly enhances the excitement about the advent of the child to come.

Many others will hear the name spoken or will read it and have that deep sense of inner authority that this name is "It." Often this sense of realization will occur while watching a movie or hearing a name on television or the radio. It also occurs frequently when reading a naming book that is filled with potential names for the coming baby.

SSENTIALS

When someone receives a name like this, it is often accompanied by a feeling of true closeness and tenderness with the baby. This often feels as if the name actually provides a bridge of closeness and oneness that contributes mightily to the prebirth bonding.

The Second School of Thought

Other people name a baby with some purpose. It might also be that the name they choose has personal qualifications of the namer. In this way of naming babies, we have a name that has passed down through generations in a family. In this case you get something like Robert Smith the Fifth. This means that Robert is the fifth generation to carry this name. This name then represents the institution of the family. Through that name, the child is inserted into that institution.

Another way naming occurs is when the namer had a very important and close relationship with another person. This is often a best friend, a beloved relative, or a teacher, someone who had a wonderful influence on the life of the namer. The baby is usually given this person's name for several reasons. One is the hope that if this baby carries this name, some of those great qualities the namer so loved will rub off on the baby. It can also be to honor this very wonderful person by placing their name upon another beloved person—the new baby.

It is also not at all unheard of to name a baby after someone in the hopes of currying favor from that person. A difficult grandparent who has money might be more willing to give it up in a will if a child bears his or her name.

Then there are the names carelessly given. Tired parents or parents relating to an unplanned and unwanted child will throw a name on them just to be done with it.

We Are Completely Equipped

We come into our life fully equipped. Like a wonderful car that is brand new, we carry a fabulous display of required equipment and special unique additions that fill us with the potential to create. Like the car that needs gas and oil to be able to perform well, we need tending and care. A car is not a living unit of energy in the same way that we are. While the name of the car may affect how successfully it will sell in the world, it has a much smaller effect on how well it performs its promised, especially-equipped tasks.

A name for a human, however, is of enormous importance. It not only will affect the ability to be successful in the world, it affects everything. Your name is the lens through which you project all the richness of yourself into life.

We Are Here to Give 100 Percent

You never see a tree wake up in the morning and say, "Oh, I'm tired. I don't think I'll leaf out today. The birds can all go somewhere else. I'm not into it." This just never happens. Trees, flowers, the ocean, mountains, animals, and atmosphere are at full performance capacity, 100 percent, every single day. So regular is this that it seems silly to contemplate a different world where nature was curtailed by fatigue, discouragement, or lack of motivation.

We rely on nature to hold this standard of excellence on a continual basis. We turn to nature for inspiration. We turn to nature to heal our broken hearts. We turn to nature for all our sustenance. We live within complete generosity—nature is constantly facilitating our quality of life and giving 100 percent of herself.

Theoretically this is the template for our lives as well, or so ancient numerology teaches. We are here to give completely of who we are and as self-knowledge develops, we can pick and choose what we give. In picking and choosing how we respond to life, we come to understand cause and effect. Like nature, we choose to evolve some parts of ourselves and cease to nurture others based on who we want to be and become.

Childhood Is for Risks and Fun

Childhood is the time when we get to put it all out there and see who we are and what we get as a result. It's when we learn to start making choices. Then as we develop, we give 100 percent still, but with greater skill, picking and choosing our own personal responses. Life then becomes the great teacher of consequence, and as a result of the consequences we further increase our skill in becoming a more evolved, better adapted, and a higher quality person.

Nature doesn't rely on names to create an energetic unit that enhances its unique participation with the fabric of life. Call an oak tree an apricot tree, and it will still be an oak. But if you fertilize it with apricot fertilizer, prune it to be the size of the apricot tree, complain because the leaves are too big, and get resentful because no matter how you prepare the acorn it doesn't taste right, you have severely limited the oak from being the wondrous, unique gift of itself. This is what happens when a baby is given a name that limits its ability to become fully who he or she is here to be. And if the child is born with a name that pushes them into carrying another's personality, qualities, or family politics, it creates a situation where the oak has to become an apricot and the aspects of neither the oak nor the apricot become well expressed.

A Name Uniquely One's Own

Numerology teaches that we should have a name that is uniquely ours. This doesn't mean that names have to be completely unique, never before seen or heard. It means that the name be seen by the namer as uniquely the baby's and that the baby emanates the name or that the name really feels right. If it happens to be a family name or the name of a beloved, okay, but let it fit the child. Numerologically it is a big mistake to have the child fit the name. What occurs is a great problem with the child developing into full uniqueness. And that limits everything, most especially the wonderful unique gift the baby is here to give.

FACTS

We need only look around to see that everything is unique. There is a law of nonrepetition in the universe, and this is certainly one of life's miracles. No two snowflakes, no two leaves, and no two hands are alike. Not even identical twins are truly identical. Each one of us is entirely unique and nonrepeatable. Each one of us has a wonderful gift to give while we are in this life, and we each have an equally demanding lesson to learn in this life as well.

But we don't want to limit the learning of the lesson. That's because it is very hard, if not impossible, for the child to assume full responsibility for him or herself, since the essence flows through a container that is an institution of expression for another. If one person holds back on the full sharing of themselves, then we are all poorer for it. We are a family of humankind, and for better or worse, we are interdependent. What one does or does not do affects the whole.

How to Manage a Tricky Task

Now what if you had a wonderful friend whose name was Sam. You would love to name your baby Sam because of the friend, but you also just love the name Sam—you just always liked it. This is different. Intent affects energy. Give a child a name with the intent of loving the unique qualities of the name, and this attitude will change the whole name unit and how it fits the baby.

If, on the other hand, you name that baby Sam because your friend died of AIDS and you want his loving ways immortalized, you then make the mistake of filling the pattern of the name with a burdensome responsibility for the child. Looking at names as individual expressions of who we are allows a flexibility in action. This flexibility is the key to engaging the baby's uniqueness in the naming, and this is the heart of numerology's teachings.

Start at the Beginning

That said, there are useful tools that can assist you in understanding the numerological qualities for the name that you know is right for your baby. You can use an intuitive experience, or you can pick a name that seems to express qualities that your baby already expresses. Either of these methods will help you to see what qualities the name you have chosen for your own reasons will bring your baby.

The first tool is to understand the cornerstone or turning point effect of the first letter of the first name. As the innocent joyous energy of your child flows through the name, very important things happen. Your child has entered this life invested by the universe with the following qualities:

- Soul essence
- Reconstructor of self-love
- Natural talent or gift to life
- A lesson to learn

SSENTIALS

This is the treasure chest of uniqueness that makes up you, your baby, and everyone else in the world. This bright and shiny spirit now flows into life. The first vibratory influence that we encounter is the first letter of the first name, and through that very first letter, the filtering of the soul starts.

Physical and Energetic Aspects

As we go into this, it's a good time to reorient into the difference between the physical aspect symbol and the energetic aspects of a symbol. The physical aspects in "A" mean the first letter in the alphabet, a vowel with several possible ways of being pronounced. It is a common sound. Although the symbols may vary, this sound is present in every language.

"A" from an energy perspective is a symbol made up of lively energetic movement, exactly like a number. The number 1 and the letter A both balance and contribute to each other. When a child is given a name where the first letter is A, this becomes the cornerstone of the person, because it is the energetic unit the baby flows first, through the first letter of the name.

Then the soul essence is shaped by the vowels. The reconstructor of self-love is shaped for life by the consonants, and talent or gift to life is shaped by all the letters of the entire name.

Because of obvious limits of last names, we will be working with the first names only. When coming into a deep understanding of your baby, you want to use both first and last names. The first name is the key to life and the last name is the karma. Middle names are controversial as to their contribution to the formula. Generally, the name that is used for signing legal documents and checks is of the greatest value for an adult chart.

The Importance of the First Letter

For our purposes, we will first focus on the first letter and how it directs the innocent energy of the baby upon initial contact. The cornerstone is just what it sounds like. It is this symbol or energetic shape that the child is founded upon. According to the shape of the symbol, the foundation functions in a certain way, giving certain characteristics to the life view and denying others. It has a great capacity to vitalize or reduce, expand or contract, stabilize or destabilize the person's life, and that means the person's entire life. It governs natural perceptions and viewpoints that have to do with the physical/material plane of life rather than the spiritual. One could see it as a cornerstone, an anchor into life, or a turning point, as all the unique potential to create turns on this letter.

FACTS

So again, we look at the shape and determine the characteristics of the cornerstone. "A" would bestow very different qualities on a child than "S" would, and both those letters would then bestow very different qualities than "P."

Cornerstone Letters and Their Characteristics

It is the spaces created by the lines as well as the lines that tell the story.

A   A triangle with a balanced midline, this letter amplifies the practical matters of Earth, especially as it adjusts and adapts. It is stable, and it represents new ideas and concepts.

B   Made up of two semicircles on a single vertical line, this letter builds by taking two things and creating a third. It is the Builder of Balance (stable) and the Bringer of Beauty.

C   A semicircle, this letter creates and coordinates. Its rocking base represents creation in all endeavors.

D   A semicircle attached to a horizontal line, this letter discriminates and directs. It is stable, and it represents patience, building, and formed and firm foundations.

E   Made up of three vertical lines attached to one vertical line, this letter engages and examines everything. It is stable and represents the qualities of moving on, change, and excitement.

F   Made up of two horizontal lines attached to one vertical line, this letter formulates, fixes the forms of life, and forms stable relationships of service and free will. It is flexible.

G   A semicircle ending in a horizontal line, this letter gives greatly to generate growth. It is rocking, bearing burdens, and it seeks the spiritual; it also represents deep inner reflection.

chart continues on next page

H   Made up of two vertical lines with one horizontal at the midpoint, this letter heightens and widens what is seen, strengthens and ennobles. It is stable, a balance of giving and receiving.

I   Made up of a line, this letter is about inspiration and intuition. It is stable, attuned to spiritual values, and has an uplifting presence.

J   This rocking letter represents the journey of justice, a balance of rebirthing amidst the changes. It's about keeping the goal in mind.

K   A vertical line bisected by two diagonal lines, this letter is kissed by spirit. It is stable, and represents knowledge from above and Earth, the unity of personal and divine will. It carries great vision and skill for uplifting humanity.

L   Made up of a vertical line and horizontal baseline, this stable letter is the long path to go, the letter of "let's get going." It represents strong convictions and firm communication skills, and it is a force for all.

M   Made up of two vertical lines joined by two diagonal lines, this letter forms two mountains of stability. It is responsible and practical, and it represents manifesting, in the sense of the maternal, close and personal service to others.

N   Made up of two vertical lines joined by one diagonal, this stable letter nourishes, nurtures, and notices. It is about change and the constant demands to move out the old and engage the new.

O   A circle, this rocking letter is the mantric "Om," open to all-knowing, complete, and represents organization. It is oriented to and sees the whole picture.

P   Made up of a vertical line and a semicircle, this stable letter represents power, pure and simple. It is the humanitarian, an authority in philosophical leadership.

Q   A circle, with a diagonal line through its base, this letter is rocking and stable, queenly. It represents quality, great vision, and the ability to give and receive in great balance. It has the power to encourage generosity in others by demonstrating broad visionary generosity.

chart continues on next page

R   This stable letter represents return to love, running to help, reconstruction, an important time to embrace unfoldings and endings, forgiveness, and compassion for all life.

S   Made up of two joined semicircles, this rocking letter is spiritual and serene; it represents the source of mankind's new template and surrendering to the highest source of wisdom.

T   Made up of one vertical and one horizontal line, this stable letter is about turning, time awareness, and timing; it represents the crossroad awareness to life and the turning points of spiritual awareness.

U   Made up of two lines and a rounded base, this rocking letter is the urn, the universal vessel of wisdom and union, and the humankind love. It shares its wisdom and love with humanity.

V   Made up of two lines, this stable letter is a vessel of universal consciousness and of value; it is visionary, vital, volunteering, the doer of great work, the builder of ideals.

W   This stable letter represents wonder, willingness, a balance between attachment and release; it is the wisher of good things and lives the law of impermanence.

X   Made up of two diagonal lines bisecting at midpoint, this stable letter possesses X-ray qualities of insight, and it directs to the material plane what it receives from the higher realms. It requires courage and strength, completely unique and unlike any other.

Y   Made up of three lines joining at midpoint, this stable letter represents yield, saying yes, having a choice, and winnowing; it offers choices to unfold the essential meaning of life at many choice points.

Z   Made up of two horizontal lines, this stable letter represents zenith, zest, and zeal. It stands for "Zoe," the ancient life force. It is gentle, benevolent, prophetic, and it needs to have the balance between giving and receiving.

The cornerstone symbol or foundation letter gives us our orientation to our gift of presence here and the type of inner strength we need to proceed through the illusion that there are blocks in life. These blocks are an illusion the life lesson distortion of perception creates.

ESSENTIALS Each letter has both a great strength and an important gift to give just by being alive. No letter is better or worse than any other. Humanity is filled with variety, and each gift has its place. Each lesson that we have, though we are absolutely unique in our approach to it, is a type of lesson that has been learned by many before us.

First Letter, First Name

The foundation, cornerstone, or turning point that is created with the first letter of the first name provides an entrance for your child into life, and it will have a tremendous impact on his or her life. Know what this letter brings to your child. Then, like you would approach any childrearing issue, support the unique way your child exhibits the gift of the letter. And then help to support the development of this gift to your child as he or she progresses through the challenges of life. It is this letter that represents their strength, and that is something they can deeply believe in about themselves. When life gets tough, as it invariably does on occasion, it is this belief and their ability to carry it out that will strengthen them. It will recenter them. It will help keep priorities straight, and they will be closer to fulfilling the promise they made in their soul, the promise of what they would accomplish here, the promise of the gift to life they would lead, the promise their soul made to the universe. No matter how hard life gets, if this promise is honored, there will be joy in the soul. This may be your greatest gift to your child: the gift of understanding true resiliency and the truth of self-trust, and it is all given through a single letter!

Your Numbers for Love, Money, and Happiness

Wouldn't it be just wonderful to open the chapter and look up your lucky number? A lucky love number! A lucky money number! A lucky career path number! A lucky life number! Well, you do have those numbers. These are the numbers you have been learning to formulate.

Lucky in Love

Your soul essence number *is* your lucky-in-love number. Have you ever heard the phrase "If you want love, then be it"? Your soul essence number is your energetic coordinate to a happy love life. Why is that, you might wonder. The soul is the essence of love. Your soul essence number—one of the nine root numbers, and one of the two master numbers—is your source of ultimate joy and love while in the midst of life and all of its beauty and challenges.

FACTS

To review, we have ten essence numbers—1 through 9, and 10, which includes everything and adjusts to a different type of 1— because Earth is a 10 vibration planet. In addition to the nine essential essences, there are the 11 and 22 master numbers.

How can you take charge of your essence number in a way that allows you to feel the effects of its joy more deeply in your life? We are talking about energy here that is identified by a number and the characteristics that are the qualities of that number. This is a flow of energy from the universe to Earth that makes up a larger flow called time.

Get It to Work for You

To connect deeply and fully with your soul essence number, you need to do some inner work. Since this is your soul essence, it is, of course, always there. It is essentially you—*the* essence of you, which you can't separate from.

However, you can deepen your skill at managing it. You can hone your awareness in living more closely to its ever present gifts. You can develop greater clarity on the components of your essential nature, and in this process of you coming to know your inner world, you will have more and more love as a part of you and your life.

Love is the great mystery, but we all seek it and it seeks us. In Kahlil Gibran's great words, "Think not that you can guide the course of love, for love—if it finds you worthy—will guide your course." Gibran surely meant "worthy" in the sense of being able to feel love, respond to it, express it, and receive it. With this in mind, let's explore some good ways to feel your essence, respond to it, express it, and receive it!

Try a Variety of Techniques

Your soul essence number is your key to love. Here are your ways to engage this love essence of you more fully in your daily thoughts, actions, feelings, and expressions. Note that of the exercises below, the final seven are particularly powerful.

1. Tap out your soul essence number with your fingertips on a surface.
2. Breathe a big breath and inwardly count the inhale and exhale so the breath is a measured breath inhaling and exhaling to the count of your soul essence number. (If your essence is a 1 or 2, count slowly. If it is 8 or 9, count more quickly, but keep it easy, relaxed, and measured.)
3. Lightly squeeze the tip of your nose the same count number as your soul essence.
4. Look at something pleasant and blink your eyes the same number as your soul essence.
5. Stand on the earth, and curl your toes into the grass the same number of times as your essence.
6. Pick flowers, collect rocks, or line up sticks the same number as your soul essence.
7. Count your steps to your essence number as you walk.
8. Write a word that you like the same number of times as your essence number.
9. Look for the symbol shapes in the world around you: circles, semicircles, triangles, straight lines. When you see one, construct it mentally into your essence number.
10. Are you the impatient type? Tap your foot or wiggle your legs to the beat of your soul essence number.
11. Doodle the symbol or joined symbols that make up your number. Look to the stars to find it.
12. Do or have done an artistic rendering of the number and just look at it each day.

13. Think about the number. Repeat it mentally over and over a few times; visualizing the number with a variety of colors.

14. Imagine a fragrance associated with your soul essence number, and breathe it while you think about the color.

15. Look into nature and see how many times you can see your soul essence number replicated in the forms of nature.

16. Count things, anything really, in a series of your essence number.

17. Tap your fingertips against your thumbs the same number of times as your soul essence number.

18. Look for your soul essence number in arts, photographs, and graphic images. Imagine if your soul essence number had a feeling to it, what would it feel like? This feeling state may change from time to time. That's fine.

19. Count in repeated counting repetitions or runs.

20. Move in rhythmic movement, synchronizing with your counting sequence. If your number had a sound, how would it sound?

21. Do you lift weights in repetitions? Curl your eyelashes? Tap your fingers on a surface? Walk to release stress? Do each one in the repetitions of your soul essence number.

Be wonderfully creative. You are learning to heighten and then automatically fine-tune your soul/love essence. Each time you draw, smell, see, hear, or taste it, you have consciously become well anchored into the flow of your soul/love essence number.

Success in Your Career

Your talent number holds your key to success. To focus on this flow line to career happiness, you can use the previous techniques. But it is particularly wise and efficient to work on honing this essence to focus it in the career environment.

Perhaps what the soul essence exercises have demonstrated to you is that the numbers are really everywhere. They are in nature—in the most lovely and remarkable ways! They are in the structure of buildings, the shapes of our bodies, the patterns of clouds, and they are etched in celestial bodies. They surround us at every level of our lives. When focusing yourself into this sea of abundance and to draw one more closely to the surface, all you need to do is practice action and awareness.

Look at the elements of your career choice, as follows:

- The practical elements: Paper, pen, computer, phone, fax.
- The mental elements: Planning, effectively communicating, a good grasp on needed information.
- The emotional elements: Good listening, not taking things too personally, the satisfaction of success.
- The spiritual elements: The knowing that you are sharing a gift given to you by the universe and that in sharing it, you give back your thank-you to the universe; the ability to rebalance from the challenges of personal life when becoming deeply engaged with your career.

For each type of element, use your talent number to enhance your working experience.

Physical Elements

- Organize your desk so that the things on its surface repeat your career number whenever possible.
- Have the form of your career number displayed on your desk.
- Draw your number with the tip of your finger as you are refocusing.
- Sitting at your desk, tap your heels on the floor the right number of times.
- Have a bouquet of flowers with the number of blooms the same as your number.
- Have pens lined up in the drawer. Get the same number as your talent number.

Mental Elements

- Plan your calendar in groups of your career number. For instance, if you are a 2 talent essence, you might organize your calendar and your goals in 2s.
- Stack your books, order your world, and create your open spaces in groups of your talent number.
- To quickly refocus, draw your talent number with the tip of your finger.

Emotional Elements

This requires some understanding of the elements that make up your talent essence number.

1	Walk or move somewhere quickly and on your own.
2	Sit down for a quick chat with someone you like.
3	Whip open a good joke book.
4	Think about the great stability of the chair, the room, the building, your bike, car, or anything.
5	Take 5 to a travel agent and get some quick information about a future trip you might take.
6	Call a friend who needs some comfort and set up a time to get together.
7	Collect favorite quotes, and either read them or add to them.
8	Figure out how you can work harder more easily.
9	Send a check off to a favorite charity.
11	Write a quick article for that tiny little spiritual press.
22	Do a quick sketch of an ideal planned community.

Spiritual Elements

Visualize or imagine your talent number, and give thanks for the opportunity to utilize this vibration for your learning and to share with life.

Unless you also know how to orchestrate the numbers to your advantage, having your numbers done or getting a very complete numerology chart drawn up does limited good. The chart becomes wonderful information that is impressive in its detail, but it is not something that is truly practical and bottom line.

The Turning Points

There is value in finding the number that is ascribed to you through the formulas. Thinking about the number or doodling it brings you into harmony with your light wave. We all know how many choices we have in each day. We all know also how those turning points of life occur. Sometimes they are obvious, like a death, but others steal in as if cloaked in darkness. It isn't until later that we look back and say, "That was a turning point!" or, "If I had known then what I know now, I would have made a different decision."

It is in these turning points we are given the opportunity to add or subtract something from our life. It is these turning points that become the end of one chapter of our book of life and the beginning of another chapter. It is in these moments in our life that we re-evaluate our decisions that have brought us to this moment in time. We can then, to a great extent, decide what to continue to engage with and what to drop away. We have these opportunities to get a new lease on our life.

We can burn up deadwood, say goodbye to that which is no longer useful, and realign with new opportunities to further the creation of the life we love to live. Turning points are moments in time when we get to alter our course, correct our relationships, and redirect our careers.

Times of Loss

The most obvious turning points are the times of loss. The bigger the loss, the more filled with opportunity is the turning point. Unfortunately, though, at these very times when we have such great opportunity to re-evaluate and reconstruct, we are usually (and understandably) so subsumed in the challenge of bearing the loss that we miss many of our opportunities to utilize the turning point creatively.

Do you remember these words of wisdom about understanding and loss?
"In every hello, there is a goodbye."
"We are all on loan to each other, and the universe calls back the loan when it is ready."
"Every cloud has a silver lining."
"One door closes, another opens."

Beginnings and endings are truly the fabric of life. The law of impermanence is the life we live, the body we inhabit, and for the most part, the part of life that everyone denies.

We act for the most part as if we can hold the ship of our life just where we want it, while in fact the ship of self is constantly being buffeted by the winds of change. Change continually challenges our ability to connect with our course and direct it in a way that our life improves. This is a huge life challenge, in fact, it is such a big one that most of us deny the constant significance of change, imminent or on the horizon. And yet we know it is out there and it always will be the most dynamic part of our life.

So we seek tools to help us when we are engaging loss on some level. Loss comes in so many different guises. You didn't make the team. You got a B instead of an A. The friendship fell apart, the child has more problems than expected, the marriage is much more work than expected, terrorists have made their impact known. Every life evolves into death. Loss is our great teacher and we have a true love-hate relationship to gain and loss.

In truth, gain can only come after loss. So the real challenge of life is to accept what is being perceived as loss and manage it in a way that you can, to the very best of your ability, maneuver through experience. This is done in the way you relate to it. Positive thinking is great, but often it is too superficial to really connect with the inner river of disorientation that occurs before we experience its benefit. That means we are bathing in a moment, a day, a week, month, or even years of loss. But if we don't have the tools to maneuver through loss, then gain cannot really occur full measure. Gain is the other half of loss. To experience both fully enables the circle of life and the necessary learning to balance and complete.

Numerology Can Help

Numerology can help because it facilitates the movement through the loss point without missing one valuable step, and, at the same time, it helps avoid your inner victim. It is your victim, not loss and gain, that is your worst enemy. Change-loss-gain is the teaching format of life. To be able to weave through the entire cycle of change-loss-gain, change-loss-gain, and so on, without becoming bogged down in your victim is an important accomplishment.

Seeing the Larger Picture

The numbers are vibrations that come from infinity and return to infinity. So each number carries a universal perspective, or the larger picture, within it. You are perfectly attuned to a few numbers, any one of which carries your key to perspective and balance and self-development.

In order to have your vibration assistance readily available to you, it is important to let your soul essence number become an ally of sorts. To acknowledge your soul essence number as a living ally within you requires an entirely balanced approach to numbers. This means both approaches have validity: physical math, and energetic numerology.

The best way to find the truth of life for yourself is to try something with one hundred percent enthusiasm. If it is for you, you will know it, and you will have a great tool for enhancing your life. If it isn't for you (and you decide this *after* you have given it a full-attention try), then pass it by. Others may benefit, but it is not for you.

Your Greatest Friend

Perhaps your most precious and certainly your most private ally is your reconstructor of self-love. Although this number is presented as a state of mind that you will automatically return to when alone, that is not always the case. When you are busy, stressed, or distracting yourself with busy-ness, your mind won't naturally rest on this vibration of renewal. It is for this very reason that knowing the vibration you carry to recenter you and to return you to perspective can prevent unnecessary aggravation from occurring.

This particular vibration has always been valuable—otherwise it wouldn't have been given to us by the universe—and it has a particular intrinsic value in times of stress and struggle. If you lived a life in which you had an hour or so to gaze in reverence at the passing clouds, you would automatically slip into your reconstructor of self-love. After cloud-gazing or watching the river flow by, a child playing, a distant mountain, or after performing any other calm or introspective activity, you feel so much better. Why? You have relaxed and renewed, you have enjoyed and received the gift of life being offered, and all of these are invaluable. But if you contemplate the thoughts that drifted in during these moments of reverie and solitude, you will find that they emanate from the orientation you are given by your number for the reconstructor of self-love.

ESSENTIALS

What if you are taking a computer break, enjoying a phone break, driving on a freeway, filled with concern, getting ready to meet the day, or just finishing it up? During these busy times your mind won't naturally just slip into your reconstructor. But if you know ahead of time, you can guide your thoughts toward this balancing point.

Meditation on Your Reconstructor of Self-Love

Meditation is a technique that greatly improves the tension between the life of the body—which wants to survive, be included, and reproduce—and the spirit, which embraces change and challenge to enhance personal growth and increase in personal quality. There are people who devote hours a day to meditation. There are also those who have a good twenty-minute meditation.

FACTS

Incorporating the numbers by embodying them through the five senses is the ancient tool for teaching numerology. As with any skill, the primary focus is not just going through the formulated steps, but to embody them. In order to succeed, you really need to feel, personally, the vast resources of life, love, and the graceful pursuit of happiness present in your life as you form your alliance with these energies and their sparkling liveliness.

In the wisdom of numerology, your meditation is your reconstructor of self-love. And there are numerologists that use the number vibration for this path back to centering and self-love.

To join in the meditative and restorative aspects of your reconstructor of self-love, you can lead your mind in one of two ways: by knowing what the book tells you about your recovery reverie, or by thinking about the root number of the reconstructor at these times, and then seeing what your mind opens into. This type of meditation will personalize the stream of consciousness for you. In the personalizing process, you will retain the useful elements of the reconstructor that are outlined in this book, but they will become very personally yours and your ally as well.

This can also help you in becoming more and more skilled in using this great resource for your deep personal enhancement and significant recovery. It can also contribute to recentering in a life that may at times seem devoid of these gentle and refining thoughts.

CHAPTER 16

1+1 = 2: Compatibility in Love

Relationship is the great knot of eternity. We all long for a rich and rewarding closeness of some sort with something or someone. Some of us have primary heart connections with work or animals or plants. And then there are those of us who as our lives go on are working out the vagaries of communication, chemistry, commitment, and continuity to create heartfelt relationships with other people.

Alone or Together?

The conundrum or riddle usually has to do with learning and growing. How does one be oneself and support the other as well? We want to develop close, trusting, continuous relationships with other people who are dear to us. Numerology does give skills and tools to address our hopes and dreams, and the magi taught how to understand basic relationship balance. What will each person bring to the table and how can we accurately evaluate success?

First Things First

The first essential step to a good relationship is to know yourself. If you don't know yourself or if you don't have a concrete self-awareness, then a truly satisfying relationship is virtually impossible to create. The first relationship tool numerology offers is the tool for self-awareness.

ESSENTIALS

As you come to better know yourself, as you accept yourself more, and as you move to become a better human being, you will learn how to comfortably share yourself. Then, at that moment, you will truly connect with someone who loves you—as you, in return, love them.

Then Comes the Other!

The deepening is a dance between self and other. So much of what happens between two people who have chemistry is electric or numerological. That energy is there from the start, from that first moment, and it will always be there. What we can do is guide the flows. We can gently nudge this wonderful and mysterious connection into rewarding, loving associations. We find our connection by combining self-awareness with a deep interest in what is best for the other and by maintaining a commitment to let what arises from this electrical brew show itself.

Love will show you yourself. Love will show you what you love to accept in yourself and what is heartrending to self-accept in your nature.

It is the great teacher in life. Through the outpouring of this most basic truth of life, we either grow through our connections of love or we wall ourselves away, severing connections because the mirror love holds up to us is too challenging to bear.

ALERT

Love is not for the faint-hearted. Love brings up all that is unlike itself. We often think of love as romantic and ideal. The seeds of the ideal are held within love, but love is also a Rotorooter that scours every area of those people brave enough to live deeply within its splendor and challenges.

Love brings the effort of great personal growth to regain loving self-acceptance. How much has your personal growth flowered into self-acceptance? The answer to that question is another one: How much do you love yourself?

The Most Basic Love

Self-love is like a very personal garden within us. We can plant our seeds of creativity, self-esteem, self-belief, and courage there. We can nourish the growth of these personal aspects. We can radiate to others our self-love and self-acceptance. But we can never have anyone enter this sanctuary within. It just isn't possible. It is our soul place. It is our most personal and private area. It is the part of us that our reconstructor of self-love returns us to. The magi taught that self-love is the igniter that enables us to love another. One cannot exist without the other, and usually they are equal. The degree to which we love ourselves is the degree to which we are able to love others. The degree to which we love another is the degree to which we love and accept ourselves.

But for that special one, the one with whom we have decided we want to share the roller-coaster of life and brave the Rotorooter, we need our ever-present tools to help us on this vital journey of relationship—the acceptance and expression of love.

Receiving Love Is the Miracle

The magi further taught that it is essential to receive the gift. We have so many choices in our culture, such abundance, that it is easy, probably way too easy, to pass from one thing or one person to another without really receiving any gift that is offered by whatever is at hand.

Receiving the gift is the first experience of living—we receive the gift of our life—the bottom-line grounding wire in all life's experiences. If you don't receive the gift, every gift to come your way, you cannot activate yourself to engage appropriately with the experience. You will be engaging only according to your own inner agenda, and that, of course, is repeating a habit, or your karma. Receive the gift, and respond as you choose. After truly receiving, you begin to loosen the ties that bind you into your karma, repetition. Your life task frees you up to work more comfortably with your desire to form and improve lasting relationships. When deepening your ability to be effective with the application of your life task, love will fill you more profoundly. Even in your darkest night you carry an unexplainable feeling of being on target with your learning challenge.

FACTS

This is the larger view of love, the approach to life that enhances the personal, intimate love with another. If you want love, be it *and* receive the gift, as it is, no judgment. Be love. Receive the gift, and respond as you choose, but be a part of it, the dance of life and love.

There Are Three Relationship Areas

Numerology can help you understand what kind of gift will be in various different combinations of numbers. If you are looking to find or deepen a relationship with a loved one, you want to work with three different areas between you: compatible, synergistic, and supportive. Compatible numbers, which are naturally sympathetic to each other, demonstrate a need for expression at a soul level. Synergetic numbers act as opposites, bringing the other person the other life view, the balanced opposite. Supportive numbers allow two people to complement each other.

The general rule of thumb is this:

* Relationship of soul essence is best in compatible numbers.
* Relationship of personality is best in balanced opposites.
* Relationship of life task is best in supportive numbers.

Another way of putting it is this:

* If you want friendly ease and cooperation, seek your compatible number.
* If you want a dynamic, passionate connection that never loses those qualities, seek your opposite number.
* If you want support to find yourself and the other, then look for your supportive flow number.

When you are looking for a valuable relationship or for skills to improve a relationship, it is useful to have an understanding of three different root numbers—soul essence, natural quality, life task—and their best possible connections.

ESSENTIALS

Relationship is complex, and out of necessity we will only be doing a broad brushstroke over this area. If you are intrigued and want to develop your understanding more deeply, turn to Appendix B, where you will find the names of wonderful books to further your quest.

Relationship Wheels

To better understand relationship numbers, we have relationship wheels that visually demonstrate how the numbers work together.

You will be introduced to these wheels in this chapter. Here is what you need to understand about them:

1. The wheels turn counterclockwise because energy works counterclockwise.
2. The number 10 is used in the chart because even though it is usually a root of 1, a 10 essence carries different qualities than a root 1 in relationship, and that needs to be acknowledged.
3. All numbers are compatible, synergistic, and supportive, some combinations more than others.
4. Each combination brings a different type of compatibility.
5. These charts show only the root number relationship. A deeper look would be done by studying numerology further or by working with an expert.
6. Respect and appreciation are always needed for the gift—no judgment.
7. The inevitable irritation that will come up is a part of the mix. When you want that person to be more like you, they can't be. That's good, not bad!
8. Each relationship works both ways.

Soul Essence Numbers for Compatibility

The soul essence relationship that nurtures and renews the soul's journey through life is often represented in the easily compatible numbers. The soul thrives in understanding, acceptance, and nonverbal communication. In soul communication, a simple act can speak volumes. The act of nourishing our souls makes the essential challenges of life more possible.

Renewing the soul in deep human contact makes it easier to rouse oneself to tackle the task of elevating personal quality. It also makes the great demands of the life task easier to reflect upon, stay focused on, and it allows us to have that all-important good progress with the lessons. To share a soul alliance with easy compatibility is an oasis of comfort and renewal. The most easily compatible soul essence numbers are illustrated in the **COMPATIBILITY RELATIONSHIP WHEEL.** Here's what each particular pair represents:

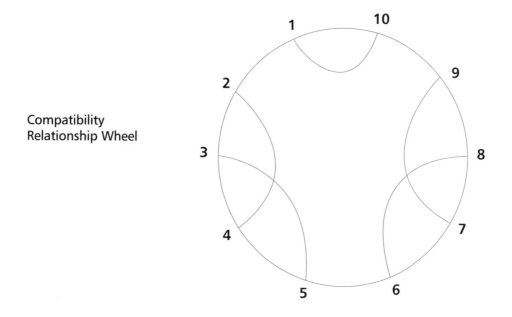

Compatibility
Relationship Wheel

1 and 10: Each understands the value and struggle of individuality, and each one has a different perspective that lends a slightly different and helpful slant.

2 and 4: Both are stabilizers and have an understanding of how that feels and what the joys and challenges are. Both support and stabilize in different ways, but the gluing quality is the same.

3 and 5: On the move, restless, and experiential, neither wants to slow the other down. The commitment is to now, to the experience, to the truth that emerges in the fast-moving, ever-changing panorama of life.

6 and 8: Successful builders of family and substance, both expect to be successful and depend on outward success to confirm the soul's success. Both bring comfort and protection.

7 and 9: These are the thinkers, analyzers, and the seekers of the culture, dedicated to the betterment of humanity and the discovery of truth through the disciplines of the mind.

Personality Numbers for Opposites

You can calculate the personality number by totaling up all the numbers (for both vowels and consonants) in your full name. When it comes to personality, what you want to look for is someone who is a balanced opposite. You love to read news and stories; he or she loves to listen to news and stories. Each will bring the other a piece that got missed, and thus the whole gets filled in. It is just like the way math and numerology come together, balanced opposites each bringing the needed other half to the table. Balanced opposites are synergistic, dynamic, and never boring. Passion stays, and interest in each other never wanes. Always opposites bring to the table qualities the other needs to complete the journey toward wholeness. The challenge is twofold:

1. Appreciate the difference instead of chafing under it.
2. Don't get lazy and let the other person carry those qualities. These are yours to learn too.

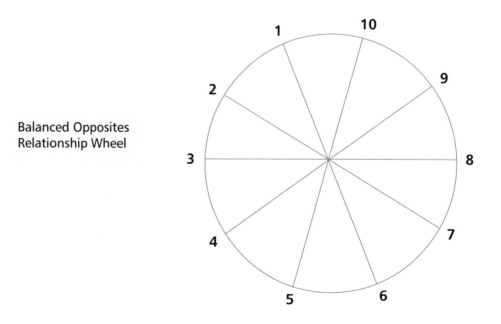

Balanced Opposites
Relationship Wheel

You can see the relationship between balanced opposite numbers in the **BALANCED OPPOSITES RELATIONSHIP WHEEL.** Specifically, here are the relationship meanings in each of the pairs:

1 and 6: The Art of Singularity meets the Art of Union.

2 and 7: The Art of Relationship meets the Art of the Dedicated Mind.

3 and 8: The Art of Pleasure meets the Art of Success.

4 and 9: The Art of Dependable Structure meets the Great Humanitarian.

5 and 10: The Art of Experiencing meets the Art of Seeing the Whole Picture.

Life Task Numbers for Support

As you learned in Chapter 9, the life task number is arrived at by totaling up the day, month, and year of your birth. Supportive numbers are those numbers that with little effort, and usually with pleasure, can support another. This alignment of the numbers is particularly important with the life task. The life task is a commitment to learn something we totally have no idea how to do. It is our lesson—how we are progressing our soul's learning.

Support
Relationship Wheel

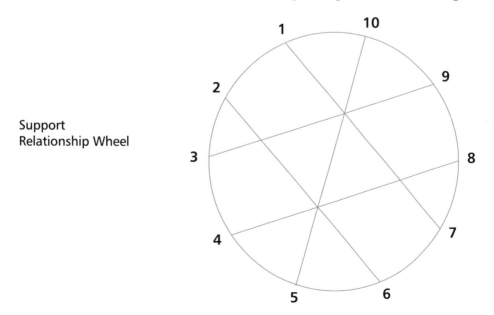

It is the centerpiece of the life, and it is hard. It is wonderful to have a relationship with another who has a life task number that by its very nature gives what is often needed support to learn a hard lesson through real-life experiences.

The supportive numbers are illustrated in the **SUPPORT RELATIONSHIP WHEEL.** For explanations of each specific pair, see the following:

1 and 7: Both are singular and walk their own path. They both know and understand the fun of being unique and the price of being alone. They both are enigmatic and share the peculiar loneliness that comes with being themselves, because no one really gets the 1 or 7 completely.

2 and 6: Both of these life tasks have to do with managing relationships with others. Neither one can be completely happy unless the skill to engage others in relationship and larger union is developed. Both can share the special unique agony of having one's own process so influenced by others. Both support and encourage each other in exploring other methods of relationship and union that may work more successfully for the others, but most especially for the 2 or 6. Both understand the pain of being subsumed in the relationship or union and the challenge of developing the right type of boundary.

3 and 9: Both numbers have a profound interest in others and at the same time an unexpected detachment. Both came to bring up the vibration of the world. Both came to do good work for themselves through others. Both have great personal pleasure in the happiness of others. Both also understand and can support each other in the struggle for continuity, patience with the process, and limits that appear to have no value at all but are there anyway.

4 and 8: The structurer and the builder, these are the confident, dependable numbers that understand the pleasure of steady building and burgeoning success. They both experience great frustration with the flaky aspects of others and wastefulness. Each brings the support that enables the other to move back into the constantly changing flow of life with renewed vigor.

5 and 10: Both see a world filled with great potential. Both feel the drive to engage it, know it, and do something with it. So many experiences, so little time. Each helps the other to see the wholeness and to increase the intensity of the experience. Neither one likes limits, and when they inevitably occur, the limits will be more tolerable in each other's company.

What about 11 and 22?

The numbers 11 and 22 are, of course, also root numbers carried by a variety of people in all the areas, and they aren't included in any of the relationship wheels because their influence is unique.

Because they are perfecting mastery level in whatever area the root numbers total to, 11 or 22, they are primarily catalytic in relationship. When a single root number is with an 11, spiritual truths and issues will emerge from within that person's nature. The journey involves a commitment to personal growth within spiritual inspiration the 11 creates. Much is true for a 22. The 22 will bring up in everyone their own personal joys or insecurities about creating and building.

FACTS

Since both numbers are catalytic to others, sometimes their contribution is appreciated, sometimes reviled. But it is always useful. The 11 and 22 need a well-developed inner strength to make their way through such mixed reactions to them. Fortunately, the mastery qualities of these numbers afford this.

Both 11 and 22 can always benefit from very close relationship with others. Each person carries a gift for themselves, and in their eyes, each gift is equal. Generally, what the 11 needs from another is warm acceptance. What the 22 needs is a place to relax and let down for a while.

In relationship, 11 or 22 essence will amplify the spiritual nature of the other person, both sides—light and dark. And the 22 will challenge the beliefs and skills that have to do with building. Each root number will bring forward its best and worst with the mastery numbers—that's the way it works. We call them mastery numbers because that is indeed what they are. Because they are masters, they bring up all that is their positive essence in another and all that is negative in the essence.

When an 11 and 22 are in partnership, they are dynamite, but must be careful to not burn themselves out.

Because of the catalytic qualities of the 11 and 22, they, more than the other numbers, have to know how to rebalance and contain. But usually, because of their level of wisdom, they can do it.

Relationships are far more complex than a relationship of the primary root numbers. But your basic flow and the basic flow of others are based in the root number. If you get that one worked out, then the nuances become easier to work with.

Missing Numbers

It is also useful to examine the missing numbers in each of your relationship numbers. For each formula, take a look at the sequence of numbers that you have written out, and take note of what digits (from 1 to 9) are missing. Remember, you are not looking at the final root numbers, but at all the numbers that make up the calculation. (For more details about missing numbers and how to calculate them, see Chapter 20.)

It is a great gift to find someone who is quite well developed in a quality that you lack or are weak in, but the gift is not an easy one to receive. First, there is usually an attraction. As their strength begins to point up your weakness, there is often an irritation on both parts. Or another response is to become dependent on the other to carry you on that one, whatever your particular weakness, just so you won't have to. Neither works. What you want to do is acknowledge, through your skill with numerology, exactly what is going on. You are missing 3s, and the other person has 3. Are they driving you crazy because they are like a butterfly flitting from here to there and you want them *here?* Use your burgeoning understanding of numbers to fill in your gap. Lighten up and fly a bit. You will have more fun. It's okay, really, and they won't bug you so much.

ESSENTIALS   If you are looking for an Opposite, but you always end up with a Compatible flow or a Support flow, relax—your natural, wise, inner nature is drawing a gift you need to receive. Let it be. Make good decisions regarding the absolute maintenance of your own quality control, and let it roll. Just keep on going. You'll get there.

CHAPTER 17

Numerology for Your Home— Feng Shui

You can use numbers for better relationships with the world you are a part of, particularly when it comes to the places where you spend your time—your home, office, place of worship, and so on. The formulas in this chapter will guide you to understanding the numerology of addresses and how it affects your life.

Numbers in Your Life

There is a big difference between numbers used for math and the numbers used for numerology. One method is material, the other electric; essentially, one is for wisdom that serves building, and one is for wisdom that serves self-knowledge. However, there are lots of areas where numbers simultaneously have material purposes and numerological possibilities. These areas have to do with the most frequently accessed areas of our lives: cars, homes, checking accounts, tax identification numbers, Social Security numbers—numbers that identify and have a powerful, though for the most part unacknowledged, effect on our lives.

Numbers used for counting and numbers used to identify have a deep and powerful effect on our lives every day. Just as the root numbers of a name can make life happy or tiring, so numbers in life can help make money, create a happier home, make you more successful in business—the list goes on. Or the opposite can happen—unacknowledged, numbers in life can create grief.

Root and Compound Influences

Every sequence of numbers has a root number, arrived at through adding up the sequence, and numerology pays a great deal of importance to root numbers. Furthermore, in more skillful numerology, every number that contributes to the root number is given careful consideration. The number and its location in the formula are significant and are considered very influential in each energetic formula. Each number in the formula sequence affects the qualities of the root number, each adding its own subtle yet powerful nuance to this energetic formula. In this way each root 8 still means power, but the slant of power is different depending on whether you got 8 by adding up 3+5 or 6+2 or 7+1:

3+5 = 8 is fun and travel to power.
6+2 = 8 is power through relations with others.
7+1 = 8 is a singular mental power.

Numbers are sequenced to contribute to the order of our lives. They also affect how we move in life, how we are received by life, and how to secure our place in life. Up to now we have focused only on the individual and the energy pattern and what that pattern coordinate means.

In this chapter we are going to approach the blending aspects. That means you, your coordinated unit, moving out into life and meeting a coordinated unit that developed separately from you for a very different reason. These energetic units were developed because of the need to order and organize for easy access the various arenas of our complex world. This includes the addresses of houses, zip codes, phone numbers, checking accounts, business identification numbers, Social Security numbers, car registrations, and license plates—the list goes on.

The way to arrive at your numerological perspective on these and the effect they have in life is to start at the beginning. What is the purpose of each one of these numbers in your life?

The Powers of Feng Shui

Feng shui is the art of placement. It heralds back to the old Chinese magi. Today, it is our most immediate resource for understanding the tremendous power and effectiveness of the art of placement. Feng shui in the hands of a true professional (choose wisely) can redirect the energetic flows in the most unharmonious structures and create for you an environment that is filled with quiet tranquility in harmony and that enhances the root number of the house.

The old magi were masters in the art of placement, using their vast understanding of numerology to guide them. Most of these arts were lost, except in Tibet and China. China's historical tolerance for an incorporation of energy wisdom into their culture is renowned.

The Connection to Numerology

As you already know, numerology developed as the art of placement. The astrologers would line up a building, a garden, or even a person being healed, according to the magnetic flows from the planets to the Earth. When the lining up was harmonious, then the structure's openings would be ultimately receptive. When the building, garden, or person was not well lined up, then the receptivity to harmony was compromised, and the effect was not optimal.

You do exactly the same thing when you are working with numerological formulas, as you are trying to understand the numbers, how they blend, what they are creating, and what you want them to create.

To work with numbers in feng shui or in numerological formulas is to conduct an orchestra. You ask the violin to get louder and the drums to get softer. You notice there is no piccolo, so you get one. Then you place the instruments in a way that they have maximum cooperation and harmony with one another. The outcome is an exquisite piece of music—your life, your home, your business, and your personal growth.

The Energies of Feng Shui

Feng shui is the single place in our world where numerology shows its magic. Take a boring, square room and fill it with the essential placements of feng shui, and you have now a room of beauty, peace, and harmony. It's magic.

The way it works may be illustrated with the following example. Say you want to build a home that is filled with warm sunlight in the mornings. As you draw up the plans for the construction, you make sure that those rooms that you will be using in the mornings all have windows that open up to the east—and voilà, you have sunlit rooms. This is exactly what happens in feng shui, except that it also helps you maximize your access to the magnetic flows of the universe.

Now let's say you want to enhance the sunlight coming into your room, so you strategically place items, things to encourage the sunlight into the parts of the room you want most to enhance. You enlarge a window, you place a plant, you use specific colors, you hang a mirror and a crystal, and you place a shimmering fountain at a spot shaded from the light. This is the art of placement, and you are doing exactly what the old numerologists did. By using your vast knowledge of sunlight, how it reflects and refracts, how it provides life-giving warmth, you have designed a room that is filled with well-placed items.

ESSENTIALS

Over time, the numerological formulas behind the art of feng shui were lost, but the appropriate placement rules have been retained. That is why we are blessed to have the guidance of feng shui in organizing and balancing the energies in our lives.

The only difference between you and the ancient magi is they understood energetic flows the way you understand sunlight. You move into your empty room and create placement to alter the space in the room to shift the outcome to be what you want—a wonderful and warm morning room. You have brought the light where you want it and provided shade where it was too invasive.

The magi did the same with interiors. They worked with the interiors of homes, palaces, places of worship, pyramids, battlefields, and ceremonial places for births, christenings, and weddings—you name it. The astrologer would design for the entrance of receptive balance and harmony, given the event. The numerologist would direct, nudge, prod, redirect, stabilize, and unite the flows of energy to facilitate the event or purpose.

Feng Shui Is a System

Feng shui is not a piecemeal art. You can't do it halfway and have it work well. Just like your sunny morning room with no plant, crystal, comfort seat, or well-placed window, the effect will be flawed. If you are going to do feng shui to understand the heart and soul of the art of placement, numerology, and what vast amounts of information have been tragically lost or hidden in past power struggles, do it completely. Get a good book, and follow the instructions meticulously. Don't leave out one thing. Then see how, by using elements in a formula, you have changed outcome by combining units of energy to create the outcome you want.

The Magic Continues

Feng shui is the voice of these wise and ancient masters speaking through the ages to us. They remind us of the resource that energy placement can be for us. They remind us of what has been lost or squandered, requesting us to come once again into the understanding of the art of placement in our homes; our places of worship and work; our schools; our bodies, minds, and spirits.

> Feng shui and the formulas in this book are your start to a whole new world of life, love, health, and energy placement. All is energy. All is being placed all the time anyway. Why not learn to direct it for the betterment of everyone?

The Numerology of Your Home

Feng shui is most often practiced in the home, which is the place where you retreat from life and the place you have downtime. But sometimes it is a strong and purposeful statement of success. Other times the owner's function for the home is primarily as a spiritual meeting place. If someone has their business at home, the home may be more of an office with a comfy bed.

The numerology of the home is done through the numbers in the address of the home. The first step with working numerology in the world is to determine what is the primary or singular goal for your residence. Once this goal is clear, then the next step is to find a house that "feels" right and has the root number in the street address that supports your goal.

If you want your house to be a home—comfy, cozy, and very nurturing—you probably don't want a root number of 22 or 8 or 1. With these root numbers, the feng shui of the home will have irreversibly woven into its energy field these "personality" components of the house.

22 Power to build, mastery creator.

8 Need to have and express personal power.

1 Singular, nonblending environment.

For a homey home, you want a final root number that ends in 6, ideally, or in 3 or 2, or, at times 4, as follows:

6 A home of rest and comfy pleasures.

3 A home that facilitates fun.

2 Relationship 1+1 = 2 is nurtured in all things.

4 Reliable, steady, solid.

A home in support of your spiritual development would have any of the following root numbers:

11 Mastery over one's spiritual awareness.

9 Humanitarian outreach.

7 The home will nurture seeking through philosophy.

For someone who loves to travel, collect art from their travels, and look forward to the next trip, 5 makes a perfect home!

The very energetic fabric of the home *is* these qualities. The house's environment will nurture and foster these qualities in the inhabitants and visitors. Here are a few additional examples:

- Do you want to hold a fund-raiser for a good cause at someone's home? Choose a home whose root number is 9. Better yet, choose an address that is 333. Everyone will have loads of fun and be more inclined to support the good cause.
- If you have a home that is a 441, then do a beautifully structured fashion show. The two 4s will make the structuring easy and the

location in the sequence means they support singular expression for a good cause.

- Are you raising money for a high school band to travel somewhere? A perfect home would be 315=9. The 3 is arts and music feeding into the 1, singular recognition, then flowing into the 5, which is travel, and finally settling into 9.
- Do you need to find a nursery school? You are lucky if you find one with 123 in its address—1+2+3 = 6, which stands for self to other to fun in a homey environment; or 136 = 1+3+6 = 10, which translates to self and fun and homey—with the 10 creating the complete 1.

The number address of the home is the most personally identifying root number for the home. The number address marks its own personal, unique singularity. It is the sequence of numbers that gives one's home a very different essential quality from the home next door. The root number of the street name is the quality that emanates from the entire street. It is the quality that subtly affects each person on that street and influences the root number of the address as well. Get the idea? It is really pretty simple. You know the value of the numbers. The values always stay the same. One influences the next, until the energetic flows settle into the root number.

Now if you have two 1s together or two 2s in the sequence, is that a mastery number not to be broken down? No. The mastery numbers exist only in the root number. So a home address of 119 = 1+1+9 = 11 (*not* 11+9 = 20 = 2).

Here is another example: 137 Maple Lane has a root number of 11 in the number address; it is a home that emanates a quiet, inner, still environment. Reading, conversation, looking for the deeper meaning in life would be very compelling pursuits in this home. The gardens would be lovely, and there would be a spiritual quality available to any guest. This would also be a great address for a church, temple, or synagogue. It would be a wonderful address for a school of theology, but not so great for a nursery school. The vibration or feng shui would naturally turn inhabitants to inward contemplation and mental pursuits.

Let's go through the 9 possible root numbers and see what they might create in their influence on your home.

1	Are you in a house or apartment that has the root number 1? This energetic unit will encourage development of your individuality and the individuality of everyone who lives there. You first, right after me!
2	You're in a space where the relationship with everything is more apparent. The way you water your plants, talk to your friends, and engage in your work will all be more personal. Just you and me, kid!
3	You have an environment that encourages light fun, the positive view, and a definite trend toward belief in the ongoing flow of life. No worries!
4	Organization, strategizing, and stable dependability emanate from this energetic unit. Count on me!
5	Time is for movement. The home may easily become a launching pad for one experience after another in the world. Action, activity. Time flies when you're having fun.
6	Warm, welcoming, and yielding to comfort. An ideal environment for the traditional, homey, nurturing space. Give me your tired, your poor, your hungry!
7	A quiet space in which the exploration of the mind, philosophy, life's purpose, and lovely traditional beauty is sustained. Develop your mind, for no one can ever take it from you.
8	Power and authority emanate from this environment. A strengthening of one's personal authority will become evident as the effects of the 8 are incorporated into the residents. Expect success.
9	Humanitarian values and a need to rest from the sorrows of life bring a balance of caring concern for others and a self-nurturing restoration for the inhabitants. There is no life without spirit!
10 = 1	This is the big picture environment. The wholeness, the details, and the overview of life's events become much easier to see, understand, and respond to individually. Diversity is the substance of wholeness.

chart continues on next page

|| This is a place for attuning spiritual awareness to all of life. Seeing and feeling spirit emanates from all things. Knowing that within joy is sorrow and within sorrow is joy. Love is life's only reality!

)) Here is where you find power to build your hopes and dreams. Hard work and personal authority become the beacon that is the magnetic draw for great success. Take a great rest after a great accomplishment!

ESSENTIALS

This is often why someone walks into a home and says, "This is it!" The pattern they feel is a perfect fit for who they are and the type of support they want from the home. If you are looking for a new home, you may be amazed at the success you will have if you use numerology as your guide.

How to Use This Knowledge

Play with the numbers—it's fun. This certainly doesn't mean that if your home address ends in another number you want to run right out and sell it. Look at the root number of your address. Let's assume that your goal for your house is as a comfy, relaxing environment where you can be completely yourself and recover from the stress of life in the world. Your root number will influence the way this homey environment affects you. This is very similar in how your name nudges you into life.

The reason sequenced numbers are also numerology is that in the very act of writing the number symbol, you leave a flow line, exactly the same flow line we talked about in Chapter 6. This flow line comes from infinity and returns to infinity. It is exactly the same line that is a part of you. Its function is shaped by the shape into which it flows. In a human, it animates the spiritual, emotional, mental, and physical. In a home, it brings its essential nature into the environment of the home. In a checking account or registration number, the same is true.

It is all energy, and these numbers are like the energy's identity tags. When you know your pattern, you can make sure that the other units of energy you engage with that are a part of your physical world are helping you continue your smooth, enriching engagement with life. An awareness of the effect numbers have on the things we will cover will help a lot.

So you have your home, where you're looking for comfort, relaxation, and protection from the outer world for a while.

What If It's Not an Easy Fit?

Any one of these root or mastery numbers is great for a home as long as the essence and the intent of the inhabitants are enhanced by the root number. But sometimes you meet a person who has just never liked their home, for no real substantial reason. Nine times out of ten it turns out that the root number doesn't fit at all well with what the inhabitant needs to rest and rebalance.

There are buildings with addresses, and many are not homes. For a business, church, small enterprise, international office, and so on, the root number that supports the original intent will *greatly* enhance success. A church or temple with a root number of 9 or 6 or 11 will have a much different inner spiritual feeling than a church or temple that has a 5 or an 8. Conversely, a business housed in a building with a root number of 22 or 8 or 5 will be a much enhanced space for a successful business.

Very, very few of us have signed contracts on buildings after getting numerology's go-ahead, but it is a good thing to consider. If your church is a 5 and your home is a 1, it doesn't mean that the church or home is a failure or that numerology now has to be wrong because it would be threatening to have it be right. Sit down quietly and evaluate the force level of your church. With a 5 root, the container of the building would be to build for movement. The church or temple might become very involved in outreach to other countries.

If you are buying a home, it helps to remember the effect of the root number and total up just the numbers of the address of the house. It will give you an understanding of how the space of the house will influence the inhabitants. If you're in a house with a root number that now concerns you, pick up a book on the art of feng shui.

It's Not Just the Home

You can rely on other numbers in your life as well—your checking account, business license, phone number, license plate, and many other numbers can help you make sense of your surroundings and establish the most favorable conditions for your success.

Money Making

It is very helpful to know the root number of your checking account. You don't want a business account to have a highly social and unfocused number. Checking accounts are for money, pure and simple. When you go to the bank, get an account that totals to 4, 8, or 22. It's that pure and simple. They might think you're a bit unusual, but you are hiring them to provide you with a service. This is just an aspect of that service they didn't know about. A checking account with a root number of 4, 8, or 22 is perfect!

Business licenses are a bit complex. Your business has a purpose or an essential nature. Here are the most appropriate numbers according to an area of work:

- Health and beauty: 6
- Counseling: 2
- Party planner: 3
- Social teacher/tutor: 7
- Attorney at law: 8
- Doctor: 9
- Meditation school: 11
- Construction company: 22

Again, you have to be a bit different and insist on your right and desire to choose your number sequence. The small amount of embarrassment it causes will be more than forgotten when your work becomes rewarding and financially successful.

Communication by Phone

The area code is the number sequence that has to do with the entire area it covers. The next three numbers have to do with the influence they place on the smaller area. The final four numbers are yours. The phone company is reasonably helpful at giving you several numbers to choose from. Take your time and total each one up. Don't stop until you get to the root number that fulfills the intent you have for the type of service you want from that phone line.

Home lines vary depending on the person getting the calls. 6 is, of course, a good general root number, but if you are bucking up your social life, get a 3. If you're in a rut, get a 5. If you are scattered, get a 4. For a business line, get an 8 or 22. Once you get used to giving this a go and getting the root number you want, it will just become a part of life to tally up the sequence and say, "I like that number!" or "Please, would you try another?"

Car vehicle identification numbers—registration and license plates—are also important. Car root numbers can either give you a car that goes forever or that is a source of endless repair, a car that is essentially safe or too accident prone. The vehicle ID number is the most critical number. For a car, a 5, 3, 4, 8, or 22 is the best. For travel, 5 is best, while 3 is for fun, 4 is for safety, 8 is for prestige, and 22 is for solid wear.

Many Other Applications

For a car that is safe, it is valuable to work with an astrologer and see if you have a retrograde Mars in your chart or another accident-prone position. If so, you definitely don't want a car that totals to 5, the Mars number. If you have a retrograde Mars and you have a 5 vehicle identification, registration, or license number, you will, unfortunately, be much more accident prone in that vehicle.

Numerology applies to it all. Numbers are everywhere. In math, in sequences, in images, in nature . . . everywhere. If you get intrigued with this intricate world of numerology, start reducing a lot of things to their root number. You will begin to sensitize yourself to their subtle but powerful influences, and you will also be more adept at sensing the significance of the following:

- Flight numbers
- Checking account numbers
- Savings accounts
- IRAs
- Time of day

- Date (day + month + year)
- Day
- Number of stairs
- The number and placement of windows

ESSENTIALS

By making numbers and their root values a part of what you routinely notice, along with colors, forms, smells, and flavors, numerology will live in you, as it was always meant to live within you. It will be a part of your daily life. As part of you, it will help you make better choices, becoming a tool for better living through numbers.

To create the formulas having to do with sequenced numbers being used to order life, just add up the sequence. The root number shows the baseline component you will be working with. Then go back to the original meanings of each root number and the two mastery numbers. These same qualities are then adjusted to fit whatever you are questioning—home, business, cars, savings or checking account. The qualities of the root numbers can be applied to anything, and they continue to be pertinent and useful.

CHAPTER 18

Timing Is
Everything!
Kronos and Kairos

T ime is how we run our lives. You may be surprised to find that there are two different but equal kinds of time: linear (Kronos) time and non-linear (Kairos) time. Each time is imperative to our ability to live a good life, so ignoring Kairos time (the kind most people find unfamiliar) is a big mistake.

Our Lives Run in Time

How many times have you heard these expressions:

- Timing is everything.
- It wasn't the time for it.
- It was behind (or ahead) of its time.
- Where has all the time gone?

- Is it time?
- Do you have the time?
- Timing in all things.

Time is what our timepieces tell us it is. We rise at seven, eat lunch at noon, meet friends in the evening at eight, and in between we have many, many schedules. All of them fit into the common understanding of the time we all share. You set up a meeting for 10 A.M., and all of you know when that meeting is to occur. As the clock announces the time, each member arrives in the meeting room ready to work.

FACTS

We all have had experiences with time being both ways—the time of order, sequence, organizing, and numbers, and the other time that emerges unexpectedly, completely disrupts our schedules, causes chaos in our organized world, and opens up unexpected events and opportunities.

But what about you? Let's say you're the member of the group who has a flat tire on the way to the meeting. You have to pull off to the side of the road to call roadside assistance service. The towing truck arrives, and there is an old high-school friend driving the truck. This is certainly an amazing reunion! The flat gets fixed, phone numbers are exchanged, and an old friend is rediscovered. Two years later, the daughter of this friend gives information to your child, and that information keeps her safe during a very scary experience.

You missed the meeting and had a difficult time being stranded on the road and having to wait for help, but this inconvenient incident brought about that chance encounter. And then, later down the road, your daughter was rescued from harm's way as a direct effect of this accidental meeting. When you look back at what happened—the flat tire, the missed meeting, the returned friend, and your safe daughter—you might say, "I reconnected with my old friend at just the right time." What kind of time is this? It has nothing to do with the clock, but from the onset it is filled with purpose and meaning.

Kronos and Kairos

The Greeks had a name for these two movements of time. The timing of humankind—clocks and calendars—was called Kronos. The timing of the universe—interruptions that lead to opportunity—was called Kairos. The trick to a balanced life was to stay open to both. Organize one's life according to Kronos time, but always be aware that there is another, more powerful force that can emerge at any time. Most important, be always ready to live in balance with the two.

To run life only by Kronos is to become a total control freak, which eventually leads to lonely self-absorption. To lead one's life only by Kairos is to have no earthly building skills and to be blown by winds of change, with no personal ground. Both of these times are meant to work together, each in accord with the other. Kronos enables human affairs to progress in a system of order and mutual understanding, and Kairos enables the universe to break up our rigid habits and insert experiences necessary for life to change.

Like a Door Opening

When that agreed-upon meeting time of 10 A.M. occurs, it's as if a door opens. Beyond the doorway, an opening is created by the intent of the participants and agreed timing, and a meeting occurs on the other side of that timing door. If the time isn't set or the intent isn't clear, then no meeting can occur, and the door to that potential remains closed.

QUESTIONS?

What is synchronicity?
Synchronicity is the signature of the gods; it means being in the right place at the right time. When Kairos opens up that door to a new experience, we engage and have an experience that was completely unplanned but full of impact.

The same analogy is true for Kairos time. It is a door of opportunity that opens, and when you step in, unexpected events occur. This is the time zone you enter when waiting for the pinpoint opportunities of Kronos time to arrive. This is the time where the greatest experience of synchronicity can occur.

The Powers of Kairos Time

When dealing with Kronos and Kairos time, the challenge is to respond well to all the experiences Kairos brings our way as we all march to the beat of Kronos time. The reason for and the ultimate challenge of Kairos time is that it is the master teacher. Kairos time is the voice of the universe, its guiding hand. There is clearly nothing in life that is as demanding or as imposing of its own will than Kairos time.

Kairos guides us to openings and closings, beginnings and endings. It is always drawing us into experience that enhances learning, deepens spirituality, and shows that there is a force of life experience and timing that goes far beyond the human ability to guide, direct, or even understand. It is the timing of great mystery, and we both love and fear it.

Kairos is the movement of life guided by another force. We can't control it. We can't really guide it. But we can be in harmony with it. When you experience harmony with Kairos time, you will notice that your timing is on. You are in the right place at the right time. You get the phone call when you *really* need it. The job opens at exactly the precise moment. You had almost given up, and then—there it was. You walk into a restaurant, and there is the love of your life. You're having health problems, and you overhear in a conversation just what you need to know to make the best decision. You're feeling glum, and as you walk across the street, you reach down, grab a flyer blowing across the street, and it is just the perfect seminar for you.

Each one of these experiences is a door opening in the movement of Kairos time. Each one gives you the nudge, guidance, or help you need to progress your life. It is also Kairos that brings unexpected loss and forces us to progress ourselves in the ways we often long to avoid.

Kairos Brings Opportunity

We control the quality of the opportunity that Kairos offers us. As much as we hate to admit it, we have no control and virtually no influence over another's life path and life choices, but we do have absolute control and even responsibility for our level of quality in how we interact with the opportunities. Both sides of the coin—the opportunities we long for and the ones we hope to avoid for a lifetime.

The challenges of life and teachings of Kairos time are universal timing. We are not able to control the timing of the big events, such as the moment of birth or death, when we fall in love, the moment we get the great job, resolve an old conflict, or face the challenge of an accident. Every one of these is controlled by the universe.

The Numerology of Time

To be in harmony with the movement of time is the ultimate goal of numerology. The ancient magi taught that Kairos time and Kronos time are both made up of numbers. Kronos is the equivalent of math numbers, or material numbers. Kairos is the equivalent of the numbers of vibration. There is no concept more rudimentary to numerology than this one.

ESSENTIALS

Kairos time is the time of energetic blending to create an outcome, numerology. We can't control outcome, but we can completely control the quality with which we interact with the Kairos process to elevate outcome. But often if we elevate our quality through appropriate creative response, the quality of the entire situation is enhanced.

It feels great to show up for that 10 A.M. meeting (Kronos time) a couple of minutes early, relaxed and prepared for whatever will happen when the door opens. The ultimate goal of numerology (Kairos time) is to help you achieve that same feeling in all of life. This does not happen by finding false security in escaping, and it does not mean engaging or adhering so closely to Kronos time that life becomes a small, self-absorbed room disconnected from the larger experience.

Kairos time is filled with vibration. That is actually what it is. Kairos is the embodiment of all the numbers we have been learning about, swirling counterclockwise, coming from eternity (the universe), whizzing the animation into life, then returning to eternity.

Our Ride on Life

It is like a big electronic bus that we all, each and every thing, sit on. We can't choose if we want to get on or not. We are *there*. But we can and do choose where we want to sit. And we do this with ultimate simplicity, with our thoughts, intent, and actions. We match vibrationally with an area in the bus of vibration, and there we are—either enjoying the view of life, driving our own experience, and laughing with others, or with our nose stuffed up the exhaust, complaining bitterly. It's your choice, my choice, and their choice. Where do you want to sit on the great bus of Kairos time? It is the position you take that gives you the perspective you have when life events occur. You get to choose; it's your call.

By understanding your numerology unit or pattern, you can have a wonderful tool for framing your experience of life and accessing behavior that may not be your typical habit (karma) and take yourself to a more pleasurable spot on the bus.

How to Pick Your Seat

Get to know your root numbers. Are you a soul 3, a life lesson 4, a personality (from the name) 9? In that case, when a life experience comes your way, force yourself to respond, first, positively; then, become dependable; finally, seek the larger reason.

By following the leadership wisdom of your numbers, you are coming into harmony with the movement of time. You are arriving at the door prepared, relaxed, and ready for life. As you continue to engage in this manner, with your numbers as your guides, you will find a miracle occurring—synchronicity. The right place at the right time. It feels as if life is being orchestrated just for you.

Or, let's say, your root numbers are 1 soul, 7 lesson, and 8 personality. Approach each challenge depending on yourself, think it through, and move forward with confidence, expecting success and trusting yourself. Look at each challenge creatively, numerologically. Yes, you must do this, even if you're hating what happened.

ALERT

If you follow your numbers using the positive aspects of the vibration, you will zip up to a new spot on Kairos time. Your perspective will become more trusting and positive. You will feel more "rightness" in the current challenge.

We grow in our skill to change, to elevate quality through those real-life experiences. It is a hard school, so if you are here—and of course you are—it means the universe knew you could do it. And the universe gave you many inner resources to accomplish the task. And the universe gave us wonderful helpers. Numerology ranks as one of the best tools, because numbers are the eternal language.

So let's look at this again.

Your soul essence number shows you how to bring your very essence into syntony with Kairos time. When this occurs, you sit on the bus in the most soul-satisfying spot for you. You achieve soul alignment by starting into the day expressing the attitudes of your soul number. This school is really a teacher for behavior modification. Just do the behaviors. You will feel "better" and more favorably charged with life and liveliness. This is your grounding wire. This gives you your location in the Kairos bus.

Learn from the Numbers

Remember, the soul number emanates your attitude, but the life task or life lesson number helps you deal with your experiences. It is applied to each challenge you have, over and over and over again. It is your door to create with new experiences brought to you courtesy of the Kairos bus.

Now that you know you have already bought your ticket, get the best spot you can! For instance, consider the following examples:

- If you are a free spirit and you have a 4 lesson, the universe wants you to tighten up the ship a bit and get more dependable substance in your experience.
- If you are a pretty serious guy, and your life lesson is a 3, you get to have fun and learn to let life bring you pleasure.
- If you're a people person and your life task is a 1, you are here to promote yourself and learn a new type of self-reliance.

Your Personality

Your personality (shown in your name) is how you impart yourself to the world. It is the pattern of behavior you are known by. Oddly enough, if allowed to develop and grow without wise guidance (as it almost always does), it actually hides what we aren't good at. So a person with self-esteem problems will become very macho. A person with inner anger will appear very sweet. An arrogant person is always masking shyness.

Guide your personality with wisdom, and it won't create a wall you're hiding something behind. It will be your vehicle of engaging that brings a full, satisfying, happy, honest you to life.

To be able to position and reposition yourself in Kairos time, follow the numbers' guidelines in establishing or re-establishing a personality that allows you to be real, honest, and perfectly aligned to opportunity as it occurs. And you'll discover a personality that is fun, first and foremost, for you! This is how it is supposed to be!

The Numbers Show Us a Way Through

This is the tool for Kairos time. Your chosen behavior is your Kairos timepiece that keeps you on target, catching each door as it opens. You use the Kronos timepiece to structure and order your life. You use your attitude timepiece to harmonize, to alter your perspective, and to open opportunity in Kairos time. You have now learned the most important tool for the life you want!

CHAPTER 19

A Life in Sync with Kairos

Since numerology is the timepiece of Kairos time, it is useful to understand the system of time that Kairos is about. Each system, the system of days, months, and years, has a corresponding numerology formula that we use to grasp its deeper meaning in the affairs of humans. You also use the formulas to increase your ability to create the life you want.

The Universe Makes Its Will Known

Kairos time is made of vibration numbers whose job is to make known what is the full potential available for development in any given day. It is Kairos time that gives us days of very different quality. Some are gentle and peaceful, and others are filled with turmoil. Our place in the vibration of time is where we gain both improved quality and a window or perspective on the event. The event is the same, but perceptions are vibrations apart.

This is why we each perceive a single event so differently. One person will see something wonderful, while the next sees only sorrow. In this context, Kairos time, the Kairos bus becomes the electronic communicator from the master—the universe. The school, or life, is managed so beautifully that if everyone were in harmony with the movement of Kairos time in the way we schedule Kronos time, we would live a life of perfect synchronicity. We would always be at the right place at the right time to have the opportunity the universe is affording us.

Earth Is the School

The school of Earth is designed for this to be the truth—for each person to feel as if life is being orchestrated just for them, each and every one of them. The possibility is there at every moment to have this experience. And with developing greater understanding on how to achieve this delicate, exquisite balance, this timing achievement can be developed and progressed throughout life.

FACTS

We have all had the experience of holding back and not stepping in. We all know that the Kairos moment goes and never returns. Like a river of opportunity, it moves on, another steps in, and our chance is lost, never to return. A firm teaching is to be present and to have the courage to engage.

The methods for achieving this form the basis of all the teachings of the best spiritual masters. The masters are those whose exquisite teachings put one in harmony with one's self. In that deep reliance on one's own truths and resources, an intuitive understanding of timing is developed. The intuitive timing that in the middle of inner peace says, "Now!"—this is the time to engage with gratitude and respect for this opportunity.

Personal Vibrations

It can be puzzling to grasp what Kairos time could actually be like. You know a lot about numerology and vibration now. The numbers come from eternity. They engage with you, and then they return to eternity. These numbers each carry specific characteristics and potential, both creative, passive, and destructive, as they mix and match through you.

 **ESSENTIALS**

You have your personal vibrational numbers. You have begun a working understanding of how to proceed through life now with numerological wisdom as your guide. Now let's define how to mesh or blend better with the calendar of events as designed by Kairos.

These vibrations arrive on Earth swirling counterclockwise as a vortex of swirling, sparkling potential. It flows through you and everyone else on Earth. It is the chi, yin-yang, aura, life force . . . you name it. These numbers each carry specific characteristics and potential, both creative, passive, and destructive, as they mix and match through you. It flows into years, designing and defining the master purpose or teaching of the year. It flows into the Kronos time of years and also months, days, hours, and minutes. Kronos gives the outer structure, or the shell; Kairos fills the interior with lessons and richness. We choose our perspective on the moment through where we have placed ourselves within our vibration. It's actually so beautifully organized and so filled with promise, the only thing lacking is our personal understanding of how to utilize this information to our advantage.

Each Year Serves Us Differently

Each year is filled with a specific purpose, experience, and teaching that everyone is affected by. In order to figure out what each year is, and how we are all influenced, each in our own way, personally, add up the year, or the Kronos number, sequentially.

Each year can be understood according to the prescribed characteristics of its root number. For instance:

1999: 1+9+9+9 = 28 = 10 = 1
2000: 2+0+0+0 = 2
2001: 2+0+0+1 = 3
2002: 2+0+0+2 = 4

So, 1999, a 1 year, was a singular year—a year of "this is who I am, and this is where I am." The year 2000 was a 2 year, when we were each taken to the bone to see what we had really created in ourselves and our life. It was a no-fantasy time, a reality year. The year 2001, a 3 year, was the first of a ten-year rebuilding cycle. That year, we sowed the seeds for a whole new life based on what we have seen about ourselves, what we want to experience—or have to experience. Finally, 2002 was a 4 year. The second of the rebuilding cycle, this year was meant to look deeply at what you've started. A deeper, more structured view of your life was available all year. It was a good time to utilize this perspective to get the foundation to your new life firm.

Here is a complete list of the root numbers derived from years:

1	Progress, venture, exploration, daring.
2	Arrangement, arguments, collecting, correcting.
3	Pleasure, pursuit, expression, creativity.
4	Diligent, grounded, without illusions, construction.
5	Rejuvenation, movement, opportunities, a larger worldview.
6	Harmony, syntony, a sense of settling in, expanded concerns.

chart continues on next page

7   Taking stock, completion starts, honing and perfecting, quality.

8   Success, expecting things, confidence, growth.

9   Grounded harmony, no escapism or violence, clearing out deadwood, making space.

11   Idealism, altruism, dreaming, vision.

22   Big ideas, big growth, big eat small, ultimate practicality.

What You Can Learn about Time

Let's say you want to find out what's in store for you in January of 2003. To calculate the root number for that month, take 1 for January and add 5 for the sum of 2003. The result is 6; that means, January 2003 will be a 6 month in a 5 year. Concerns will be for the group, community, health, and well-being in a year that will just be starting to accelerate.

For the rest of the month/year root numbers, refer to the following list of Universal Kairos Month numbers:

1   New, ideas, pioneer, get started.

2   Collecting, sowing, communication.

3   Fun, friends, activity, operations.

4   Exacting, training, skill, steady building.

5   Increase, expansion, new, activity.

6   Health and well-being, community support, education, balance in all things.

7   Analysis, serve higher authority, still mind, perfection desired.

8   Grow, large, organize, form, succeed.

9   Put things in order, discriminate, discover, eliminate.

11   Church, synagogue, temple, spiritual values expressed, secretive.

22   International, work to improve, tireless energy, formulate.

The Universal Kairos Day

Each day further carries its own opportunities to expand self-knowledge. The formula for this is as follows: year root number + month root number + day root number. For example: The Universal Kairos Day number for January 1, 2003, would be calculated as follows:

year root number:	2003 = 5
month root number:	1
day root number:	1
	5+1+1 = 7

This means that January 1, 2003, is a 7 day with much activity, particularly in cities. A 7 day is a good time for analysis and making decisions. The following are the Universal Kairos Day numbers and what they stand for:

1 New ideas, me, strength of individual purpose.

2 Quiet, simmering, lethargy, building for the next day.

3 Nervous, ups and downs, active, pleasure seeking, escapism.

4 Detail, steadying force, moving along, low boiling point, turning points.

5 Speculate, expand, group activities, worldview.

6 Homey, arts, music, group needs prevail.

7 Improve, analysis, perfection, active groups, inner peace.

8 Big success, wheeler-dealer, scheduling.

9 Friendship, tolerance, public concerns, humanitarian ventures.

11 Spiritual layer to the lack of energy of a 2 day.

22 A strong drive to create from the structure implied in the 4 day.

Designing Your Personal Year

Your personal year is how to best take advantage of the opportunities being offered to everyone that year by honing your understanding of its deeper value for you. Your personal year is the sum of the following three numbers:

- The root number of the current year
- The root number for your birth month
- The root number for your birth day

So if you were born on October 3, 1947, and it is the year 2003, you would do the following calculations:

Current year:	2003 = 5
Birth month:	October = 10 = 1
Birth day:	3
	5+1+3 = 9

For this person, the year 2003, with its interior demand to expand and take risks, will have a deep and continuing humanitarian focus. This year will motivate an intertwining with the soil of life, separating the wheat from the chaff, and getting everything in order.

Refer to the following numbers for your own personal year:

1 Speak for yourself. Have your own ideas, paddle your own canoe, pioneer new aspects of life, take the leap, energize.

2 Attract what you need to nurture your new aspect of life, stay open, engage with enthusiasm, partnership. Pay attention to the small new starts.

3 Friendship, fun, social, happy and cheerful, vacations, keep centered, new life effects coming forward.

chart continues on next page

4   Work, focus, demand dependable action, dig deep, fertilize and prune your life's events, make steady decisions, action. Sense of purpose and destiny available.

5   New, new, new—people, situations, jobs, progressing, expanding. Adapt to change! Destroy habits and ruts that don't energize and revitalize.

6   You will be needed this year. Much warmth, settling down. Root into your life. A year for deeper meaning, truth, and rich engaging.

7   Hindsight put to good use, great personal growth based on inner reflection, no casual associations, deeper meaning in your life in all areas springs from self-awareness.

8   Launch forward, hard work, effort, new projects, own personal power, seek success, be fair and just.

9   Clear out deadwood, stay focused on lightening the load and bringing your life up to date, finishing, completing. Nose to the reality grindstone, no escapism.

11   Inner, visualize ideal, the bottom floats up and spiritual insight brings new purpose and light to personal perspective. Don't accept the challenges as opposing limits—find the key.

22   Practical, dream for reality, drive for the larger good, your opportunity to give that gift to the world.

Kairos Ebbs and Flows

Kairos time is a vortex of counterclockwise vibration. It has waves, and it is in these waves that it flows. You know how you feel when you are in harmonic rhythm with another person. It is as if the two waves that you together represent are cresting and ebbing at the same time. It is heaven, until one wave begins to flow a bit differently. The rhythms are no longer connecting easily. Instead, they can actually begin to crash together. That might be caused by different times for different experiences for different lessons. You and your rhythm in accordance to Kairos time is exactly the same. That means in one year you might flow, when in another you ebb.

Kairos Years: Ebbs and Flows			
1	flow	7	low ebbing
2	ebb	8	high flow
3	flow	9	both are yours
4	ebb	11	ebb
5	flow	22	flow for all
6	ebb		

During the 1 year, the challenges of your life lesson will be particularly evident. For instance, if someone is learning problem solving, there will be lots of problems to solve in the 1 year. Someone learning how to flow along with life will have many challenges to their rigidity. A person learning an aspect of progressing instead of becoming habitual may have a complete life change thrust upon them. So in the 1 year, we can get a good look at our bottom-line lesson.

FACTS

Since we are all here learning a slightly different lesson than everyone else, it is useful to personalize your reflections on past years for yourself. In this way, you can better see how it is that you interact with Kairos and how Kairos moves you.

The 2 year shows how to now take these newly found skills out into life. The 3 is to find the fun in them. The 4 is to make them dependable. The 5 is to move them into the world. The 6 makes them a comfort. The 7 learns the mental process for seeing how they fit into the larger scheme. The 8 makes the skills a success in the world. The 9 serves humanity and weeds out the rest. After this sequence is complete, the cycle goes back to another 1. Remember, deep in your soul you know these things very well. The numbers first jog your memory of what feels right, and then they show you how to fly.

CHAPTER 20

Numerology and the Karmic Wheel

There are millions of people in the world who believe in karma. What is karma? How does it affect you? Does everyone have it? How do you find out what your karma is? Numerology shows the way to karma through numbers.

What Is Karma?

The idea of karma has been interpreted differently by various people and cultures, but there are a few basics that everyone agrees with. The belief in karma is accompanied by belief in reincarnation, which assumes that the world is a school for learning that each soul, or energy, returns to in different forms for the purpose of self-development.

Learning Isn't Easy

The ancient magi taught that it's a very hard school, hard because we are developing four areas of ourselves—the physical, emotional, mental, and spiritual. We are learning through the challenges of the life experience more about who we are when we respond emotionally, mentally, physically, or spiritually in any given experience.

For instance, if someone bangs into the side of your car, do you put your car in reverse, back up, and then drive forward and bang them? Do you cry and swear in the front seat? Maybe you get a piece of paper and write down their license plate, insurance company, and get the name of witnesses. Or do you pray?

If your friend needs someone to talk to, but you are very busy, do you go for a run? Do you take a minute to listen because your friend is a big priority? Do you watch your friend's face as he/she talks, thinking about your other concerns? Or do you talk to your friend about spiritual attitudes that might help?

You have just gotten a letter from the IRS saying you're going to be audited. Do you go work out? Sit down and cry? Call your accountant for an appointment? Go to a spiritual adviser for advice?

You have just found out your animal friend is very sick and dying. Do you take them out in nature to see the trees and flowers again? Do you put your head next to them and grieve? Do you talk to them about all the good times and how much you're going to miss them? Do you start to put in place the needed environment to give them a peaceful passage?

Each one of these situations is an everyday occurrence. Each gives an opportunity to choose a reaction and the sequence in which you would react. The goal is *always* to deal with the event in a way that we have improved our quality according *to our own standards.*

Judging Others

Think about someone you know who is very opinionated or judgmental. Are they open? Are they easy to communicate with? Nope. It is as if their opinions and judgments build an invisible wall that they sit behind. Behind this wall they feel some sort of safety from an alarming world, and they build comforting habits to live within.

We can never judge a person accurately. *Never.* We don't ever have enough information about anyone else but ourselves to be accurate judges. We can only gain clarity about ourselves. There is also an interesting thing that happens, with judgment done at one's leisure as opposed to happening in court.

This type of behavior, which is used repetitively in every situation, is an often-used response to the challenges and events that come our way. Initially it brings a feeling of enhanced personal safety by being able to judge the world. But as judgment of others gets used as a habit, in most situations it limits the precious ability to choose our responses and creates, in turn, a rigid response to life. This then limits the growth of personal quality because life is not responded to as a constantly changing gift to be embraced for our own enhancement.

Many Responses Are Available

There are many, many responses to any given event. Each one of us will have our own personal reaction. Some of our reactions will bring us forward-moving growth, but others will keep us more stagnant in the same old pattern of behavior.

Many say karma is punishment and that we get karma for misdeeds. So when someone says, "I guess it's my karma!" usually what they are saying is, "I guess it's my punishment or consequence for a misdeed."

Generally we all do a life just like you are doing this one. Basically you're a great person. When was the last time you rocketed out of bed saying, "Well, today I am going to be a miserable jerk . . . all day!" Occasionally, if ever! No, we get up each day and do the best we can with who we are. The people who are true jerks—committed to it with conscious intent—are few and far between. They can do a lot of damage, get a lot of press coverage, but that is because they are showing aberrant behavior, out of the norm.

FACTS

The ancient magi taught that behavior repetition is *the* most negative condition and a state to be avoided at all costs. To the degree that behavioral repetition occurs, that is the degree by which opportunity for personal growth—new and fresh insights— diminishes. This continues, until over time the opportunity for self-knowledge can stagnate, completely hooking the person into an endless cycle of repetition, or nongrowth—the karmic wheel.

We All Have Karma

We all have something we are learning. Otherwise, we wouldn't be in this life. We wouldn't be having all these experiences. We wouldn't be able to build a life in order to see our abilities to create, build, and contribute. Yet we get lost. The ability to respond appropriately according to our own choice in any given situation gets limited by our habitual, therefore seemingly safe, responses. Or we begin to build the wall between us and the beautiful challenges of life with our increasing judgment. Have opinions, certainly! Know how you want people to treat you, of course! But don't judge the rightness or wrongness of anything in life. If it is here, there is a place for it, and respect its place. Fight it if you choose, destroy it if you choose, but don't do it because you have judged it as wrong. Fight against it, destroy it, because it is you—but for no other reason. To do otherwise brings about two karmic creating behaviors:

1. **Judgment.** The act of judging creates karma because over time the repetitive behavior this increases will take over any joyous spontaneity.

2. **Restricted free will.** Your ability to choose your reaction with free will becomes greatly compromised because you have given your reason for responding as caused by the other person's behavior, as if you are caught in a net thrown over you by them. You therefore are controlled in your response, forced to respond in a certain way because of them.

When you don't do this, and—instead—you recognize that if this person is here and their behavior is a part of life, that this may be beyond your own wisdom to understand but that there is a reason for it all. If you accept that, you give up the moral judgment and say, "Okay, based on my new shiny attitude here, how do I choose to respond for me, for myself?"

Is This Hard?

Oh my gosh, yes! That is why we dodge and dart around it. All of us to some degree avoid personal responsibility in our actions. The most common evasive techniques are the following:

- **Self-righteous rage:** I smashed his car because he hit me first.
- **Self-absorption:** I wanted to listen to my friend, but I couldn't stop thinking about my life.
- **Self-protecting judgment:** Those jerks are auditing me. I don't deserve this!
- **The victim:** I am suffering so much over my animal friend's illness, I can't do anything.
- **The escape artist:** Oh well, it's all meant to be, so I am not going to really engage with any of it.
- **Denial:** This life event doesn't fit with what I believe life should bring me, so I am going to ignore it until it goes away.

These are common reactions to life's events. And they are reactions guaranteed to create repetitive reactions—unthinking, habitual reactions to life—karma. This is because these are some of our favorite ways to not fully engage and be present. Full presence does not ever repeat.

Karma and Life Lesson

But if we all do them, then there must be some common problem somewhere. The problem is our karma. The problem solver is our lesson. The lesson, or karma, when understood, points out what we need to do to break the repetition and be able to have the personal freedom required to make our own choices in how we respond to events. And then have the freedom to enhance our growth with the self-knowledge that comes—*on its own*—after we have truly chosen our own response. Karma is where we repeat an old soul-denying behavior, for in repetition the soul cannot shine. What comes forward instead is an ever-strengthening personality characteristic that takes itself *way too seriously*, and the joyous response to life and its opportunities is subsumed in the repetitive behavior. The life lesson breaks up the repetition. You do something new, and that means you respond to the event with a new, fresh approach. First there is a fear about putting yourself out there in an unfamiliar way. Feel the fear, and do it anyway. Then comes the amazement that life is changing. You are rearranging your vibrational unit to create a desired outcome! Over time, life becomes more wonderful to you. You break your repetitions, and those around you are more inclined to do the same. Or you might choose to be with those who behave less repetitively. This is karma repetition. This is freedom—the life lesson.

Repetitions and the Rhythms of Life

Consider the difference between habits of repetition and the rhythms of your life. Behavior repetition is a way of relating to every single situation as if it is the same situation or requires the same old response. These are deeply entrenched psychological behaviors that stem from the past. We all have these habits, and they do the same for each one of us. They prevent growth, true joy, and spontaneity from occurring.

Rhythms are very personal and intimate aspects of our lives. Your rhythm in life is how you came into syntony with the symphony of life. Your rhythm is an internal sense of centered groundedness that has nothing to do with the outer world. You find your rhythm alone. Your reconstructor of self-love helps, and doing things in private and at your own pace and timing helps. Your rhythms are the personal time you express as you move through the larger musical score of life.

Habits—Healing or Hurting?

Your habits are the connections you have built with life. Habits tend to stay in place because you never re-evaluate them. They are a structure that you live and hide within. They indicate how much you have given up on life and your personal quest for growth and self-knowledge.

The magi taught that the learning in our lifetimes is a step-by-step process. It takes many lifetimes to complete the process, not because we are stupid, mean-spirited, escape-oriented people and therefore tied to a karmic wheel, but because the school of Earth is filled with the opportunity for self-knowledge, so much opportunity that it takes many lifetimes to fully reap the benefits. This is not a curse. It is a blessing.

QUESTIONS?

Is living life a blessing?

Yes, and that blessing grows as we accept the following:

1. Life is hard.
2. When you realize life is hard, it gets better.
3. You're here by your own choice.
4. Embrace each opportunity.

Learning your missing numbers will give you the key to filling in the areas of yourself you need to know to create this thankful attitude within.

Appreciating life makes living life so much easier. Cursing it makes it so much harder. With knowledge of your life path, you gained some understanding into your life lesson. Now you will receive the tools for how to identify behaviors within you that need to be enhanced for the life lesson to really take hold. As you do this, you will find that you've freed yourself from your karma or your stultifying repetitions.

Only you can do this. There is not another person in the world who can do this one for you—not one. You have complete, ultimate responsibility for this job of knowing yourself, and you get the complete and ultimate inner joy in your accomplishment of yourself.

Personal Freedom at Last

It will be you who has the freedom to choose how you want to respond. It will be you who seems to slow down time enough to allow for this. It will be you who sees your life progressing, flowing into arenas of unexpected occurrences. It will be you who lets life be the great adventure and love it. It will be you who turns away from the empty promise of safety—you will understand the useless repetitions required to maintain it. It will be you who looks to nature to be inspired in your increasing understanding of how nature demonstrates ongoing stability within dynamic change.

These two seeming opposites will become teachers in your own life—stability as a result of how you relate to change, not repetition to fake safety. It's a big challenge. The magi taught that it is the ultimate challenge of life. But you're up to it, and you're ready for it. You must be; otherwise you wouldn't be here, at this time, in this place. Let's get to it!

What is it you need to know to continue progressing in your life task? If you're repeating, and of course you are, you need to get the tools to fill in what you don't yet know about yourself so you can diminish the areas of repetition in your life. You need to understand your gaps. Those are the areas of your development that remain hidden to you. For when each part of you is fully engaged, repetition is absolutely not possible. It can't happen because you are present, pure and simple!

The Missing Letters

The missing letters are just that—letters that you are missing in your numerical sequence. To determine missing numbers, take your name, and write down the number values of the vowels above them and the number values of the consonants below them.

VOWEL VALUES:

Full name: _____

CONSONANT VALUES:

Now, place a mark for every number in your name next to the following column of numbers: Next to 1, write down how many times 1 appears in the number sequence of your name, then do the same thing for 2, and so on. Remember, you are not working with the root numbers—all you are doing is counting how many times each number appears in the sequence. When you find a number not represented, then write a 0 next to it. The 0 symbol represents the space waiting to know itself, in other words, a wholeness not yet fulfilled.

When you have compiled your list of numbers, take a look at those numbers that are missing from your name (that is, the numbers with a 0 next to them). They represent all that you still haven't learned in your life. The following sections will give you explanations for what it means to miss particular numbers.

If You Are Missing 1s

You come into this life with an area of self-development that wants to strengthen. The challenge is to stand alone, to stand on your own two feet for your own beliefs and standards. You are wanting to create a life in which you are self-centered in the healthy way. You want experiences that encourage self-exploration. Your unique, never-to-be-repeated self wants to bubble to the surface. If this process is not allowed to fill in, you will lead your life through others. You might make everyone a part of your family. You might live through your kids instead of getting a life. You might define yourself through your work, saying to yourself, for instance, "I am a doctor," instead of "I am a woman, who is also a doctor." You might perform your life, like this: "I am a religious person, and I obey every law of my faith," instead of seeking to become a person who uses the rules of life to express your unique self and take on the rules rather than performing the rules perfectly.

ESSENTIALS

As you become more adept at finding yourself within the outer system, your unique attributes will become more clear and trustable to you. You may often find that when you need support the most, there you are, alone, struggling to get to your own feet, finding out about . . . whom? You!

If You Are Missing 2s

You are here missing some vital information on how relationships are conducted. You may get too close or dependent, or you may absolutely not know how to need, nurture, and build a relationship with anything. This often shows up as a true fear of responsibility. To take on responsibility for another (not a job, that doesn't count!), whether that's a plant, a cat, a dog, a needy person, a child, a parent, or a love partner, all requires a commitment to learning about maintenance and an acceptance of the sort of wonderful messiness of relationship. This requires the skills that the 2 vibration brings.

The ability to communicate, not just to state yourself honestly, that is half of the picture. But there's also listening to the other, empathizing with their life view, and then finding a workable common ground. The 2 also brings an awareness of how your life and the life of the other is enhanced through the interaction and the deepening over time of the relationship. The 2 also shows the type of healthy security that is born through a well-developed relating skill. The 2 demonstrates how to be touched deeply by someone or something other than yourself.

With no 2s in your sequence, you will be inclined to engage with others, but you will always feel untouched by true closeness or intimacy. You may attempt to protect yourself from the pain of this by limiting your commitment to half of your responsibility for keeping things going and deepening. Plants get watered not when they need it, but when you want. Pets get cared for at your convenience and people have to fit into your life and be extremely flexible with their needs, otherwise you tend to withdraw. Life will bring you experiences that vividly demonstrate that no person is an island, and you will learn that the skills of interconnecting are crucial to the fulfillment of a long life.

If You Are Missing 3s

Since the 3 is fun, light-hearted, and convivial, to miss 3s indicates a nature too inclined to take oneself, or life, or another life view *very* seriously. Every situation, large or small, will be seen as serious. A light perspective on how to progress and proceed in life will be subsumed in the heavy seriousness or just the complete lack of familiarity with a light approach to life. The first, the heaviness, will generally be expressed as a serious, even severe person. The lack of knowing how to be lighthearted will often show up as shyness. Sometimes this is really crippling shyness.

What the person is looking for is a ticket to the bus of how to move through life. They are looking for the oil to smooth out the trip, over and through it all. Laughter and pleasure provide movement and restore a belief in life, even in the worst times. The 3 is what brings this to life. Without the 3, the individual struggles to understand the who, where, what, and how of pleasure in life. They will constantly be tripping over themselves unable to see the joy because of their own self-preoccupation. Life will bring challenges that will offer only one solution for happiness—lighten up!

If You Are Missing 4s

A person missing 4s will have a very limited understanding of how to get from life the gifts that are there for them. As a result, it will be hard to find their place in it all. Subject to moving from one thing to another or always feeling yanked from one event to another, they have no clue as about how to steady themselves in the profusion, structure themselves and their relationship to the experience, and then integrate what has happened and how it affects them.

Life will seem out of control and beyond their ability to affect it. In a sense, they are in their boat on the sea of life, but they have no idea how to use the oars or the compass.

A person who lacks 4s can become involved in relationships where the other is very structured, even rigid. They will also be drawn to jobs where the job description is very, very clear—even a job that is limiting will be okay with them—or they will be terrified of a structured person or job. It is usually the case that one or the other is true.

The missing-4 person is here to find their own personal rhythms in life and then to structure themselves in a way that those rhythms are steadied and deepened. Then the next step is to create a life where the person's inner rhythms are in a structure that creates harmonious and dependable relationship with others, jobs, and life in general. The missing-4 person is seeking to understand the value of inner structure to be able to express oneself well and the value of outer in life structure. These structures then create dependability rather than rigidity.

Life will bring many challenges to organize, become dependable, and create a flexible structure in order to cope with the events creatively.

If You Are Missing 5s

A life devoid of true excitement for the adventure is the challenge. To have the 5 missing means the person looks at others to shake and move the world, others to provide the adventure, others to provide the zest and vitality. Someone without 5s can be a shrinking violet in social situations. He or she can be the person who sets their course straight in life, does each step in a completely predictable way, lives life organized, predictable, and surprisingly noncreative. They don't try the new Thai restaurant because they always eat the same type of food. They watch the same shows, develop deep predictability, and don't seem to miss at all the elements of change, diversity, and adventure.

What this person has is an undeveloped area having to do with the value of creativity and change. They generally have no idea how to incorporate change into their lives in a way that they take hold of the new experience and enhance their lives.

Missing 5s will bring to themselves life experiences in which the only way they will be able to understand the gift within the experience will be to accept it. In the acceptance of it, they will begin to open to the inevitability of change. Then they must reinstate their ordered life with this new situation in the mix. Over time the missing 5 may come to accept that life is an unknown adventure and find pleasure in the unexpected.

If You Are Missing 6s

The family becomes only a launching pad for the missing 6. This person has no understanding of how deeply important the human family unit is, and he or she is very able to take generously from family support and never give a bit back. This is not because they are selfish. It is a true blind spot. They simply don't see how very much they need a good family.

Nor do they see how much they want a good family. They may go through all the steps. They have parents, maybe a mate, maybe kids, but the missing 6 will see everyone as unique individuals. This view is not just first and foremost, it's how their perception is and where it stops.

The understanding of connecting and creating a unit of comfort is virtually off their screen.

The missing 6 needs to see that not only are they not an island, they are also deeply and completely connected to the family of humankind. And while this connection is for their benefit, it is not for their benefit exclusively. It is a process of give and take that is rich with human love.

The missing 6 will have life experiences that point up *very* clearly that family and extended family are a foundation to healthy living.

If You Are Missing 7s

The person missing 7s will have a very hard time problem solving life's dilemmas. In order to get a handle on how to react creatively to the challenges of life, we need workable philosophies. The missing 7 will resort to dogma, because the ability to be philosophically rich is absent.

The reason for education will not be evident. Experience will be the primary teacher. Complex life events having to do with loss or gain will generally be diminished in their potential power to facilitate now necessary changes.

It may be very hard for the missing 7 to get ideas across so they are understood by others. Life events can be confusing and bewildering.

A missing 7 will tend to hook up with analytical people to get a needed balance.

Life will bring the missing 7 very clear illustration of why education, philosophical theory, and traditional tried-and-true ways are needed.

If You Are Missing 8s

The missing of 8s in your formulas will create dilemmas surrounding how to put yourself in the world with confidence. This goes from a casual walk down the street to entering a high-pressure, unfavorable experience. An 8 person expects success and walks that expectation everywhere. Missing 8s means that the true, deep confidence that oozes from every pore and instills everything around it is missing. A missing 8 may also not have a clear understanding of their effect on the world. A missing 8 can do amazing things and be remarkably untouched by the success of those achievements. Even more significantly, this person might not know how to build on the successes to enhance self-confidence.

In life, the missing 8 will be given experiences by life that demand inner strength be found and focused. It is through these real-life experiences that the missing 8 will begin to fill in this gap of confidence. Ideally this is the accepted confidence of knowing one's value to the world. The other thing to be learned is the quiet inner confidence that whatever life dishes up, the missing 8 now knows the inner resources are there. Nothing seems as unsettling, and it all becomes a part of life.

If You Are Missing 9s

This person will not be aware of the spiritual rhythm of life and growth that knits us all together. Life will appear to be without deep, intrinsic spiritual value. The meaning of life will become something other than serving humanity with love and patience. Finding the heart, that is, the spiritual awareness within the service may not be possible. Service may take on a doormat-like quality, since the spiritual reason for service to engage others with love, support, and acceptance to challenge one's ability to improve personal quality gets lost.

The spiritual reason for service might get lost in the inability to serve without becoming the victim of the served. Humanity can be seen as a pathetic waste of time, period! There is no conception of service of the other as a means of evolving in oneness. True contempt can develop for concepts of oneness, humility, and service as a way of life.

A missing 9 will have experiences in life that will encourage, if not force, the recognition that we are joined together as a universal family. The missing 9 learns that what happens to one, happens to us all.

If You Are Missing 11s or 22s

It is common to miss the mastery numbers, and it means that the person has not yet reached mastery in either of these two levels of life—spiritual mastery and material mastery. To carry one of these root numbers at the end of your sequence doesn't mean you can kick it and coast now. Usually, having a mastery number means you will draw to yourself all the challenges required to get the mastery number in the first place. This is done so you can continue to perfect your responses to the challenges that you got an A in before. Now you get to go for A+, or better. Watching a mastery number go through a challenge using the skill the double number brings is an inspiration to behold. It is a process to learn from for all of us who lack them.

This issue of missing numbers and the problem it creates really points up the inherent problem with nicknames. The shorter the name, the more missing numbers. The fuller the name, the more vibration the individual has to work with. A nickname can limit a person so much that they actually are working with a deficit. They lack so many of the vibrations they came to develop that their potential for personal development is greatly at risk. We love to abbreviate so many names, but looking at the habit through the lens of numerology, we see that it is a risky business.

Numerology Tables

This appendix will help further your insights regarding numerology's powers of synchronicity. It includes the Life Task Calendar and a chart describing the numerology within book page numbers.

Life Task Calendar

Here is a chart with the years from 1920 to 2010 that provides the particular vibration of each year and the meaning behind it. Remember that the new year starts on winter solstice, December 21, so if you are born on December 22, 1968, your birth year is 1969.

1920 = 12 = 3   Allows for fun and love of the changes of life, to lighten up, a nature disinclined to change.

1921 = 13 = 4   Balance of the self is required to be truly creative for others. Steady building.

1922 = 14 = 5   Hard work and creating success pulls one out of self-pity or a too-rigid viewpoint.

1923 = 15 = 6   Home and hearth becomes a place of freedom and happiness instead of sacrifice and disappointment.

1924 = 16 = 7   Use mental seeking and intelligence to break up rigid beliefs and standards.

1925 = 17 = 8   Create personal power not through the group's standards but through standing solidly and flexibly alone.

1926 = 18 = 9   To be spiritually respected is not the same as having a rich, loving, and vulnerable personal life.

1927 = 19 = 10 = 1   Stand not on the edge of the culture, but join in the center of it all as your own person.

1928 = 20 = 2   Being on the side of life gives perspective, but true happiness is found in taking your spiritual evolution into the depth of connecting with others—no detachment. Relationship on all levels.

1929 = 21 = 3   An inborn depth, but not an understanding of how things connect together. Pleasure in life as a tool for building a life one connected step at a time.

1930 = 13 = 4   Learning the power to create for the world has more to do with the ability to stabilize and balance in the midst of impermanence than with force of personality.

1931 = 14 = 5   Fritter away your time, and your life has no value. Go deep, find a truth and belief, stick with it, and create fabulous success. Build tried and true values.

1932 = 15 = 6   Great personal joys at home and in the world of humankind are gained through equality, flexibility, and the wisdom that then flows from acceptance and love.

1933 = 16 = 7   The intellect and seeking wisdom must be activated to increase an understanding of oneness of all humanity, the 1933 included! Break up all the aspects of the ugly ego.

1934 = 17 = 8   A strong sense of self serves a limited purpose if humanity, friends, and family are not loved, accepted, and encouraged.

1935 = 18 = 9   The spiritual awareness of the unity of all things inspires the loss of self-centeredness and draws a retiring nature into the world.

1936 = 19 = 10 = 1 A very large and full person showing their family, all of humanity, a more spiritual approach is possible in the most personal way. Warm and approachable.

1937 = 20 = 2 No relationship is truly meaningful until you have a complete love of yourself. Relationships that exhaust, limit, and consume time must be resolved through a very jovial inner contentment. Being a part of the group is easy. Be involved with your own inner rhythms and unique value—for you.

1938 = 21 = 3 A light-hearted approach to change and all the wonderful gifts it brings allows a new approach to stability. Not fixed, but flexible.

1939 = 22 A personality of great power learns that success comes from a blend of inner power and inspiring building of security and comfort for self as well as others.

1940 = 14 = 5 A forceful, often intense personality learning balance and compromise are the tools for success.

1941 = 15 = 6 Create a home that is a haven, with emotional balance, and turning disappointments into triumphs. Making relationship workable and positive.

1942 = 16 = 7 Don't let yourself fall into the same old downward-turning thoughts. Take those thoughts by the reins and turn them positive. Reflect on yourself with self-love and bind your accomplishments.

1943 = 17 = 8 The powerful personality pulls out of the negative in-turning group or family experiences and pursues the path of freedom through self-knowledge.

1944 = 18 = 9 The world doesn't need another teacher to respect. The world needs a loving, embracing member of humanity. Be loving first, respected later.

1945 = 19 = 10 = 1 The strong, complete self is here to become a member of the family of humanity, messy though it looks!

1946 = 20 = 2 The separate person now needing to find comfort in the heart of the culture.

1947 = 21 = 3 Connection with life requires a light-hearted and yet compassionate appreciation of the whole—and your part in it, within it, connected to it, in the center of it.

1948 = 22 A power source of stability, learning to be flexible and let change improve things.

1949 = 23 = 5 Hard work won't produce true inner happiness unless it is done with attention to bringing joy, creativity, satisfaction, and pleasure to the 1949 worker.

1950 = 15 = 6 Home and hearth are within. The world, family, and friends can contribute, but the true home is the unshakable world of self-love.

1951 = 16 = 7   A seeking, curious mind has been given you to help you out of outdated beliefs, strong opinions, and a distrust of life's lively flow of uncertainty.

1952 = 17 = 8   Strong, strong will who will miss the joys of life if every occasion is met with "my way or no way." A building of inner confidence to match the power.

1953 = 18 = 9   A spiritual nature facing the struggle of living lovingly and not controlling everything. A great capacity for an unusual person with loving ways. The control issue must be resolved before the maturing of the spiritual nature can occur.

1954 = 19 = 10 = 1   An aspect of enlightenment is carried in the inner world. This must be expressed without restraint to everyone in all aspects of life—no hiding out. The embodiment of generous warmth deeply engaged with the systems of life.

1955 = 20 = 2   The struggle of where individual fits into the relatedness and relationship while maintaining and building boundaries around the self. The learning is true happiness with oneself while in relationship, not doing relationship, not having them do you.

1956 = 21 = 3   Underscoring the world of connection is the pleasure of being a part of it all. Be it.

1957 = 22   Power building. Great stabilizer. Learning openness, fun, and trust in the flowing changes of life.

1958 = 23 = 5   A shaker-mover motivated by relationships and the desire for light-hearted fun comes to terms with the winds of change and redefines stability.

1959 = 24 = 6   Learning the art of balance as it relates to family and comfort. No extreme positions will have true homey value.

1960 = 16 = 7   Use your mind, your intellect, to solve your way out of your pea soup of self-pity.

1961 = 17 = 8   Personal success is the method with which to pull yourself out of unpleasant situations or victim attitudes.

1962 = 18 = 9   Spiritual development of a unique personally power type must be expressed openly, not through something.

1963 = 19 = 10 = 1   Self—the respected self—must find the key to join the family of human love and equality.

1964 = 20 = 2   Relationship with one's self built on self-love, with no fear of what people think is essential to inner peace.

1965 = 21 = 3   If you take life with a loving, light heart, finding the common ground of joy and sharing, life is a pleasurable bouquet, with you in the happy middle of it.

1966 = 22   A powerhouse of creativity and building. Unwilling to let the vagaries of life undercut the mission. Needs to let others help, not just take it all on themselves.

1967 = 23 = 5   Shake out that lack of assurance, meet the world, and build a life filled with all the aspects of a human life well lived and well loved. It all is one—you find the common touching points.

1968 = 24 = 6   Take the comforts and challenges of home and hearth, and sculpt them into a life in which you can express yourself without reservation, a life in which you are loved, valued, and nurtured for yourself, not for what you provide.

1969 = 25 = 7   Rigidity, being too sure about what is right and proper and just and good, can be made flexible and willing through your exploring, ranging, restless mind. Develop new attitudes, and look at everything from all sides.

1970 = 17 = 8   Hard work, rigid standards, and service for the sake of standards can lead to inner loneliness. Join life as an accepting member. Give only what you are receiving. Relax and jump into the flow of it all. It feels great!

1971 = 18 = 9   A very strong personality with deep spiritual convictions. Find ways to emanate what you know rather than working hard at it.

1972 = 19 = 10 = 1   Here to teach. A deeply gentle person who knows what the world would benefit from knowing. Get out there and do it.

1973 = 20 = 2   A relationship to people. The world must change from deeply personal and engaged to more spiritually motivated, respecting the life choices of others, supporting rather than changing it, loving rather than overly guiding others.

1974 = 21 = 3   You are here to enjoy your life as a deeply spiritual expression of inner joy and outer appreciation.

1975 = 22   The force and harmony of the master of the material world.

1976 = 23 = 5   Hard work creating and maintaining stability turns into the fun and excitement of enjoying all the aspects of life.

1977 = 24 = 6   Balance produces a wonderful living environment.

1978 = 25 = 7   Using a penetrating intellect and developing discernment to find the art of delicate balance and steady growth.

1979 = 26 = 8   Personal power used as a tool for bringing a profoundly emotional nature into the beauty and connection of life.

1980 = 18 = 9   A naturally spiritual person, taking all dogma out and finding great personal spiritual growth without systems of belief.

1981 = 19 = 10 = 1   The self approaching each new experience in life new, fresh, no habits or beliefs that are outdated.

1982 = 20 = 2   A great spiritual companion learning to be in relationship to the world by bringing all he/she knows into practical form and teaching.

1983 = 21 = 3   Only through fun and shared pleasure can true security of the self in life be found.

1984 = 22   The power to build creates inner freedom and spiritual clarity.

1985 = 23 = 5   A shaker and mover who needs to get settled. Restlessness must change to intelligently applied curiosity that can build the life.

1986 = 24 = 6   Homelike atmosphere is achieved by investing in building a life and not letting group issues undercut a wholesome life.

1987 = 25 = 7   Great wisdom is applied to find personal freedom from human dilemmas.

1988 = 26 = 8   The power of being right and knowing what is best becomes power to live life with only the self to evolve. Embracing the whole.

1989 = 27 = 9   A deeply felt spiritual nature must trust the emotional connections in life and learn to trust again, become fully human with a defined goal.

1990 = 19 = 10 = 1   Me. I am here to build with power and force, blending in with no fear.

1991 = 20 = 2   We are all together here, but now we must leave this comfort and go into the world to contribute.

1992 = 21 = 3   Through seeing equality in everything, myself included, I can play in life and demonstrate loving personal authority at the same time.

1993 = 22   Protection and guidance as their nature, the learning is to let others be responsible for their own lives. It takes up all of one's time just being responsible for one's own personal quality.

1994 = 23 = 5   Stable service is a well-learned lesson. Stability is only a value when it frees you to express yourself as you choose. Leave behind confining aspects of work.

1995 = 24 = 6   The confusion about service and self with loved ones becomes heard through the balanced embrace of change. Let life show you the way.

1996 = 25 = 7   The stillness and intelligence of your mind will show you new ways to find the balanced life you seek.

1997 = 26 = 8   Emotional force and wisdom channeled to create problem solving, growth from intensity. Lighten up and create a life of gentle order and connection.

1998 = 27 = 9   Spiritual wisdom rests as a well within. True wisdom creates comfort and well-being wherever it goes. Bring yourself out of the well. Use the water of your wisdom to fertilize and nurture your garden of life—no pulling out of life for fear of it!

1999 = 28 = 10 = 1   Seek the ever-expanding you, enhanced by change, now able to know yourself better and better with each new approach to life and life's events.

2000 = 2 To be deeply wise brings more information than one can easily tolerate. Let each person learn and grow from their own chosen experience. Don't worry or rescue; trust the wisdom of forces higher than you. Be at peace, happy.

2001 = 3 Spiritual growth doesn't occur when one takes oneself too seriously. Join in the family of man. It is a feast. No one is left out. Everyone is equal at the banquet table.

2002 = 4 Personal authority and being respected holds limited true love. Belong as a member of this large and wonderful family. Your separation is your own perception only.

2003 = 5 Experiencing all that life has to offer is wonderful, but until you put the experiences in to form a stable, satisfying experience, their value is fleeting.

2004 = 6 Love and comfort are everyone's jobs. Contribute without reservation to the world with harmony with what is your goal.

2005 = 7 Life is a changing, ever-changing, experience. Dance in it, enjoying your uniqueness. Relax, and build your world for you.

2006 = 8 Expect success from your efforts, but over time learn to find your own beliefs, uniquely yours. Be flexible, engage the process of life as your teacher here to serve your personal freedom.

2007 = 9 Structure and guidelines provide tools for spiritual sharing, but your true spiritual sharing comes from becoming one with the ocean of compassion, love, and equanimity.

2008 = 10 = 1 You can go your own way, but you must always understand the effect you are having and what it is creating. Be willing to change, because love asks it of you.

2009 = 11 Spiritual masters often go through many lessons to demonstrate spiritual behavior in real life events. Carry your life experiences with loving acceptance.

2010 = 3 Deeply loving and spiritual, this nature sees all and loves all. Must not lose the sweet joy for living because of concern for others. Be wise and loving, but most of all enjoy your life.

On the Pages of a Book

Numbers provide guidance. Here is how to seek the guidance of numerology with the help of a book. Pick a book that is important to you, that you have had for a long time, and that may relate to your problem. As you flip through the book, focus on your problem, question, or whatever it is that you need guidance with. When you have your intent well in mind, let the book fall open or find a page with your hands that "feels" right. Look at the page number. The following lists the explanations for any of the numbers you get:

1 This day is designed for you. Seize it!

2 Life is your gift. Be in harmony with each experience.

3 Look into each experience for the joy held within.

4 Plan your day so you have a practical, well-thought-out approach to the on-coming events.

5 You are free to shake and move and enjoy today.

6 Your heart is full. Embrace every experience of the day.

7 You can rely on your inner guidance with complete trust.

8 Feel success is hand in hand with you throughout the day.

9 You are sustained by the universe. Feel that soft hand of support in all you do.

10 The entire picture is available to you if you focus on it today.

11 In each moment spiritual truths reside. See the light in each experience today.

12 Share something you are good at with another today in the name of fun.

13 You are at the center of all changes. Each change carries great gifts. Trust this natural order in all of life.

14 Use steadfast beliefs as your route to freedom.

15 You have several choices—choose the one that is best for you and it will be best for those you love.

16 The natural beauties of life will lead you to your inner wisdom.

17 You are using inner wisdom to create your success. Go for it.

18 Spiritual truths come through the equal sharing of power with others.

19 You have a spiritual responsibility to improve who you are in this situation.

20 Balance in all things. No extreme positions.

21 You are to share in the abundance of life with everyone you meet today.

22 The power to create is yours, but first know where you are going and be organized.

23 Fun, friendship equals travel—a look on life as a whole new experience today. Even if it is the same old life, find the new.

24 Are you finding yourself unable to be happy? Find the comfort in self-acceptance and this will bring you a step closer to who you want to be.

25 You, traveling through life as a connoisseur of the finest the day offers.

26 When was the last time you laughed in joy and felt how strong your heart becomes? Laugh today.

27 Quiet moments of inner silence will give you the answer you seek.

28 The day will be yours as you give action to your creative ideas.

29 You are the perfect balance of male and female within you. Appreciate your focus and your creativity.

30 Live of course and laugh a lot.

31 Don't hide your joy and uniqueness under a basket—radiate.

32 Enjoy another person deeply. Letting yourself really get to know them is often better than traveling (and a lot less expensive!).

33 There is no comfort as wonderful as true inner joy. It comes in the small pleasures.

34 Time to enjoy the pleasure of learning something new. Anything, big or small.

35 There is the power of pure joy in doing what brings you inner freedom.

36 Sometimes understanding brings a wise spiritual detachment.

37 Creative mental productivity will enhance you today.

38 Harmony is best found today by trusting your natural, powerful instinct for the positive viewpoint on anything that happens.

39 There are few things that combine as well as joy and love of humanity.

Appreciate each person today—even the jerks. They let you see your goodness.

40 In order to progress today, you must have a plan of action.

41 A plan of action applied in exactly your own way will bring you a new sense of inner freedom.

42 Want a productive day that contributes to your comforts? Put yourself into today with extra discipline.

43 Incline, stasis, decline all have their place in life. Be wise enough to let go of what is over.

44 Today you are the stable, responsible force that brings success to others.

45 Your experiences will provide a life view that is useful for others.

46 Resonate with your soul today, and see life in its complete wholeness. Everything is in its right place. See it and believe.

47 Use your imagination. Create in it an attainable dream, and take your first step toward it.

48 Hard work flavored with a type of discipline that improves your life brings great joy.

49 What is real, what is fantasy? Apply your beliefs, and reality will show you which is which.

50 Loosen up. This is a day for spontaneous responses. Trust yourself and find yourself.

51 A day to take all the potential that surrounds you and make it into the gift it is.

52 Your seeking mind needs you to be open to many new ideas today.

53 A day filled with the new, the interesting, and the joyful brings the greatest success.

54 Take some time to explore something you are interested in but have not yet done.

55 You are the sum total of every experience you have ever had. You are awesome!

56 This is a day to demonstrate your deep commitment to providing consistent guidance to others all of life's changes.

57 Take that traveling mind of yours, and let it rest on what you love to do or think about or read.

58 The power to change yourself will be in every experience today.

59 Life is to enjoy. Don't make your own suffering. Martyrdom is not cool. Party down in the rubble of crumbled expectations.

60 Life is filled to overflowing with sensuous luxury. Wrap yourself in it today.

61 Surround yourself today with an aura of self-contained goodwill.

62 Everyone is an equal part of humanity. This truth is where true power lies.

63 Spiritual humanitarian values can be passed easily today to others by noticing in them something you truly like and find pleasure in.

64 There are many familiar and new things that happen each day to contribute to your happiness. Today, appreciate the changes and how necessary they are.

65 Everyone has a piece of truth and wisdom. Yours comes from what you love

and the experiences you and only you have had. Share them!

66 Live today as if every need you have is filled. Be a cup overflowing for others.

67 The form through which love of others and a seeking mind pour is teaching and learning. Teach another. Learn from another. Be grateful.

68 To find the innate power in beauty makes all of life a pleasure trip.

69 Was there ever anything more lovely than a perfect balance of sensuality and spirituality? The warm glow and the bright light. Be both today.

70 Your seeking mind will find the truth in truth's time.

71 Seek. There are no answers, only better and better questions.

72 Your unique style can bring a new sense of inner worth.

73 Your inner voice is filled with the joy of life as your birthright. Trust the complete wisdom of this intuitive knowing.

74 Get information, understand it, run it by another, make up your mind.

75 An exploring mind, a curious mind, is a happy mind.

76 Use your intelligence to identify the larger need, then share what you know with calm assuredness.

77 Set the balance today by allowing the mystery of life to be alive in your awareness.

78 Turn your mind and desire for success today toward self-support and self-nurturing.

79 This is a day to bring into your awareness the great circle of birth-life-death-birth-life-death. Remember the eight, on its side, the symbol ∞ (infinity).

80 There is enormous inner power in the resolution of karmic debt. Today, if something doesn't make sense, be your best, improve your quality, and let the karma flow to completion.

81 Today serve others with your own brand of power.

82 Do you feel as if you are under someone's thumb? Are you suffering under an unjust authority? The solution to freedom and life lies within your grasp. Take charge. You are not a victim, don't act like it.

83 Today you are attracting a lot. Enjoy seeing your life reflect you today. Don't like your life? Change your thoughts and actions.

84 So much is happening! Let it change you so you can be even happier with yourself.

85 The true source of power and creation in life is the absolute acceptance of impermanence.

86 There are times to take yourself seriously and times to laugh at yourself. Laugh today.

87 This is a day to seek within yourself something you love to do or would love to learn to do.

88 Growth is not possible without inner reflection and integrating the effects of the day upon you. This is the path to wisdom.

89 No power is complete unless you serve a source higher and holier than yourself—there are many to choose from.

90 Acceptance of life as it is and acceptance of life as it could be are a spiritual balancing act. But today you can do it.

91 You are the master of your life, both material and spiritual. Take the rudder.

92 Your standards are yours and yours alone. Know what they are and then live up to them—they are yours!

93 What brings you a moment of spiritual attunement—nature, music, prayer, closing the deal, running? Then do it!

94 In order to share what you believe, you must get organized.

95 Life is filled with variety and inspiration. Decide to see it today.

96 Food, luxury, and the good life can be an expression of spiritual truths. Enjoy with no guilt, doubt, reservation, or fear.

97 Your mind will direct your spiritual growth if you allow a state of inner quiet to be present within.

98 Power and prestige have no value without a love of humanity.

99 You are one with all and all is one with you.

100 Valor is the first requirement for a life well lived.

101 Body/mind and spirit create the perfect human possibility. Live up to your potential.

102 Through the eyes of an innocent child truth is exposed. Trust your innocence.

103 To know yourself and your joys is two-thirds the learning. Now put in boundaries that exist as a result of self-knowledge.

104 In order to be able to be appropriate in your responses to all, the opportunity presented to you requires ever increasing clarity.

105 As you journey through your own inner life, self-acceptance is the key to the warmth of inner love.

106 You have to look at yourself in the mirror each day and be happy with what you see. The only way to ensure this is to always speak your truth with honesty and simplicity.

107 Let your instinctive inner nature show you how to have a wonderful day.

108 There is no sure path in life, and all paths in life are the sure path. Relax.

109 There are no mistakes. There are no failures. There is only self-knowledge.

110 Have you ever wished you had a personality characteristic that you admire in another? Well today, be it, make it yours.

111 Spirit guides your every step. You make the final choice on how to step. Listen to your inner voice and make a well-thought-out choice—joy.

112 To help another in the most practical of ways is a blessed gift to you and them.

113 Life gets tough. Life gets easy. One becomes the other. Be at peace, it all fits.

114 In order to progress in life you have to have a clear understanding of what you are doing, and why, and where you are going. Keep clarity as your goal.

115 The spiritual, literary, and poetry masterworks have something to offer you today.

116 Your home is within. Be at peace with yourself, and in this acceptance of yourself there is no fear.

117 This is a day to move ahead—your path will be smooth.

118 Sow your seeds today for future projects.

119 Walk hand in hand with the universe today. Feel the companionship of this source of life and love.

120 There is absolutely nothing like a good friend to laugh and cry with. Make a connection to someone whom you love.

121 Your body benefits from your love and care. Give your body great care and appreciation today.

122 You can create what you can conceive of, but it must be reasonable and attainable. Create reasonable goals, celebrate their attainment, and then create the next goal.

123 Be creative in letting others know what you need to be secure. Ask for what you want, and then work gratefully with what you get.

124 You are the one who steps into the opportunities that present themselves. Keep your eyes open and step lively!

125 Allow your experiences to express through you in a way that you are clear, honest, and full of integrity in your communication.

126 Shame and guilt erode the person, the couple, and the family. Let spiritual wisdom set you free to live shame- and guilt-free.

127 There is no past. There is no future. There is only today!

128 The opportunities presented to you will give you great satisfaction.

129 Dance with life. For life is like the dance. It's only happening when you are doing it. Keep dancing with delight.

130 Be like the tree bursting with life because of its deep roots. The tree takes all that nature gives it, integrates it, and makes it work for the tree's greatest good. Be like the tree.

131 Love is your nature. Inner light is the guidance. Meditate to bring the two together within you.

132 You are a part of a network, a community, a nation, a world, and a universe. You are never alone. You are a member of a universal family, valued and unique.

133 Seek perspective in all you do today.

134 The turtle never got anywhere without sticking its neck out.

135 Love everyone, trust few, guide your own life.

136 You are unique in the universe. If you don't share fully who you are, we are all poorer from your withholding. Be yourself!

137 At every moment we only create what we need. If you have something in your life you don't want, figure out how not to need it anymore.

138 Inner acceptance emanates confidence.

139 Re-evaluate yourself. What gives you pleasure? And your spiritual values? Get rid of what doesn't work anymore!

140 Boundaries that are healthy give the freedom to be yourself. Create boundaries, not restrictions.

141 Re-evaluate past decisions. Hindsight helps make a choice about a decision easier when we are in a similar situation. It is a tool for learning, not self-chastisement.

142 This is a day to be true to yourself. If you aren't sure how you feel about something, take a moment before you respond, or buy some time until you are surer.

143 Responsibility is your key to life. Wear your responsibilities happily and gratefully. Without them you would be entirely alone and lonely.

144 Evaluate your life for truths that make up your personal foundation of beliefs. Today be true to them.

145 To live a life well is to embrace your personal experience, understand the larger connection, and seek the meaning for you.

146 This is your day to be at home and confident with whatever occurs.

147 Your life is filled with magic and mystery. Watch it and love it. Look for it everywhere.

148 Authority has to do with seeing the talents of others and utilizing those talents well to support the goals you have set.

149 There is in the tarot cards the card of the fool. This is your card for today.

150 There can be many different routes to the creation of a happy, comfy home. Appreciate yours today and enjoy the uniqueness of your own path and what you have created.

151 This is a day to mind your mental. Direct it well. What you think and where you direct your thoughts become your life.

152 If your life seems too limited, then get out there and get into the banquet!

153 Are you using escapism as a coping tool? Take vacations once in a while, but at all other times become a reality addict—love the truth of life.

154 Nature is life's great teacher. Are you perplexed? Observe how nature works. It tells you the rules for a happy life.

155 There are several levels of reality. The one we all see and an unseen realm. Each one is a wonderful expression of life in its variety and uniqueness.

156 Today being able to see your faults as dear, even treasured aspects of your whole nature, is a great step toward self-acceptance—and improving yourself as well!

157 Your whole day depends on how you start it. Take time to spend a few minutes to adjust yourself into a new day!

158 Would you like to be more comfortable and dependable for others? You can be enhancing the structure in your life.

159 You are a part of a *huge* family of humans and you have an important place within the universe. You are a member of a large and loving family.

160 Are you giving yourself mental moments to relax in a miniature inner vacation? Think of a place you love, and in your mind, put yourself there—on a mini-vacation.

161 In your daydreams you hold the keys to your personal strength and contributions to life. Bring them, one at a time, into action.

162 Today is a sweeter day, filled with friendship and the great wonder of all that makes life beautiful.

163 Be at home in your life, have great fun, and feel how complete your life and happiness are!

164 Closeness requires security and trust to bloom. Are you giving what is required to enhance the closeness with others?

165 Nurture yourself within every experience you have today. Every event or experience has a gift for you in it . . . find it.

166 Sometimes it is necessary to rewrite our personal rules and bylaws for happiness. Today is a perfect day for this.

167 Today it is important to just come into the journey of a day in balance and equanimity.

168 Power can enhance or suffocate. You must learn the difference.

169 You have two very different natures—your body's nature, which wants security and survival, and your spirit, which wants to experience, to grow. You need to integrate both so your learnings go deep and become wisdom.

170 There is only one source of power, and that is your relationship to the universe.

171 This is a day to take some time to keep an inspirational phrase with you.

172 Look at yourself in the mirror. Gaze deeply into your own eyes. Accept all you see in love.

173 Life on Earth continually moves within nature's rhythms. Blend your life to the natural rhythms.

174 Great works have been created every single day for centuries. See the great works in daily life that surround you.

175 Experience is the foundation on which you stand and build from each day. No matter how hard or easy, treasure each one, for it has made you who you are today.

176 Spirit combines with the practicalities of life through acceptance of all the opportunities life has provided. Take a delighted advantage of each one!

177 You create your world, your life, through your thoughts. Are you being kind to yourself?

178 To know the truth of your strength, you must seek the experience to know yourself. Don't shirk from the experience of life, love, and productivity.

179 The best you create today will be your source of belief in yourself and your personal power.

180 The power of spirit is in the knowledge of the self and knowing the quality of us all. Power means nothing until it is tempered with the respect for the equality of all life.

181 Seek to see the whole picture today, otherwise you might miss important elements and details.

182 There is no faith, love, or support like the love of an animal for a human. Open your heart to your animal friend and find a perfect love.

183 Timing is everything. Take charge of yours.

184 The sweet taste of success. Use your power today wisely, don't be a victim or a tyrant.

185 Today what you say will be very meaningful to another.

186 Your life is the result of each decision you have made. Be responsible and use opportunity wisely.

187 The wisdom of the universe comes through life events and your intuition. Trust them both.

188 There may be an issue today you feel very stubborn about. Be flexible, and see both sides.

189 Guidance can't help you unless you ask first for help.

190 No matter how it looks, all is as it should be. Be at peace.

191 Your ideas are wonderful. Make them practical too.

192 You are a treasure chest of wonders. Use each experience in life to discover another personal quality.

193 From the smallest experience and the simplest phrase wisdom is exposed. Share what you know.

194 Take a look at the places in life that are spiritual, and now the places that are practical. Appreciate them both. And now see the times they blend into a beautiful expression of life.

195 Sometimes security becomes too important. What are you sacrificing to keep your life secure?

196 To find true comfort in life you must have a balance between what you are willing to give and what you are willing to receive.

197 Don't be pushy about what you want. Finesse, not manipulation, is the tool.

198 In the karmic learnings of life, we all experience everything in all our lives. In this life we don't get away with anything. Be humbled by this reality.

199 Is there an area of your life you would like to rebuild? Start today.

200 You are in relationship to everything in life. You are alone and joined, both at the same time.

APPENDIX B

Further Resources

This appendix can help you expand your explorations of numerology with the help of books and Web sites that offer various systems and approaches to numerology. While it is certainly not exhaustive, it does highlight some of the best resources out there.

Further Reading

Numerology and math have been with us since our very beginnings, through all the stages of human evolution on Earth. As a result, numerology has developed many branches. You have, available to you, a number of books that explore different numerological systems.

There are many books on the market, and I have overlooked, I am sure, some wonderful ones. This list in no way represents the only good books out there for you to find and learn from. It simply points the way into avenues of research that can help expand your skill.

This appendix is divided into sections. It gives sources that are available for a continued exploration of the numerology system explained in this book as well as other systems that developed throughout the world. Don't spend lots of time worrying about which one system is correct. These systems evolved over thousands of years, and they all have the same root that grows into different branches. Through this exploration, you will find the basic truths of numerology that are worldwide. Should you decide to become, over time, accomplished with numerology, those universal bottom lines will help you to sift through the vast inaccuracies that have unfortunately developed as well-meaning but poorly trained individuals have contributed their knowledge to the system.

Truth is a wonderful thing. Should you decide to explore, beyond your current learning, your truth about and belief in life as portrayed through numerology, this study will open vast expanses of wisdom for you.

- The most basic book—and many feel the only other one necessary for development of skills—is *Your Days Are Numbered: A Manual of Numerology for Everybody* by Florence Campbell (Devorss & Co., 1983). Florence Campbell wrote a classic. Published originally in 1931, it has had numerous reprintings because the demand for its accuracy and simplicity has stayed constant over time.

- *Numerology—Spiritual Light Vibrations,* by Jeanne (Your Center for Truth Press, 1986), is an amazingly generous sharing of years of accumulated skill as a highly qualified numerologist. Jeanne's work stands on Campbell's and develops it. In addition to this wonderful book, Your Center for Truth Press also offers Jeanne's computer software that will assist you in doing numerology charts. For more information, contact this company at P. O. Box 4094, Salem, OR, 97302-8094.

- *Numerology, Key to Your Inner Self,* by Hans Decoz, with Tom Monte (Perigee, 1994), is a complete book with formulas, philosophical framing, and additional uses, an excellent tool for expanding and deepening your curiosity. Decoz is clear and concise in constructing the world of numerology as a tool for decoding the order of nature.

- *The Book of Numerology: Taking a Count of Your Life,* by Hal A. Lingerman (Red Wheel/Weiser, 1994), is a book that has a slightly different view on numbers—how they blend and how to use them and their rhythms in your life. It is good for finding the common ground and variations in the formulas and conclusions.

- *The Secret Science of Numerology: The Hidden Meaning of Numbers and Letters,* by Shirley Blackwell Lawrence (New Page Books, 2001), is an in-depth look at numerology and how it works.
- *Numerology Made Easy,* by W. Mykian (Wilshire Book Co., 1982), brings a slightly different perspective to numerology.

The Chaldean System

- *Chaldean Numerology, an Ancient Map for Modern Times,* by Leeya Brooke Thompson (Tenacity Press, 1999), is an interesting look at the ancient Chaldean culture and numerology. Sharing her years of experience in a book that expands already learned information, Thompson brings an ancient form of numerology to life.

The Chinese System

- *The Everything® Feng Shui Book,* by Katina Z. Jones (Adams Media Corporation, 2002), is an introduction to the Chinese art of feng shui.
- *Feng Shui Made Easy: Designing Your Life with the Ancient Art of Placement,* by William Spear (Harper San Francisco, 1995), and *The Personal Feng Shui Manual: How to Develop a Healthy and Harmonious Lifestyle,* by Master Lam Kam Chuen (Owl Books, 1998), are the two don't-miss books to begin to grasp the connections of numerology and feng shui.

- *The I-Ching or Book of Changes,* translated by Richard Wilhelm and Cary F. Baynes (Princeton University Press, 1967), is the hands-down best example of numerology and wisdom combined to assist human affairs. It is not a numerology instruction book, but it does demonstrate a method of numerology in action.
- *Nine Star Ki: Your Astrological Companion to Feng Shui,* by Robert Sachs (Sterling Publications, 2002), is a useful blend of numerology, astrology, and feng shui, even though it is marketed as an astrology book.

The Mayan System

- *The Mayan Factor: Path Beyond Technology* by José Argüelles (Bear & Co., 1987), is an interesting view of numerology through the eyes of a man who has studied Mayan mathematics. In his book, Argüelles presents a system of cyclical time versus our familiar linear time.

Online Resources

The Internet is chock full of numerology sites. If you type in "numerology" into any search engine, you would get hundreds of thousands of results. Here are just a few good examples of what's out there.

✐ *www.decoz.com* is the site of Hans Decoz, author of *Numerology, Key to Your Inner Self.* Decoz offers an excellent site with many different offerings in the area of numerology.

✎ *www.2near.com/edge/numerology* is a Web site run by John Kostura; it offers a numerology calculator as a no-charge download.

✎ *www.bon-usage.com/english_software/ numerology* offers software for people in search of a practical and complete tool to support their development of skill, expertise, and precision.

✎ *www.chcp.org/vnumbers.html* is a good site for extending understanding of numerology to the Chinese approach.

✎ *http://dir.indiamart.com/indianservices/ astrology.html* offers the East Indian perspective of numbers and their value in your life. This Web site also offers software, consultation, and a list of numerologists who are available for consultation.

✎ *http://sacredspiral.topcities.com/numerology* is a good resource for books on the subject of numerology. In addition, it offers Mayan numbers and their meaning.

Additional Resources

You have available to you for assistance in your life a master numerologist. Gregge Tiffen does not teach classes, but he has tapes. He uses his vast skill to assist his clients in understanding the deeper meaning of their life and how to direct yourself in life to gain the maximum growth and rich benefits available to you. Visit Tiffen's Web site at ✎ *www. g-systems.com*, or call G Systems at 972-447-9092 for more information.

Appendix C

A Sample Numerology Reading

The following appendix presents a fictitious numerology chart that you can refer to as an example as you create a chart for yourself or another person. It is in the act of actually doing the chart that the numbers, both their personality and influence, become more understandable as you find your balance between linear information and intuitive knowledge. The name we'll be working with is Megan Eaton.

Soul Essence

The first step is to calculate the soul essence, which is done by adding up the value of the vowels written out above the name:

$$5 \quad | \quad 5 \quad | \quad 6 \qquad = 18 = 9$$

M E G A N   E A T O N

At a soul essence level, Megan Eaton is a server of humanity. When someone carries this essential essence, they are usually loved by many and draw toward themselves many people. This is because, deep within, everyone senses this 9 person is here for others, and the 9 essence has the strong drive to assist them with their life and problems.

Megan attracts many, and she suffers from confusion about whether the person is drawn to her as a person or is drawn to what she can do for them. It can be a problem for Megan not to engage with people who are takers. She doesn't have the greatest boundaries between herself and others because her inner essence moves to serve as one with all humanity.

Her sweetness and soul commitment to this leaves her blending or merging immediately with others in order to sense the need of the other and be able to respond to it in a soul-touching way. Her deep and complete commitment to sharing all her knowledge and wisdom does not come from a compulsion to know or be right, that is, from her ego. It instead comes from her ability to grasp in an instant what the other person needs in order to feel uplifted. She knows when to give a kiss and when to give a kick. Her internal wisdom is vast, and she shares with endless generosity.

Megan must guard against becoming exhausted by the needs and demands of the world. She needs to have a place in her life—a room, garden, quiet space, a view—where she can let go and recenter. This must be done alone. Recentering doesn't need to take a long time. The time spent here is determined by her degree of exhaustion from life. When she is in this place, she has to develop the discipline to not keep going over in her mind all the things that are troubling her or troubling others. She has to provide for herself a quiet time of personal nurturing and refreshment. This requires both self-knowledge and flexibility—self-knowledge to know what will be restorative, and flexibility to respond to her current state of life fatigue with a variety of ideas or activities that help. The reconstructor of self-love provides much wisdom for this part of her challenge.

Megan is never so happy as when another has improved his or her lot. She believes to her toes that when one is doing better, so are we all, and vice versa. This is another aspect of the boundary issue. It is not always clear to Megan where she stops and the other person starts. Because her essence perceives humanitarian union at its highest potential, this is always what she puts out there and strives for. In order for this to feel like a success, though, the world has to respond favorably. If she sees a child crying and comforts the child, it is wonderful and fulfilling for her if the parent is grateful. But if the parent becomes irate, even if Megan knows that this reaction has completely to do with the parent's own inner frustration and not with Megan's soothing of the baby or with their perception of her worth as a person, it will give her a soul pain. She needs to recognize that she has no control over the results of her humanitarian gestures, nor should she expect it. Recognizing this can free her up to be more of who she is. To nurture the child in a way that satisfies her soul's standards, she has to be open, and she has to learn to tolerate this level of openness and then recover from the soul pain that her true openness inevitably encounters. This is what her quiet space is for. The 9 soul essence that she carries opens amazing doors to life. She is able to see and relate to the most wondrous aspects of humanity, and also the foulest. She can feel the impact of both.

Megan serves us all as a 9 essence. Her most important task is to recognize she is here as a soul restorer to others—often a thankless job—and she must learn to make her boundaries of self so firm that she doesn't suffer. She needs to have two groups of people in her life. The first, and by far the larger, will be her work. These can be family, friends, fellow workers, and strangers. These are people who need her for something, and they will always take a toll on her. The second group, usually a precious few, consists of her true friends. These are people who love themselves and as such have no clinging demands or projections on her.

Instead of always being in service and demonstrating the force of love, with these friends she is free to be herself and enjoy a deep sharing of love for its own sake.

Life Focus

The life focus number is calculated by adding up the digits of the person's birth date. Megan's birth date, or touchdown time, is August 26, 1964:

$$8/26/1964 = 8 + 2 + 6 + 1 + 9 + 6 + 4 = 36 = 9$$

That is, the total of Megan's touchdown time is 9—a double 9. As her soul pattern of 9 flows into her life focus, they are both the same essence.

Megan is here as a truly committed balm, salve, or healer to humanity. Her life focus has to do only with others. Deep in her soul's truth, she carries a firm, unshakeable belief that she is always safe and cared for, that she may always be provided for, and that it is others who are more at risk. She feels the pain of others before she feels her own. She feels another's pain as her own. And as she lifts the other's pain from herself, the other feels mysteriously better.

Megan trusts intuitive wisdom and believes in the power of love and good. Her favorite day is to be on-call, as needed. Her preference is not to focus, create a list, and accomplish predecided-upon tasks. She prefers to function in Kairos time, and, like a wave on the sand, to be there as needed and then move on.

This enormous commitment to being a filled-with-light drop in a sea of humans can make paying bills, balancing the checkbook, arriving on time, and being basically reliable in linear time very tough. She will need to learn balance between the world of structured responsibility and of being where she is needed according to universal guidance saying: Now, right here, focus on that person. She can become completely swept up in these moments.

Her capacity to be present, bring love and caring, and provide a needed uplift is unsurpassed. But her essential personality must help her stay within her boundaries or else she will have no real sense of self separate and distinct from her work. It is very important for her to have a few precious friends who love themselves so truly that they ask nothing from her. Here she can relax and be a normal human. If she doesn't have a friend who doesn't "need" her, this should be her top priority, for without this, she won't really have her own life of personal love and human richness.

Birth Year

Her birth year is 1964. In this year, a 2 year, the primary challenge is to leave behind an attachment to coming to understand one's personal worth through how the world reacts. For instance, I am respected, I will be a loving person/I am not respected, I will not open my love until I am. Or: I am excluded from the group and this keeps me from being a happy person. The folks born in this year are learning how to become a part of humanity without needing to be respected first or continually welcomed. They are learning how to belong and the truth of the inclusive qualities of love.

Megan brings a great healer in to a birth year focus of feeling not a part of humanity. She feels very called upon as a healer, but in her most personal issues—family, relationship, children—she is at a loss about how to make these essential parts of a human life hers as well. She is much better equipped to provide encouragement to others, to see them happy and full-hearted, then go home to crawl into bed alone—perhaps relieved to be alone, but not able to be just a woman, partner, friend, or mom.

The sweet, ordinary pleasures of life seem to slip between her fingers. She must find ways to contain her needs as her own, needs that are the same as everyone else's. Being a healer does not mean that in these most personal areas she is whole. She must join into the family of humankind, give up her attachment to being the healer, not put everyone in her personal life also into her professional life, for if she does not, she will never get to be just a human. She needs to accept the invitation to return to the culture, the family of humankind. She is a flow of humanity. She can have boundaries of self-definition, but she must not hold the position of the healer who knows but resists the pressure from all sides to be magical and step off the position or pedestal.

This step into life is done as an ordinary person, for deep within, that is exactly what Megan is. But her love of humanity and her ability to heal combined with the needs of others make her special (so she will help them), and it can overwhelm her and make it so hard just to be another member of life. This is Megan's challenge—join in and don't be select, separate.

Personal Talents

To calculate the personal talent number, write out the numbers underneath each letter of the full name and add them up together:

M	E	G	A	N		E	A	T	O	N	
4	5	7	1	5		5	1	2	6	5	= 41 = 5

Megan has the talents of a 5. With the strong 9 here and the 1965 entry year, Megan would be an amazing speaker. She can do motivational speaking because by the very nature of her energy she connects immediately to her audience and them to her. It would be absolutely essential for her to believe completely and wholeheartedly in what she was imparting. Virtually incapable of deceit, she must know her words are helping. So much of Megan's strong 9 inclines her toward success with the public if she can focus her skills. She would succeed in the following roles:

- Motivational speaker or spokesperson
- Minister
- Writer
- Energy worker or masseuse
- Advocate (a perfect Erin Brockovich type)

- A charity fund-raiser speaker
- Foundation representative
- Travel guide
- Reconstructor of Self-Love

With these wonderful talents that have to do with the public, her reconstructor of self-love will add the resource Megan *really* needs. How to be with herself, at peace in her self, and filling with pure inner self-knowledge gained from inner reflections, particularly in times of adversity.

To calculate the reconstructor, add up the numbers under the consonants that are written out below the name:

M	E	G	A	N		E	A	T	O	N	
4		7		5				2		5	= 23 = 5

A mover-shaker, Megan's route to self-love and nourishment has to do with personal freedom, with feeling unlimited and able to move out across the world and do whatever she wants, whenever she wants. This is the freedom this humanitarian needs to restore herself. On her own, she can think about traveling and going to different places, from shopping in Paris, to going to Africa and talking with the Masai. If she doesn't have the resources already, she will be able to develop them, probably by her motivational speaking. When she's deeply in her reconstructor of self-love, she would be a part of humanity as travel, fun, adventure, but without responsibility for making them feel better.

This is a woman who comes filled with love for humanity and given what is required to bring into the material world the concrete expressions of her ideas. However, in order to do this, Megan has to learn to time manage and prioritize. She needs form and grounded information to complete the tasks. She must learn boundaries, and monitor her energy output. The wonderful dreams of the 5 seem pleasurable, self-inspiring, and totally renewing instead of overwhelming responsibility.

In her leisure time Megan will enjoy conferences of shakers-movers on the very edge of creating better lives for people. She will be a powerful speaker at these events and imbue others with the absolute rightness of these ideas. She will need to be careful to be practical, not just inspirational. And she will need to keep her private world of the 5 private and not open to all the world for review, criticism, and comments. The 5 is her private nurturing world. It gives her force in the world and a belief in the big picture.

However, her whole success as a creator and inspirer rests on getting focused, practical, and within boundaries. Without these disciplines in place, Megan will be a loose cannon. She will be trying to do good, but without the focus, she can cause harm.

Key and Karma

The key and karma are calculated through full name analysis. The key is the sum of the vowel values and the karma is the sum of the consonant values. The key and karma serve as the final definition of Megan's self-package for her lifetime.

5	1		5 1		6	= 18 = 9 (KEY)
M	E G	A N	E	A T	O N	
4	7	5		2	5	= 23 = 5 (KARMA)

Looking at the name from the perspective of key and karma, Megan's key is her humanitarian spirit of brotherhood for all. This is where her gifts and joys lie. This is her great pleasure, to be a humanitarian. Her last name, her karma, is her lesson, or where she has started repeating a behavior over and over again and where it is time for her now to progress to a new behavior.

Having a 9 key and a 5 karma means her great flowing spirit must be brought into practical form. She has to find ways to create in her own life first the world she knows could exist. Then the quality and standards of that personal life must never be compromised for the empty promises of power and position.

Megan must—and her name forces it—balance her key inspirational qualities with her attitudes toward affecting the world around her. She must not resort to superficial wisdoms or platitudes in order to avoid the hard work of making her vision real. Nor can she make the vision real for others but ignore her own life of love, honesty, and human emotional connection. Hers is a life of balance, finding the fine line between seeing the possibilities and then finding the opportunities that allow the possibilities to unfold into reality.

The Eaton karmic 5 indicates her problem is to be superficial and changeable. She inspires, but has trouble getting her feet dirty in the mix of life. She needs to really get down and get it done. But with her 9 essence and 5 reconstructor of self-love, this enables her to make a connection with anyone and everyone she meets. Megan Eaton never meets a stranger.

This woman, should she really exist somewhere, is a powerhouse of potential and in this life must become a powerhouse of dedicated and practical work to make her vision real. She can permeate her personal life with it and from there change the world, one project at a time.

Index

THE EVERYTHING TAROT BOOK

By M. J. Abadie

The ancient art of reading Tarot cards is one of the most universally popular methods of interpreting the self and the future. Written in easy-to-follow language, *The Everything® Tarot Book* features everything you need to know to complete Tarot readings for yourself and others. It includes comprehensive explanations of each card, no matter what Tarot deck you own. More importantly, it provides a wide range of sample spreads—some classic, some unique—so that the many mysteries and wonders of the Tarot are yours for the asking!

Trade paperback, $12.95
1-58062-191-0, 304 pages

OTHER *EVERYTHING®* BOOKS BY ADAMS MEDIA CORPORATION

Everything® **Dessert Cookbook**
$12.95, 1-55850-717-5

Everything® **Diabetes Cookbook**
$14.95, 1-58062-691-2

Everything® **Dieting Book**
$14.95, 1-58062-663-7

Everything® **Digital Photography Book**
$12.95, 1-58062-574-6

Everything® **Dog Book**
$12.95, 1-58062-144-9

Everything® **Dog Training and Tricks Book**
$14.95, 1-58062-666-1

Everything® **Dreams Book**
$12.95, 1-55850-806-6

Everything® **Etiquette Book**
$12.95, 1-55850-807-4

Everything® **Fairy Tales Book**
$12.95, 1-58062-546-0

Everything® **Family Tree Book**
$12.95, 1-55850-763-9

Everything® **Feng Shui Book**
$14.95, 1-58062-587-8

Everything® **Fly-Fishing Book**
$12.95, 1-58062-148-1

Everything® **Games Book**
$12.95, 1-55850-643-8

Everything® **Get-A-Job Book**
$12.95, 1-58062-223-2

Everything® **Get Out of Debt Book**
$12.95, 1-58062-588-6

Everything® **Get Published Book**
$12.95, 1-58062-315-8

Everything® **Get Ready for Baby Book**
$12.95, 1-55850-844-9

Everything® **Get Rich Book**
$12.95, 1-58062-670-X

Everything® **Ghost Book**
$14.95, 1-58062-533-9

Everything® **Golf Book**
$12.95, 1-55850-814-7

Everything® **Grammar and Style Book**
$12.95, 1-58062-573-8

Everything® **Great Thinkers Book**
$14.95, 1-58062-662-9

Everything® **Travel Guide to
The Disneyland Resort®,
California Adventure®,
Universal Studios®, and
Anaheim**
$14.95, 1-58062-742-0

Everything® **Guide to Las Vegas**
$12.95, 1-58062-438-3

Everything® **Guide to New England**
$14.95, 1-58062-589-4

Everything® **Guide to New York City**
$12.95, 1-58062-314-X

Everything® **Travel Guide to Walt Disney
World®, Universal Studios®, and
Greater Orlando, 3rd Edition**
$14.95, 1-58062-743-9

Everything® **Guide to Washington D.C.**
$12.95, 1-58062-313-1

Everything® **Guide to Writing
Children's Books**
$14.95, 1-58062-785-4

Everything® **Guitar Book**
$14.95, 1-58062-555-X

Everything® **Herbal Remedies Book**
$12.95, 1-58062-331-X

Everything® **Home-Based Business Book**
$12.95, 1-58062-364-6

Everything® **Homebuying Book**
$12.95, 1-58062-074-4

Everything® **Homeselling Book**
$12.95, 1-58062-304-2

Everything® **Horse Book**
$12.95, 1-58062-564-9

Everything® **Hot Careers Book**
$12.95, 1-58062-486-3

Everything® **Hypnosis Book**
$14.95, 1-58062-737-4

Everything® **Internet Book**
$12.95, 1-58062-073-6

Everything® **Investing Book**
$12.95, 1-58062-149-X

Everything® **Jewish Wedding Book**
$14.95, 1-55850-801-5

Everything® **Judaism Book**
$14.95, 1-58062-728-5

Everything® **Job Interview Book**
$12.95, 1-58062-493-6

Everything® **Knitting Book**
$14.95, 1-58062-727-7

Everything® **Lawn Care Book**
$12.95, 1-58062-487-1

Everything® **Leadership Book**
$12.95, 1-58062-513-4

Everything® **Learning French Book**
$12.95, 1-58062-649-1

Everything® **Learning Italian Book**
$14.95, 1-58062-724-2

Everything® **Learning Spanish Book**
$12.95, 1-58062-575-4

Everything® **Low-Carb Cookbook**
$14.95, 1-58062-784-6

Everything® **Low-Fat High-Flavor
Cookbook**
$12.95, 1-55850-802-3

Everything® **Magic Book**
$14.95, 1-58062-418-9

Everything® **Managing People Book**
$12.95, 1-58062-577-0

Everything® **Meditation Book**
$14.95, 1-58062-665-3

Everything® **Menopause Book**
$14.95, 1-58062-741-2

Everything® **Microsoft® Word 2000 Book**
$12.95, 1-58062-306-9

Everything® **Money Book**
$12.95, 1-58062-145-7

Everything® **Mother Goose Book**
$12.95, 1-58062-490-1

Everything® **Motorcycle Book**
$12.95, 1-58062-554-1

Everything® **Mutual Funds Book**
$12.95, 1-58062-419-7

Everything® **Network Marketing Book**
$14.95, 1-58062-736-6

Everything® **Numerology Book**
$14.95, 1-58062-700-5

Everything® **One-Pot Cookbook**
$12.95, 1-58062-186-4

Everything® **Online Business Book**
$12.95, 1-58062-320-4

Everything® **Online Genealogy Book**
$12.95, 1-58062-402-2

Everything® **Online Investing Book**
$12.95, 1-58062-338-7

Everything® **Online Job Search Book**
$12.95, 1-58062-365-4

Everything® **Organize Your Home Book**
$12.95, 1-58062-617-3

Everything® **Pasta Book**
$12.95, 1-55850-719-1

Everything® **Philosophy Book**
$12.95, 1-58062-644-0

Everything® **Pilates Book**
$14.95, 1-58062-738-2

Everything® **Playing Piano and
Keyboards Book**
$12.95, 1-58062-651-3

Everything® **Potty Training Book**
$14.95, 1-58062-740-4

Everything® **Pregnancy Book**
$14.95, 1-58062-146-5

Everything® **Pregnancy Organizer**
$15.00, 1-58062-336-0

Everything® **Project Management Book**
$12.95, 1-58062-583-5

Everything® **Puppy Book**
$12.95, 1-58062-576-2

Everything® **Quick Meals Cookbook**
$14.95, 1-58062-488-X

Everything® **Resume Book**
$12.95, 1-58062-311-5

Everything® **Romance Book**
$12.95, 1-58062-566-5

Everything® **Running Book**
$12.95, 1-58062-618-1

Everything® **Sailing Book, 2nd Ed.**
$12.95, 1-58062-671-8

Everything® **Saints Book**
$12.95, 1-58062-534-7

Everything® **Scrapbooking Book**
$14.95, 1-58062-729-3

Everything® **Selling Book**
$12.95, 1-58062-319-0

Everything® **Shakespeare Book**
$14.95, 1-58062-591-6

Everything® **Slow Cooker Cookbook**
$14.95, 1-58062-667-X

Everything® **Soup Cookbook**
$14.95, 1-58062-556-8

Everything® **Spells and Charms Book**
$12.95, 1-58062-532-0

Everything® **Start Your Own Business Book**
$14.95, 1-58062-650-5

Everything® **Stress Management Book**
$14.95, 1-58062-578-9

Everything® **Study Book**
$12.95, 1-55850-615-2

Everything® **T'ai Chi and QiGong Book**
$12.95, 1-58062-646-7

Everything® **Tall Tales, Legends, and Other Outrageous Lies Book**
$12.95, 1-58062-514-2

Everything® **Tarot Book**
$12.95, 1-58062-191-0

Everything® **Thai Cookbook**
$14.95, 1-58062-733-1

Everything® **Time Management Book**
$12.95, 1-58062-492-8

Everything® **Toasts Book**
$12.95, 1-58062-189-9

Everything® **Toddler Book**
$14.95, 1-58062-592-4

Everything® **Total Fitness Book**
$12.95, 1-58062-318-2

Everything® **Trivia Book**
$12.95, 1-58062-143-0

Everything® **Tropical Fish Book**
$12.95, 1-58062-343-3

Everything® **Vegetarian Cookbook**
$12.95, 1-58062-640-8

Everything® **Vitamins, Minerals, and Nutritional Supplements Book**
$12.95, 1-58062-496-0

Everything® **Weather Book**
$14.95, 1-58062-668-8

Everything® **Wedding Book, 2nd Ed.**
$14.95, 1-58062-190-2

Everything® **Wedding Checklist**
$7.95, 1-58062-456-1

Everything® **Wedding Etiquette Book**
$7.95, 1-58062-454-5

Everything® **Wedding Organizer**
$15.00, 1-55850-828-7

Everything® **Wedding Shower Book**
$7.95, 1-58062-188-0

Everything® **Wedding Vows Book**
$7.95, 1-58062-455-3

Everything® **Weddings on a Budget Book**
$9.95, 1-58062-782-X

Everything® **Weight Training Book**
$14.95, 1-58062-593-2

Everything® **Wicca and Witchcraft Book**
$14.95, 1-58062-725-0

Everything® **Wine Book**
$12.95, 1-55850-808-2

Everything® **World War II Book**
$14.95, 1-58062-572-X

Everything® **World's Religions Book**
$14.95, 1-58062-648-3

Everything® **Yoga Book**
$14.95, 1-58062-594-0

*Prices subject to change without notice.

EVERYTHING KIDS' SERIES!

Everything® **Kids' Baseball Book, 2nd Ed.**
$6.95, 1-58062-688-2

Everything® **Kids' Cookbook**
$6.95, 1-58062-658-0

Everything® **Kids' Joke Book**
$6.95, 1-58062-686-6

Everything® **Kids' Mazes Book**
$6.95, 1-58062-558-4

Everything® **Kids' Money Book**
$6.95, 1-58062-685-8

Everything® **Kids' Monsters Book**
$6.95, 1-58062-657-2

Everything® **Kids' Nature Book**
$6.95, 1-58062-684-X

Everything® **Kids' Puzzle Book**
$6.95, 1-58062-687-4

Everything® **Kids' Science Experiments Book**
$6.95, 1-58062-557-6

Everything® **Kids' Soccer Book**
$6.95, 1-58062-642-4

Everything® **Kids' Travel Activity Book**
$6.95, 1-58062-641-6

Available wherever books are sold!
To order, call 800-872-5627, or visit us at everything.com

Everything® is a registered trademark of Adams Media Corporation.